Brief Contents

Contents

Introduction

Mentoring, or guiding, a less-experienced person to greater professional effectiveness, with a responsive, professional relationship-based approach, can help educators to meet higher program and teaching standards to benefit children and families. An old idea with new relevance, the mentoring process today is individualized to meet the needs of both emerging and experienced teachers as they encounter and reflect upon real-world challenges in early childhood classrooms. In a time when many teachers are feeling exhausted, blamed, and under attack because of rising standards and lower levels of support, the relationship-based mentoring process offers a way to nurture teachers toward professional growth with respectful and satisfying ongoing professional relationships.

The Timeliness of Mentoring

Change is occurring in the field of early childhood education. It is encouraging to many of us who have spent a lifetime in this profession to observe the increasing recognition of the importance of the role of the early childhood teacher. The growing professional respect for a diverse and multidisciplinary profession that equally values nurturing and teaching is long overdue. Many feel that our profession is at a defining moment in which we are now more valued and understood by the general public and by many policy makers but are still struggling to have our own practices match a professional vision for the highest quality programs for all young children (Goffin & Washington, 2007).

Mentoring is a professional-development strategy designed to bridge the gap between our professional vision and our actual practices. It refocuses us on the traditional early childhood value of relationships at the center of teaching practice (Bellm, Whitebook, & Hnatiuk, 1997a, b). A mentor understands why emotional intelligence (Goleman, 2006) is essential in establishing learning relationships. Acting as a professional ally who focuses first on observed strengths, a mentor allows for safe conversations with the teacher about what is happening, how it is affecting children, and ways to investigate and try out needed changes (Gardenswartz, Cherbosque, & Rowe, 2010). Mentoring has been specifically defined by the National Association for the Education of Young Children (NAEYC) and the National Association of Child Care Resource and Referral Agencies (NACCRRA) as follows:

> A relationship-based process between colleagues in similar professional roles, with a more-experienced individual with adult learning knowledge and skills, the mentor, providing guidance and example to the less-experienced protégé or mentee. Mentoring is intended to increase an individual's personal or professional capacity, resulting in greater professional effectiveness (Lutton, 2012, p. 84).

Mentoring as a form of job-embedded professional development (e.g., collaborative sharing of best practices, reflecting together about observed teacher–child interactions, conducting teacher inquiry into questions of interest) is especially suited to help teachers to meet professional standards while differentiating their practices for specific children and partnering with local communities (Schienfeld, Haigh, & Schienfeld, 2008).

Mentoring has also shown promise in helping a diverse group of working teachers who are being mentored in their classrooms to simultaneously receive college credit for courses with practicum experiences (Chu, Martinez-Griego & Cronin, 2010). Coaching is a closely related role that emphasizes all of the relationship-based skills of mentoring but also implies a specific focus, such as implementing literacy goals, and is facilitated by a professional with relevant expertise (Lutton, 2012, p. 85).

We are in an era when educational requirements for early childhood teachers are increasing in most publicly and privately funded early childhood programs. A national dialogue about ways to implement effective early childhood professional-development strategies is occurring. Quality rating and improvement systems (QRIS) are being developed and strengthened, with incentives for caregivers and teachers to engage in research-based practices (Connors-Tadros & Carlson, 2011, p. 36). Linking teaching practices to research into programs that have resulted in positive outcomes for children will continue to require that teachers engage in professional-development opportunities (Buyssee, Wesley, Snyder & Winton, 2006; Hanft, Rush & Sheldon, 2004).

The field of early childhood education has entered a time when a commitment to accountability and assessment means that teachers must understand what children know, and they must also be able to use that information to plan instruction. The priorities of federal legislation such as the *Race to the Top–Early Learning Challenge Grant* have tied competitive funding to a state's ability to create quality-rating and improvement systems for childcare providers and efforts to measure children's and program's progress at improving learning outcomes.

These requirements exist within a field that has a firm commitment to the right of children to play and consensus that children learn best through exploration, while being respected and listened to (Smith, 2006; Mardell, Fiore, Boni & Tonachel, 2010). The complexity of our current early learning environment cries out for skilled mentors and coaches to support teachers to resist a "false dichotomy . . . between play and learning." (Zigler, 2009). Instead, supporting playful inquiry-based learning and being able to explain and document reasons why play supports learning requires careful professional reflection and planning. Professional development is needed for teachers who are carrying out investigations of everyday practices in order to examine and improve their teaching and learning (Stremmel, 2012, p. 112). Supporting teacher inquiry into children's learning offers pathways to renewal for teachers, mentors, and everyone involved in our field (Stremmel, 2012, p. 114). Mentoring relationships, together with other learning-community study groups or higher education courses, offer the possibility of increasing the quality of programs while differentiating the adult learning process for every teacher.

Experiences in working with a variety of programs have demonstrated to this author the ways in which teaching practices change when a respected mentor works alongside another adult student or mature teacher. Mentors (who might also wear the hat of college instructor, director, or colleague) who listen to the experiences, dilemmas, and interests of teachers are especially effective when they offer ongoing feedback and encouragement to strive for the highest standards, in ways that respect the cultural, community, and program context of the teacher (Chu et al., 2010; Chang, 2006; Alvarado, 2004).

In contrast, many of us have had the experience of teaching, or taking workshops, at conferences that were "one-shot" experiences. Even though these sessions may be engaging and full of needed information, later observations and self-assessments often reveal that little or no long-term change in teaching practices has occurred as a result of attendance and participation (Guskey, 2000). Individualizing the learning of adults to a focus on analysis of practices, coupled with a knowledgeable guide, is one way to influence teacher learning and, ultimately, have a positive impact on the children they care for and educate (Stichter, Lewis, Richter, Johnson, & Bradley, 2006; American Research Institute, 2001).

When a teacher works with a mentor who supports a focus on the teacher's actual interactions with children and provides assessment tools to increase the teacher's awareness, the subsequent changes in teaching behaviors can affect child outcomes (Hamre & Pianta, 2007). Although much more research is needed into the effectiveness of mentoring as a strategy to improve teaching practice (Whitebook & Ryan, 2011, p. 7), recent studies suggest that professional development that includes mentoring and coaching leads to more changes in the behaviors of teachers than programs implemented without mentoring (Pianta, Mashburn, Downer, Hamre, & Justice, 2008; Ramey & Ramey, 2008). A recent professional literature review (ACF/OHS/NCQTL, 2012a, b; Snyder, 2012) involving 101 coaching studies about early childhood teachers from 1995 to January 2011 revealed that over three quarters of the studies involved practices also associated with a recent model developed at Vanderbilt University. This model, known as *Practice-Based Coaching*, involves shared teacher–coach goal planning and action steps, focused observation, the use of data to guide reflection, feedback on teaching, and general support provided over time. Positive child outcomes documented in studies using similar practices included "increased participation and engagement, increased social skills and fewer challenging behaviors (and) increased literacy and language" (ACF/OHS/NCQTL, 2012a, pp. 2–4).

Benefits and Characteristics of Effective Mentoring

Examining the specific features of effective professional development is one way to align the mentoring or coaching process with research-based qualities and characteristics. This growing body of study of effective professional development indicates that professional learning should

- be ongoing, intensive, and practice focused;
- include self-assessment; and
- be associated with specific criteria or expert feedback that is aligned with instructional goals, learning standards, and curriculum materials (Darling-Hammond, Wei, Andree, Richardson & Orphanos, 2009; Trivette, Dunst, Hamby & O'Herin, 2009).

High-quality mentoring fits all of those criteria and also has been shown to lower staff turnover, decrease the isolation of caregiving (Kagan, Kauerz, & Tarrant, 2008), and increase the emotionally responsive involvement of teachers' interacting with children (Howes, James, & Ritchie, 2003). The Quality Interventions for Early Care and Education (QUINCE) project's *Partners for Inclusion* model is showing results that ongoing mentoring and consultation increase family childcare teacher effectiveness after 6 months to 1 year of monthly visits, as measured in scores on the *Family Child Care Environment Rating Scale–Revised* (Harms, Cryer, & Clifford, 2007) and the *Early Childhood Environment Rating Scale* (Sylva, Sirai-Blatchford, & Taggart, 2006) literacy measures (Bryant, 2007; QUINCE, 2009). This study and others indicate that the power of a mentoring relationship is influenced by variations in the intensity, continuity, individualization, and focus of the professional development facilitated by a skilled early childhood professional working with a less-skilled or less-experienced teacher (NCCIC, 2009; Weber & Trauten, 2008).

The mentoring process should help teachers to contrast their actions with their desired results through focus and reflection on their daily practices and interactions. This involves a set of mentoring communication, inquiry, and leadership skills and relevant competencies (e,g., adult learning, building relationships, assessment and planning, the change process, professional ethics) that are as essential to fostering professional growth as expertise in specific content areas such as math or early literacy (Minnesota SMART, 2005, 2007). Ways of being that promote dialogue and reflection, and that foster inquiry into what teachers, families, and communities value, is required in the tool kit of the mentor. Identifying mentors or mentoring teams who understand the communities that they work in because they share common experiences or collaborate with others with the knowledge and perspectives that they lack is essential. Finally, recent research has found that child-centered beliefs and attitudes are significantly associated with higher quality care in home-based settings. Professional development that is effective in engaging—and in some cases, in modifying—family childcare providers' attitudes is being cited as essential for raising quality (Forry et al., 2012). Individualized mentoring has the potential to support reflection and to change beliefs and caregiving strategies over time.

Mentoring seems uniquely suited to engaging in professional development within and among specific programs, institutions, and early learning systems. The key tools of mentoring are the ones long valued by effective teachers of young children: listening, observing, and responding to the interests, feelings, and thoughts of others, with sensitivity and humility. Deep content knowledge and experience in the field are, of course, also required. Content knowledge, although necessary, is not enough to change teacher practices, without expertise in the process of mentoring.

Teachers usually do not learn and grow in isolation or gain from decontextualized theories that they can't apply. Instead, skilled mentors know that all learning is situated in a specific context (Lave & Wenger, 1991). Understanding the interrelationships and intersections among a school or organization's teachers, classrooms, and programs is also required for change and learning to take root (Opfer & Pedder, 2011). Learning communities or communities of practice facilitated by a mentor who works with a cohorts of teachers to examine their collective beliefs, gather information with a specific focus for inquiry, and put new learning into practice have the possibility of sustaining teacher development (Dickinson & Brady, 2006; Lave & Wenger, 1991; Zaslow et. al., 2011). Finally, when mentoring or related approaches are used as a part of a quality-improvement initiative, organizational system levels and the needs and involvement of individuals, classrooms, collective groups, and programs must be considered (Tout, Isner, & Zaslow, 2011).

Audience for This Text

This text may be useful as a resource to support

- the collaborative work and professional development of emerging community-based mentors and coaches;
- educators with early learning content knowledge and experience as teachers of young children who also want to gain the skills of the adult educator;
- mentors in a co-learning pair and/or participants in a professional-learning community interested in supporting peers in inquiry methods of teacher research;
- higher education faculty examining mentoring and leadership as one aspect of a professionalism, administration, or field-based practicum course;
- early-learning program administrators interested in a personal study of their dual roles as supervisors and mentors to their staff; and
- coaches using a specific or prescribed research-based coaching model who need a foundation in relationship-based professional-development knowledge, skills, and strategies.

Groups who are in preparation for creating a mentoring system for early-childhood teachers involved in a QRIS or similar quality-improvement initiative may use this text as a companion to other mentoring protocols when offering foundational professional development in relationship-based mentoring competencies. The last three chapters also address a planning and leadership-development process needed to sustain the gains made in any mentoring effort. The mentor in this text is viewed as a co-learner and co-investigator with the teacher. Although they may have related but different roles, goals, and purposes, as well as different knowledge and specialized expertise, both teacher and mentor are equally important parts of the mentoring process.

This text will broadly support all who work in roles facilitating the professional development of teachers of young children. Degreed early-childhood teachers also need mentoring. They are often not required to complete student teaching as a prerequisite for completing their degrees, and unlike K–12 teachers, are frequently not afforded an induction period of intensive support by supervisors and peer teachers (Whitebook & Ryan, 2011). Instead, due to the low education levels of teachers in the birth-to-5 early education field, a newly degreed teacher may encounter unrealistic expectations from employers. Mentoring is needed to retain new and experienced early-childhood teachers and to help them to explore their roles effectively. Mentors may also wear multiple hats as supervisors, directors, or program managers and may need to clarify and reflect on what roles best support teachers in meeting licensing, accreditation and other quality standards. By working through the text's reflective exercises and dialogue starters, readers can develop essential skills in the following areas:

Relationship-Based Professional-Development Strategies and Approaches

These strategies and approaches include examining the differences and similarities in values, goals, and roles associated with mentoring, collaborative teacher–researcher partnerships, coaching, consultation, supervision, and evaluation. The stages of teacher and mentor growth and leadership development are reviewed. Chapters specifically support the reader to be able to:

- explain the purpose of mentoring and the qualities of an effective mentor and identify relationship-based professional development strategies and models;
- analyze ways in which the role of the supervisor contrasts with the role of a mentor, coach, or consultant; and
- support emerging mentors and leaders from underrepresented groups by partnering with early-childhood leaders in a local community.

Educational Interactions and the Process of Inquiry

Methods for implementing the process of collaborative inquiry in professional-learning communities are explored through the tools of observation, dialogue, goal setting, implementing a plan, and critical feedback. Readers will learn how to

- identify and use appropriate observation and assessment techniques to gather information for developing teacher, program, or other professional goals;
- demonstrate skills for engaging in a cycle of educational inquiry as a collaborator and guide with an early childhood teacher;
- identify, facilitate, and evaluate effective communication strategies for mentoring and other adult professional-development relationships;
- understand the ongoing, organic, or iterative nature of the mentoring process; and
- apply reflection and evaluation strategies for mentor–teacher partnerships.

Sustaining a Focus on Valuing Equity, Diversity, and Culturally Relevant Practices

The individual, program, and systems levels are examined through discussions of cultural competency, responsiveness, and ways to value multiple perspectives. In all aspects of the mentoring process, the text notes the importance of recognizing what mentors and teachers know and do not know about the cultural, language, and community contexts. Rejection of practices that assume that the goal of early care and education to promote a monocultural and monolingual society is consistent in the text (Paris, 2012, p. 93). Concepts are explored that support readers to

- identify personal biases interfering with effective teaching and mentoring;
- describe and integrate the principles behind cultural competence, social justice, and anti-bias practices; and
- identify ways to support the development of leadership and mentoring practices that are responsive to the community and cultural context.

Adult-Learning Theories and Approaches Applied to the Mentoring Relationship

Ways to analyze and explore a variety of methods to gain an understanding of one's own and other's practices in teaching and in the mentoring relationship are described. The developmental process of change in a professional early-childhood teacher–mentoring relationship is reviewed from many perspectives in order to show readers how to

- describe selected theories of adult development and learning and analyze the implications for fostering a responsive teacher–mentor relationship;
- explore reflective critical-thinking practices and use a variety of methods to gain an understanding of one's own and others' practices in teaching and mentoring relationships.
- describe the developmental process of change, resistance to change, conflict, and transformation possible in a professional early-childhood teacher–mentoring relationship.

Professional-Development Leadership and Planning for Mentoring Systems

The connections between facilitating individual teacher curiosity and problem-solving and the broader needs of an overall professional plan for learning and development are examined within a system of professional development. Ways to grow a diversity of early childhood leaders who facilitate a learning-community approach to early education are emphasized. Specifically, when the reader completes a self-study or course by using this text, he or she should have a growing capacity to consider these categories of mentoring skills and knowledge and should

- be able to identify the steps to focusing on specific teacher questions or topics;
- establish bigger goals linked to desired child and/or program outcomes;
- construct with mentee an overall professional-development plan;
- transition to a satisfactory conclusion of a mentoring relationship and bridge to new support networks; and
- engage in leadership for professional-development systems planning.

This text may be used in an early childhood course designed to meet specific National Association for the Education of Young Children (NAEYC) Standards and Guidelines for Professional Development (Lutton, 2012). A focus on Standard 6—Becoming a

Professional from the NAEYC Standards for Early Childhood Professional Preparation Programs is especially related to the content of the text. Standard 6 indicates that

> . . . students [referred to as *teachers* in this text] identify and conduct themselves as members of the early childhood profession. They know and use ethical guidelines and other professional standards related to early childhood practice. They are continuous, collaborative learners who demonstrate knowledgeable, reflective, and critical perspectives on their work, making informed decisions that integrate knowledge from a variety of sources. They are informed advocates for sound educational practices and policies.
>
> 6a: Identifying and involving oneself with the early childhood field
> 6b: Knowing about and upholding ethical standards and other professional guidelines
> 6c: Engaging in continuous, collaborative learning to inform practice
> 6d: Integrating knowledgeable, reflective, and critical perspectives on early education
> 6e: Engaging in informed advocacy for children and the profession
>
> (Lutton, 2012, p. 26)

The text addresses the central issues in mentoring of improving program quality and teaching practices, relationships, inquiry, and leadership. This is not a text with one answer for all programs or people. The underlying assumptions are that technical assistance to programs, adult-learning experiences or early childhood college practicum experiences for teachers, and other forms of professional development do not produce long-term transformational change in teacher practices unless a knowledgeable, experienced, and trusted person first listens to the teacher's concerns and offers empathy, identifying questions to investigate, and encouraging reflection on practices. Adults, like children, learn best when their understanding of teaching and learning is built on ways that make sense in their context and their culture and is embedded in supportive professional-development relationships over time.

Section I: Relationship-Based Learning

Section I (Chapters 1–4) emphasizes relationship building and an understanding of the cultural and community context, communication skills, and adult-learning strategies needed to support the professional development of an early childhood teacher. Differences and similarities in the approaches and goals associated with mentoring, coaching, consultation, and supervision are examined. When readers have completed Section I, they will be able to

- explain the concept, goals, and possible outcomes of mentoring;
- describe the roles and responsibilities of mentors and participants;
- explain the differences between mentoring and related approaches and supervision;
- describe differing assumptions and adult-learning theories underlying mentoring approaches;
- apply strategies for building professional relationships;
- use effective communication strategies in mentoring;
- identify examples of transformative and culturally responsive mentoring approaches; and
- explain common stages of mentor and teacher development.

Section II: Mentoring for Inquiry, Reflection, and Leadership

Section II (Chapters 5–8) explores the role of the mentor to join with an early childhood teacher to listen to concerns and discover areas of interest. Strategies shared are inspired by the schools of Reggio Emilia, where teachers document (photography, videotaping, written notes and transcripts) children's actions, words, and dialogue to make meaning by interpreting their documentation with colleagues and mentors over time. Emphasis is on developing mentoring with teachers and programs to identify needs and interests. These final chapters examine key elements of mentoring for early childhood leadership explored though an examination of reflective supervision and the process of change. When readers have completed Section II, they will be able to

- explain the role of the mentor in facilitating a teacher's cycle of inquiry;
- describe ways to join with an early childhood teacher to explore questions and interests;
- understand and adapt to a teacher's readiness for change;
- explain the differences between observation, critical reflection, and interpretation of information gathered in the early childhood program setting;
- review methods to plan for changes in teaching strategies and program approaches;
- identify ways to transfer skills from teaching to mentoring and leadership;
- identify strategies for creating a system of mentoring that meets the needs of a community and fits the cultural context;
- explain ways to mentor for reflective supervision, decision-making, and program change; and
- provide strategies for facilitating a program for or systems approach to collaborative observation, reflection, and action.

Being a part of a mentoring relationship is rewarding because it holds the possibility of awakening curiosity in both the mentor and the mentee, or protégé. Having feelings of dissatisfaction with the present but no clear pathway to the future is a powerful ally of the mentor. These feelings may change to a sense of increased energy and direction through the spirit of collaborative inquiry at work in a mentoring relationship. The potential of this relationship cannot be achieved without attention and consideration of the skills, knowledge, and investigations required. This text hopes to help you in your preparation for that professional journey.

Reflection
....

- What characteristics of mentoring for professional development and learning do you feel are important to support your learning or the development of other staff, teachers, or colleagues?
- With what national, state, or local trends in early childhood education program accountability are you involved in or aware of? What purpose might mentoring for personal and professional development serve in the current educational context or in your setting?
- After reviewing the topics in this text, select several that are interesting to you to further your learning. Identify topics with which you are familiar or those that you are have experience in applying in work with other early childhood teachers, children, and families.

References
....

Administration for Children and Families (ACF), Office of Head Start (OHS), National Center on Quality Teaching and Learning (NCQTL). (May 2012a). *What do we know about coaching?* Retrieved from http://eclkc.ohs.acf.hhs.gov/hslc/tta-system/teaching/docs/What-Do-We-Know-About-Coaching.pdf

Administration for Children and Families (ACF), Office of Head Start (OHS), National Center on Quality Teaching and Learning (NCQTL). (May 2012b). *Practice based coaching*. Retrieved from http://eclkc.ohs.acf.hhs.gov/hslc/tta-system/teaching/docs/practice-based-coaching.pdf

Alvarado, C. (November 2004). Authentic leadership: Lessons learned on the journey to equity. *Zero to Three*, 32–39.

American Institute for Research. (2001). *Putting the pro in protégé: A guide for mentoring in Head Start and Early Head Start.* Washington, DC: American Institute for Research (Head Start Bureau Publication # 105-98-2080).

Bellm, D., Whitebook, M., & Hnatiuk, P. (1997a). *Early childhood mentoring curriculum: A handbook for mentors.* Washington, DC: The National Center for the Early Childhood Work Force.

Bellm, D., Whitebook, M., & Hnatiuk, P. (1997b). *The early childhood mentoring curriculum: A trainers guide.* Washington, DC: The National Center for the Early Childhood Work Force.

Bryant, D. (November, 2007). *Delivering and evaluating the Partners for Inclusion model of early childhood professional development in a five state collaborative study.* Presentation at the meetings of the National Association for the Education of Young Children, Chicago, IL.

Buyssee, V., & Wesley, P. (2005). *Consultation in early childhood settings.* Baltimore: Paul H. Brookes Publishing Co.

Buyssee, V., Wesley, P., Snyder, P., & Winton, P. (2006). Evidence-based practice: What does it mean for the early childhood field? *Young Exceptional Children, 9*(4), 2–10.

Chu, M., Martinez, B., & Cronin, S. (2010). A Head Start/College Partnership: Using a culturally and linguistically responsive approach to help working teachers earn college degrees. *Young Children, 65*(4), 24–29.

Chang, H. (2006). *Getting ready for quality: The critical importance of developing and supporting a skilled, ethnically and linguistically diverse early childhood workforce.* Oakland, CA: California Tomorrow.

Connors-Tadros, L., & Carlson, B. C. (2011). Integrating quality rating systems and professional development systems in early childhood. In C. Howes & R. Pianta (Eds.), *Foundations for teaching excellence.* (pp. 25–26). Baltimore: Paul. H. Brookes Publishing Co.

Darling-Hammond, L., Wei, R. C., Andree, A., Richardson, N., & Orphanos, S. (2009). *Professional learning in the learning profession: A status report on teacher development in the United States and abroad.* Dallas: National Staff Development Council.

Dickinson, D. K., & Brady, J. P. (2006). Toward effective support for language and literacy through professional development. In M. Zazlow & I. Martinez-Beck (Eds.), *Critical issues in early childhood professional development* (pp. 141–170). Baltimore: Paul H. Brookes Publishing Co.

Forry, N., Iruka, I., Kainz, K., Tout, K., Torquati, J., Susman-Stillman, A., Bryant, D., Starr, R., & Smith, S. (2012). Identifying profiles of quality in home-based child care, *Issue Brief OPRE* 2012-20. Washington, DC: Office of Planning, Research and Evaluation Admin. for Children and Families, U.S. Dept. of Health and Human Ser. Retrieved from http://www.acf.hhs.gov/programs/opre/cc/childcare_technical/reports/identifying_profiles.pdf

Gardenswartz, L., Cherbosque, J., & Rowe, A. (2010). Emotional intelligence and diversity: A model for difference in the workplace. *Training and Development 63*(2), 44–49.

Goffin, S., & Washington, V. (2007). *Ready or not: Leadership choices in early care and education.* New York: Teachers College Press.

Goleman, D. (2006). *Emotional intelligence: Why it can matter more than IQ.* New York: Bantam.

Guskey, T. (2000). *Evaluating professional development.* Thousand Oaks, CA: Corwin Press.

Hanft, B., Rush, D., & Sheldon, M. (2004). *Coaching Families and Colleagues in Early Childhood.* Baltimore: Paul H. Brookes Publishing Co.

Hamre, B., & Pianta, R. (2007). Learning opportunities in preschool and early elementary classrooms. In R. Pianta, M. Cox, & K. Snow (2007), *School readiness and the transition to kindergarten in the era of accountability* (pp. 49–83). Baltimore: Paul H. Brookes Publishing Co.

Harms, T., Cryer, D., & Clifford, R. (2007). *Family Child Care Environment Rating Scale–revised*. New York: Teachers College Press.

Howes, C., James, J., & Ritchie, S. (2003). Pathways to effective teaching. *Early Childhood Research Quarterly 18*(1), 104–120. In C. Howes & R. Pianta (2011). *Foundations for teaching excellence: Connecting early childhood quality rating, professional development, and competency systems in states*. Baltimore: Paul H. Brookes Publishing Co.

Kagan, S., Kauerz, K., & Tarrant, K. (2008). *The early care and education teaching workforce at the fulcrum: An agenda for reform*. New York: Teachers College Press.

Lave, J., & Wenger, E. (1991). *Situated learning: Legitimate peripheral participation*. Cambridge, UK: Cambridge University Press.

Lutton, A. (Ed.). (2012). *Advancing the profession: NAEYC standards and guidelines for professional development*. Washington, DC: NAEYC.

Mardell, B., Fiore, L., Boni, M., & Tonachel, M. (2010). The rights of children: Policies to best serve 3, 4, and 5 year olds in public schools, *Scholarlypartnershipsedu, (5)*1, 38–52. Retrieved from http://opus.ipfw.edu/spe/vol5/iss1

Minnesota SMART (Sharehouse, Mentoring, Assistance, Resources, Training), Minnesota Department of Human Services. (2005, June). *Growing Smarter: Understanding and Planning for Relationship-Based Professional Development Among Child and Youth Care Providers in Minnesota*. Retrieved from: http://mnsmart.metrostate.edu/docs/MNSMART_Final_Report.swf

Minnesota Sharehouse, Mentoring, Assistance, Resources, Training (SMART), Minnesota Department of Human Services. (2007). *General Core Competencies for all Relationship Based Professional Development Strategies*. Concordia University. Retrieve at http://www.mncpd.org under the tab "Relationship Based Professional Development" and scroll down to "General Core Competencies."

National Association for the Education of Young Children (NAEYC) and National Association of Child Care Resource and Referral Agencies (NACCRRA). (2011). *Early childhood education professional development: Training and technical assistance glossary*. Washington, DC: National Association for the Education of Young Children. Retrieved from http://www.naeyc.org/GlossaryTraining_TA.pdf

National Child Care Information and Technical Assistance Center (NCCIC). (2009, May). *Relationship based professional development: models, qualifications, training, and supports*. Retrieved from http://nccic.acf.hhs.gov/poptopics/rbpd.html

Opfer, V., & Pedder, D. (2011). Conceptualizing teacher professional development. *Review of Educational Research, 81*(3), 376–407.

Paris, D. (2012). Culturally sustaining pedagogy: A needed change in stance, terminology and practice. *Educational Researcher,* American Educational Research Association (AERA), 41(3) 93–97.

Pianta, R. C., Mashburn, A. J., Downer, J. T., Hamre, B. K., & Justice, L. (2008). Effects of webmediated professional development resources on teacher-child interaction in pre-kindergarten classrooms. *Early Childhood Research Quarterly, 23*(4), 431–451.

Quality Interventions for Early Care and Education (QUINCE) Research Team, Delivering and Evaluating On-Site Consultation in a 5-State Collaborative Study, presentation, National Association of Child Care Resource and Referral Agencies Public Policy Conference, March 2009.

Ramey, S., & Ramey, C. (2008). Establishing a science of professional development for early education programs: The Knowledge Application Information Systems theory of professional development. In L. M. Justice & C. Vukelich (Eds.), *Achieving excellence in preschool literacy instruction* (pp. 41–63). New York: Guilford Press.

Schienfeld, D., Haigh, K., & Schienfeld, K. (2008). *We are all explorers: Learning and teaching with Reggio principles in urban settings*. New York: Teachers College Press.

Smith, P. (2006). Evolutional foundations and functions of play: An overview. In A. Goncu & S. Gaskins (Eds.), *Play and development: Evolutionary, sociocultural and functional perspectives* (pp. 21–49). Mahwah, NJ: Lawrence Erlbaum Associates.

Snyder, P., Hemmeter, M. L., Artman, K., Kinder, K., Pasia, C., & McLaughlin, T. (2012). Early childhood professional development: Categorical framework and systematic review of the literature. Manuscript submitted for publication.

Stichter, J., Lewis, T., Richter, M., Johnson, N., & Bradley, L. (2006). Assessing antecedent variables: The effect of instructional variables on student outcomes through in-service and peer coaching professional development models. *Education & Treatment of Children, 29*(4), 665–692.

Stremmel, A. (2012). Reshaping the landscape of early childhood teaching through teacher research. In G. Perry, B. Henderson, & D. Meier (Eds.), *Our inquiry, our practice: Undertaking, supporting and learning from early childhood teacher research(ers)* (pp. 107–116). Washington, DC: NAEYC.

Sylva, K., Sirai-Blatchford, I., & Taggart, B. (2006). *Assessing quality in the early years: Early Childhood Environment Rating Scale (ECERS-E).* London: Trentham Books.

Tout, K., Isner, T., & Zaslow, M. (2011, February). Coaching for quality improvement: Lessons learned from quality rating and improvement systems. Child Trends for the Children's Services Council of Palm Beach County. Retrieved from http://www.childtrends.org/Files/Child_Trends-2011_04_27_FR_CoachingQuality.pdf

Trivette, C., Dunst, C., Hamby, D., & O'Herin, C. (2009). *Characteristics and consequences of adult learning methods and strategies.* (Winterberry Research Synthesis, Vol. 2, No. 2). Asheville, NC: Winterberry Press.

Weber, R., & Trauten, M. (2008). *Effective investments in the child care and early education profession: A review of the recent literature.* Oregon Partnership Research Project, Oregon State University, Family Policy Program. Retrieved from http://www.hhs.oregonstate.edu/hdfs/sites/default/files/Lit_Review.pdf

Whitebook, M., & Ryan, S. (2011). *Degrees in context: Asking the right questions about preparing skilled and effective teachers of young children.* Preschool Policy Brief, 22 (pp. 1–15). National Institute for Early Education Research, New Brunswick, NJ. Retrieved from http://nieer.org/resources/policybriefs/23.pdf

Zaslow, M., Halle, T., Tout, K., & Weinstein, D. (2011). Early childhood professional development definitions and measurement approaches. In C. Howes & R. Pianta (Eds.),(pp. 3–24) *Foundations for Teaching Excellence* (pp. 3–24). Baltimore: Paul. H. Brookes Publishing Co.

Zigler, E. (2009). Foreword. In K. Hirsh-Pasek, R. M. Golinkoff, L. Berk, & D. G. Singer. A mandate for playful learning in preschool (pp. ix–xiii). New York: Oxford University Press

Acknowledgments

Thank you to the early childhood teachers and teacher-educators who helped me understand what adults need in order to learn and grow through professional development. A special thank-you to Barbara Martinez-Griego; Sally Holloway; and the Early Childhood Teacher Preparation Council, Mary Garguile, Barbara Yasui, and Drs. Brenda Boyd; Eileen Hughes; Kristen French; Maria Timmons Flores; and all of the members of the former Seattle-area Culturally Relevant Anti-Bias Leadership Group.

A huge thank you to my editor, Julie Peters, for her guidance.

I would also like to thank the reviewers of this text, including Julie Bullard, University of Montana Western; Erin K. Gallagher, Children's Services Council of Palm Beach; Barbara Haxton, the Ohio Head Start Association; Kim A. Horejs, Fox Valley Technical College; Elisa Huss-Hage, Owens Community College; Flora L. Jenkins, Michigan Department of Education; Diane McCormack Nunez, Rio Salado College; Katherine McCormick, University of Kentucky; Calvin Moore, Jr., JCCEO Head Start; Linda Olivenbaum, California Early Childhood Mentor Program; Mary Perkins, Educational Service District 113; Lindsey Russo, SUNY New Paltz; Bob Sasse, Palomar College; Rosa L. Trapp-Dail, Howard University; and Wendy Valentine, United Way of Massachusetts Bay.

Finally, a special acknowledgement goes out to my grandson, Jack Chu, who inspires me to work to support quality childcare for young children everywhere.

● ●

CHAPTER 1

Relationship-Based Professional Learning

The chapter supports your growing capacity to

- experience the power of reflection;
- define the terms and purposes of relationship-based (RB) professional development (PD);
- identify the roles and functions of a mentor and mentee, or protégé;
- compare the differences and similarities between mentoring and supervising;
- choose ground rules or agreements to structure a learning relationship;
- describe qualities and characteristics of mentoring;
- analyze what matters in relationship-based PD competencies; and
- plan to demonstrate relationship-based PD competencies.

What does it take to have a successful professional-mentoring relationship? How does mentoring fit into professional development that strengthens early childhood teaching and program practices? This chapter examines these questions and the terms, goals, benefits, roles, and responsibilities associated with a collaborative mentoring relationship. Mentoring is also explored as a process occurring in learning pairs of mentor–teacher (i.e., as protégé or mentee), small groups that may contain mentoring teams, and in collegial, colearning relationships. The ways that supervision differs from and is similar to mentoring are examined. Mentor competencies identified in this chapter reflect the knowledge and skills needed to understand teachers in their unique role as learners.

> *"By allowing time with a mentor before class, (childcare) providers were able to share ideas and network with each other. With a focus on building relationships and learning, teachers were more willing to share some of the more difficult aspects of their work. Learners commented on their growth and how their perspectives on child guidance were changing."*
>
> Laurie Cornelius, Clark College, Vancouver, Washington,
> reflecting on the *Bridges to Higher Education* mentoring component
> of child-guidance professional-development college courses, 2007–2008.

Learning About the Learner

● ●

A mentor to early childhood teachers must be a respected, knowledgeable, and experienced person who is skilled in supporting and nurturing the growth of someone who is less experienced. Promoting professional and personal growth involves a collaborative, culturally responsive, and respectful professional relationship. A mentoring relationship begins with listening. Shelly Macy, early childhood teacher–educator from the Northwest Indian College in Bellingham, Washington, notes, "Only after being listened to are practitioners likely to be able to listen to an outside resource. . . . They already have tons of information from their work, and a listener who is interested as they share is invaluable. Listening, listening, listening . . . is especially important where there are cultural differences between mentor and teacher" (Chu, 2008). When the mentor is skilled at observing and listening, the teacher (as protégé, or mentee) tends to feel acknowledged and understood. Then can begin the task of promoting the teacher–researcher skills of analyzing practices and engaging in the ongoing inquiry into the daily work with children and families. A blossoming mentoring relationship begins with learning about the learner.

The power of mentoring lies in individualizing a learning relationship to solve relevant problems in the work or college practicum setting. Mentors, who are open to the point of view of the teacher, (a) alter their strategies to fit the situation, and (b) see themselves as serving others (Rush, Shelden, & Hanft, 2003). Qualities that are needed to accomplish these two very ambitious tasks and that must be recognized by the mentee teacher are competence ("I can learn from you"), flexibility ("I need to talk to you about something not on the plan"), ethicality ("I know you are confidential"), honesty ("I never realized I was doing that"), and most of all, caring ("I like talking to you, too!").

Mentors must have the disposition to learn how to use their influence or professional power *for* the mentee through facilitation of shared learning. Using power *over* a mentee, as when a supervisor directs change to occur, must be clearly differentiated from a process of mentoring involving learner choice. Using power *over* a person may feel to that person more like an oppressive external force (Sullivan, 2010, p. 9) than support for learning.

Finally, *delivering content* without knowing a teacher, a program, a school, or the cultural and community context is the opposite of relationship-based learning. Valuing the accumulated knowledge of children, teachers, programs, and communities is at the heart of a relationship-based mentoring process. When teachers feel that a mentor understands and values their knowledge and skills, they are often more ready to join with the mentor to move toward an imagined future that adds research-based evidence to their resources. To be an effective mentor is to recognize that learning is influenced by and embedded in the lives, values, cultures, and working conditions of the teacher (Opfer & Pedder, 2011, p. 376; Nabobo-Baba & Tiko, 2009).

Experiencing the Power of Reflection

Throughout the chapters, reflective writing and discussion starters are integrated into the text to stimulate you to think about your interests, views, and contributions to the mentoring relationship. The opening questions will help you to identify your current needs and your understanding of the concept of mentoring. Begin now to practice the idea of *parallel process*, or acting in the same way that you want the adult students, colleagues, or teachers whom you supervise or mentor to be treated and to treat others (Scott Heller & Gilkerson, 2009, pp. 11–12). First, reflect and consider the topic of mentoring by responding to the reflection questions throughout each chapter. Here, the concept of *reflection* is used to mean a method of encouraging the process of actively thinking about the knowledge, skills, and practices that a teacher uses. A mentor or coach employs reflection for the purpose of supporting an early childhood teacher's development. Pausing to reflect as you read will prepare you for future mentoring relationships that will require the same sort of process—making visible or discussing often unwritten and unspoken questions and assumptions. In this way, you will practice reflecting on and posing questions before making plans and finding solutions. Identifying your intense interests now will also allow you to move around in the book and find sections that you want to read, based on your current needs.

REFLECTION

Reflecting on the questions that follow will provide you with insight into your own learning needs. *Keep a reflective journal* or write directing in the "reflection" areas as you use this text to explore how mentoring fits into your professional role. Experiencing the power of reflection yourself will support you as you mentor other teachers.

Begin by brainstorming what comes to mind, and supply multiple endings to these sentences.

1. Mentoring is . . . . [or] Mentoring includes . . . .

2. Mentoring is not . . . . [or] Mentoring should not emphasize . . . .

3. Next, compare your brainstormed lists with Table 1.1, and consider the following questions: What did you write that should be included in the table? Do you disagree with anything in the table? Why? What are the areas that you excel in? What do others notice about you that would support the role of mentor? Which ideas in Table 1.1 could you use more information about or more practice in doing?

Understanding the importance of the items in the left-hand column of Table 1.1 ("Mentoring is or should include:") will help mentors to gain the skills and knowledge necessary to grow professional learning relationships with teachers. Likewise, recognizing the pitfalls inherent in the thinking and actions delineated in the column on the right-hand side of Table 1.1 ("Mentoring is not or should not emphasize:") reminds mentors to monitor their practices for an overuse of choices that often break trust and collaboration. Teachers who are seeking to learn and grow as professionals need mentors willing to do the same.

Table 1.1   What Is Mentoring?

Mentoring is or should include:	Mentoring is not or should not emphasize:
• A dynamic process of both challenge and support	• Evaluation
• Relationship building	• Punitive outcomes
• Personal and professional growth	• A high-stakes test
• Formal or informal partnerships	• Direction by others
• Connecting research-based skills and knowledge to new practices	• Excessive information, without time for reflection and discussion
• Culturally responsive practices that respect the accumulated knowledge of cultural groups	• No input from the teacher
	• Only one point of view
• Assisting to develop strategies	• Views in conflict with the values of the cultural and community context
• Observation, reflection, and self-direction	• Technical information without discussion of how to adapt it or apply it
• Setting goals and clarifying expectations	• Harsh or critical communication style
• Accountability and agreement on process by mentor and teacher	• Simple solutions or only one perspective about complex situations
• Understanding the complexities of a teacher's context	• One-size-fits-all approach to delivering discrete skills and knowledge
• Understanding the prior knowledge, beliefs, and experiences of the teacher	• Agreement and harmony all the time
• Periods of disequilibrium	• One-time event without follow-up or application to a work setting
• Searching for practices to fit goals	• Inducing feelings of being overwhelmed, misunderstood, or alone
• Reflecting on dilemmas over time, with frequent feedback	• Prescriptive protocols without explanation or individualization to fit the context of a specific teacher
• Negotiating the frequency, duration, and other aspects of the professional-development process	

REFLECTION

Think about someone who mentored you. Reflect on or discuss the following questions:

1. What did he or she do that you appreciated?

2. What characteristics did he or she have?

3. Was the mentor assigned to you or chosen by you?

....
Connections
....

Revisit the list of topics at the beginning of this chapter. Consider the following questions:

1. What do you hope to learn? What is it about the topic of mentoring and coaching development that interests you?

2. How do you see a mentoring relationship as a part of your current or future work with teachers of young children and families?

3. What are you wondering about?

....

Now, reflect on what you want to discover in the remainder of the chapter. Review the book's table of contents, and check to see whether your interests are explored in other parts of the book.

Definitions, Purposes, and Terms Used in Relationship-Based Professional Development
....

A common characteristic of professional-development methods and roles examined in this book is that they are all *relationship based*. A professional relationship-based approach facilitates program quality improvement by focusing on learning processes that support a teacher's construction of understanding rather than by focusing only on evaluation of skills or on compliance with technical information. In many ways, the approach is similar to working with children, in which case teachers focus on developing children's construction of knowledge rather than focusing only on meeting discrete instructional goals.

Many professions have a period of professional induction or apprenticeship to support the application of foundational knowledge, abilities, and dispositions to the work setting. Examples include an internship at a law firm or a hospital residency in a medical program. In early childhood education, experienced caregivers, teachers, and administrators benefit from an educational approach that incorporates individualized support to encourage observation, critical reflection, multiple perspectives, and new ways of thinking about working with children and families. Bridging practices from course content to implementing these ideas in daily practice usually requires the support of someone with greater knowledge and experience than the teachers possess. Despite a considerable investment of federal, state, and foundation funds in early childhood professional-development activities, most of such activities are still short term and are found to be of limited value (Barnett, Epstein, Friedman, Sansanelli, & Hustedt, 2009). Mentors who model, coplan, and provide feedback—with repeated opportunities to practice strategies—are engaging in practices associated with better retention of new teachers (Darling-Hammond, Hammerness, Grossman, Rust, & Shulman, 2005, p. 409; Goe, 2007) and are key to the implementation of curricula reform (Strickland & Riley-Ayers, 2007).

Researchers and educators have noted a lack of consensus in the field of early childhood education regarding characteristics and definitions of professional-development approaches such as mentoring, coaching, and consultation (Ramey & Ramey, 2005). A lack of common language in the literature has caused confusion about what the purpose and processes are as indicated by various terms. The *mentoring, coaching*, and *consultation* definitions examined in this chapter are based on the glossary of professional development terms (Lutton, 2012, pp. 84–86) developed by the National Association for the Education of Young Children (NAEYC) and the National Association of Child Care Resource and Referral Agencies (NACCRRA). Their work was informed by feedback from early childhood professional-development leaders from 44 states, as well as from prominent research and education organizations and agencies.

However, these terms likely will continue to evolve because different disciplines (e.g., mental health, higher education, workforce development traditions) and program approaches may favor one term over another, even when practitioners are discussing the same strategies for professional development. If we are to value professional and personal diversity and early childhood education's multidisciplinary heritage, then we probably will have to remain comfortable specifically explaining our approaches and philosophy beyond just identifying the terms we use. Documenting mentoring and coaching methods—including their sequence, scope, frequency, duration, and timing—is important for those in our field to be able to evaluate the relative power of each adult instructional choice. Many research studies, however, do not clearly identify what specific mentoring and coaching methods are used with teachers (ACF/0HS/NCQTL, 2012).

This book uses the term *teacher* to refer to all certified teachers, childcare providers, aides, assistants, and other staff who work in early care and education settings. Young children view all adults in their programs as teachers, and this text will share their point of view. The terms *mentee* and *protégé* are used interchangeably. However, this book most often will refer to the *mentor–teacher relationship* as an intentional way of avoiding any association with a subservient or hierarchical mentoring relationship. In the author's experience, many teachers dislike the terms *protégé* and *mentee* and prefer to be thought of as a professional (teacher) joining with another professional (mentor) who is supporting their growth.

Definitions of relationship-based professional development terms used in this book follow.

Mentor: A respected, experienced person who supports and nurtures the growth of someone who is less experienced.

This general term implies a relationship that is longer range, ongoing, and mutually agreeable. Mentoring is " . . . a relationship-based process between colleagues in similar professional roles with a more-experienced individual with adult learning knowledge and skills . . . providing guidance and example to the less-experienced protégé or mentee . . . [that] is intended to increase an individual's personal and professional capacity, resulting in greater professional effectiveness" (Lutton, 2012, p. 84). The mentoring process should involve a mentor–teacher match that is based on a mutual respect for professional, personal, and cultural values and goals. Since 1988, the California Early Childhood Mentor program has trained experienced, qualified early childhood teachers to supervise student teachers who are assigned to the mentors' birth-to-age-five and before- and after-school program classrooms. Selection is based on professional qualifications and a quality review of the mentor's classroom. This book will use the term *mentor* to focus on common strategies that should be foundational to any relationship-based professional-development approach.

Coach: A person with specific expertise or skill who helps identify and develop skill in another.

Although, in general, the term *mentor* is used very broadly, the term *coach* is often employed to identify "a relationship-based process led by an expert with specialized and adult learning knowledge and skills, who often serves in a different professional role than the recipient(s) . . . to build capacity for specific professional dispositions, skills, and behaviors and [who] is focused on goal setting and achievement for an individual or group" (Lutton, 2012, p. 85). The term *coach* is used in the field of sports and in public school educational settings. Many primary schools have a tradition of teachers' supporting their peers by serving part-time as literacy or math coaches. These teachers usually are recognized by their peers as having expertise and educational qualifications in an area in which other teachers are requesting professional development.

Consultant: A person who facilitates the resolution of specific work-related issues involving people or programs.

The term *consultation* is often used in reference to a "collaborative, problem-solving process between an external consultant with specific expertise and adult learning knowledge and skills and an individual or group from one program or organization" (Lutton, 2012, p. 86). Consultation is common also in the areas of physical and mental health and facilitates the "resolution of an issue-specific concern . . . or addresses a specific topic" (p. 86). In Washington State, for example, local county public-health-department nurse consultants are contracted by childcare centers to support infant and toddler teachers to establish and maintain a healthy and safe environment and meet the special health needs of enrolled children. Consultation may be short term to resolve a specific problem or may involve longer term relationships in order to advise a program quality-improvement process. Consultants are often brought into a program during a time of crisis. The author acted as a childcare consultant at a childcare center after a toddler was accidentally scalded by coffee from a teacher's cup. A review of program policies and practices led the center to meet licensing and insurance requirements designed to prevent any further harm to children.

What Category of Professional Development Is This? It Depends on Whom You Ask!

Higher education instructors tend to refer to education that may include seminars combined with field experiences in early childhood programs to describe the category of teaching and learning programs—for both preservice and in-service teachers—that they facilitate. Educational courses leading to college credit often also include research- and evidence-based practices and the underlying history, theory, and philosophy of a subject area that give participants a depth and breadth of understanding. College courses complying with NAEYC's 2- and 4-year degree requirements should be both knowledge oriented and practice focused. This means that a focus on the "application or use of knowledge and skills related to the

(NAEYC) standard" are "best learned, practiced, and assessed in field experiences" (NAEYC, 2012, p. 14). Courses with an explicit focus on practice have been found to have direct positive influences on teachers' use of effective practices (Hamre, et al., 2012).

Instructors from a *training* background (e.g., Child Care Resource and Referral Agency trainers, program specialists in Head Start) usually work with groups of teachers because these groups have specific technical and content knowledge that address an identified need. Trainers tend to use the term *technical assistance* when referring to helping teachers put theory into practice. NAEYC and NACCRRA use *technical assistance* as an overarching term to describe the category of professional development that includes mentoring, coaching, and consultation (Lutton, 2012, p. 83). This book will focus primarily on the skills, knowledge, and related dispositions and competencies needed in a mentoring or coaching professional-development relationship. The term *mentor* will be used when discussing common competencies needed in relationship-based professional learning.

Focus First on the Teaching–Learning Relationship

Mentoring may be only one small part of the many professional responsibilities of experienced teachers, directors, college professors, and others in the field of early childhood education. However, increasing awareness of the power of mentoring in the areas of professional "collaborative problem-solving and change" (Buysse & Wesley, 2005, p. 5) has expanded opportunities for part- and full-time mentoring positions as state and other systems organize around program quality improvement (National Child Care Information and Technical Assistance Center, 2010). Mentoring tends to be least successful when the mentor and/or the teacher do not understand the purpose, role, and goals of relationship-based professional development. Regardless of nuances of the professional-development role as defined by NAEYC and NACCRRA (Lutton, 2012), it is the author's experience that the underlying assumptions about how adults learn affect any approach to a teaching–learning relationship.

Identifying the Roles and Functions of a Mentor and Teacher (as Mentee or Protégé)

Confusion, vagueness, and uncertainty about the roles of mentor and teacher (as mentee or protégé) will cause this form of relationship-based professional development to be less successful. Clear understanding of the roles and responsibilities of each role is essential. Consider the following:

A mentee, or protégé, (referred to as *teacher* in this text) is

- usually less experienced in some professional areas than the mentor is. In other areas, the protégé may be more experienced or knowledgeable.
- a colearner and co-investigator with the mentor.
- responsible for agreeing to work with a mentor.
- interested in sharing his or her learning needs and shaping the process of mentoring.
- willing to participate in professional dialogue or professional development sessions about his or her practices.
- responsible for keeping appointments and commitments with the mentor.
- willing to tell the mentor concerns, frustrations, or questions about the mentoring process.

- willing to detail and negotiate other specifics, as needed.
- interested in joining with another professional whom he or she feels has valuable professional perspectives that support, guide, teach, or facilitate learning.
- committed to improving teaching practices.

This list of mentee, or protégé, characteristics hints at the pitfalls of the mentoring process that can arise when these characteristics and conditions for learning are not present. Learners who have no choice in who mentors them, how they will learn, what topics are explored, or the times and places of the mentor–teacher meetings may not persist in this form of professional development.

Connections

1. Identify ways to share mentoring characteristics with a teacher seeking mentoring for professional development. One way is to embed these characteristics into a mentoring contract that specifies action items for which the mentor and the mentee are responsible. Jot down ideas for communicating mentee expectations.

2. Consider how shared choice and power can be supported even in a strict research-based mentoring protocol. Replicating with fidelity an early-literacy protocol, for example, usually still allows for flexibility in scheduling mentoring meetings. When mentors demonstrate respect for a teacher's basic needs and his or her point of view by listening to concerns and questions, more opportunities for learning about effective practices may arise. How do you think mentee choice might be supported?

Differences and Similarities Between Mentoring and Supervising

The need to foster a safe learning environment requires the mentor and supervisor to be explicit and clear about their unique roles. If the same person is performing both roles (e.g., evaluation of job performance and providing support for learning), it is especially important to identify the function being performed at any one time. In other words, always identify the differences between a suggestion, a choice, and a requirement. Mentors need to be able to answer the questions "Is this a brainstorming session, or am I evaluating you? Is this confidential, or will your response be reported to someone?" Learning and growth are hampered when adults do not feel safe to explore ideas and new practices with a trusted guide.

Mentoring is usually designed as a function very separate from supervision and evaluation in order to allow a teacher to feel comfortable sharing his or her struggles and challenges. However, the reality of many early childhood settings today is that one person may be asked or required to fill both roles. Supervisors acting in the role of mentor and mentors asked to share observations of a teacher's performance should carefully examine potential ethical dilemmas resulting from their acting in the two roles at the same time.

REFLECTION

How would you disclose to a teacher your different roles and functions of mentoring and supervising if you held both roles at the same time? Consider the criteria in Table 1.2 in your response.

Table 1.2   The Different Roles and Functions of Mentoring and Supervising

Mentoring Involves Guiding, Reflection, and Analysis	Supervision Involves Evaluation, Hiring, and Salary Issues
Teachers should know what, if any, parts of their work with mentors are not confidential.	If a mentor has any involvement in hiring, promotion, or other employment-related decisions, it must be disclosed to the teacher.
The role of mentor is not, for example, to evaluate teachers for promotions, but to examine with a teacher an evaluation process that a supervisor will implement.	In a positive program climate, the performance of a teacher is supported through clear division of roles, and transparency in the multiple duties performed by one person. A supervisor acting as a mentor would encourage reflection on a classroom dilemma of the teacher's choice.
Mentoring is also involved in guiding reflection on, for example, a videotape of a teacher managing child transitions to help her to improve proactive guidance strategies.	A supervisor conducting a mandated annual performance review would need to clearly disclose the purpose and function of his or her observations and conversations with the teacher, especially those upon which evaluation will be based.

Clear roles and responsibilities for administrators is one of the important characteristics of high-quality mentoring and induction practices (New Teacher Center, 2011). Supervisors, directors, and administrators also play an important role in supporting teachers in their ongoing on-the-job learning and in their work to increase the buy-in of other staff and stakeholders (Villani, 2009, p. 212). Administrators or supervisors who host internship and practicum students and allow their teachers to act as mentors often reap the benefits of fostering a learning community atmosphere that benefits everyone.

REFLECTION

Write the words *mentor, supervisor, both roles,* and *gaps* across the top of a piece of paper. Divide the paper into four columns under these words. First, brainstorm ideas that apply to the functions, roles, and influences of the different roles of the mentor and supervisor. Then, add ideas that are common to each role. Move items that seem to be common functions or roles into the third column. Finally, consider gaps that neither role provides in supporting the professional development of teachers of young children. Expand on the chart started here as you consider what is needed to support growth in teaching practices. Come back to this chart after you read the entire book, and consider what responses you would add or change.

Professional Development of Teachers in the Context of Supportive Relationships			
Mentor Role	**Supervisor Role**	**Both Roles**	**Gaps**
Guiding, facilitating	Evaluating, hiring, and firing	Modeling ethical and effective practices	Peer support as colearners

Review what you have written. Check to see whether the following apply:

SOME CHARACTERISTICS ARE THE SAME

The differences between these two roles may have been hard to distinguish, because a supervisor may also be a mentor. Both roles involve modeling ethical practices, which should improve program quality and teacher skills. Professionals in the mental health field, infant-toddler specialists, and other family-support professionals working with young children are increasingly looking at reflective supervision (Scott Heller & Gilkerson, 2009) as a way to encourage staff to think about and learn how to use their interpersonal skills most effectively. More broadly, supporting informal and formal professional apprenticeships has been a longstanding practice for teachers who educate young children. The influences of the program or the community context on the roles of mentor and supervisor may also include emerging leadership positions, which include combinations of both roles or roles that have some areas of overlap (Elliott et al. 2000, p. 13). The bottom line is that the teacher, as mentee, must understand the roles and functions of each person in order to feel safe enough to learn.

MANY CHARACTERISTICS ARE DIFFERENT

Although a supervisor may use mentoring techniques, the role of supervisor may conflict or interfere with mentoring or with the desire to explore multiple perspectives on a topic. The need on the part of the teacher mentee to speak openly could be hampered by his or her knowledge that the supervisor has the responsibility to hire, fire, promote, evaluate, and make other employment judgments regarding the teacher. Although a mentor who is not the protégé's supervisor may be involved in assessment of the performance of the adult with whom he or she is working, the mentor does not usually have the same power as the supervisor or use assessment information for the same purpose. Mentors may assess what a teacher understands and make evaluations to promote improved practices with children, whereas supervisors often evaluate teachers for purposes of promotion or demotion.

IDENTIFY BROAD GOALS FOR AN EFFECTIVE LEARNING RELATIONSHIP

Although the specific goals of early childhood teacher-mentoring programs will vary, the broad goals often include

1. promoting professional and personal growth in the context of a collaborative, culturally responsive, and respectful professional learning relationship;
2. strengthening the teacher's ability to join with others, solve problems, and construct knowledge through a process of listening, observing, dialogue, analysis, reflection, and ongoing inquiry into the teacher's daily work with children and families;
3. supporting the teacher as a learner and a professional as he or she develops and maintains the ability to solve problems in his or her work setting by applying research or evidence-based promising practices. The evidence may also come from his or her own teacher research or may be obtained by applying and adapting strategies successfully used by other teachers in similar settings.

Specific outcomes from these overall goals may be in improved classroom practice, improved program quality, and more positive developmental outcomes for children. Additionally, administrators who value teacher professional development may support staff retention and facilitate credential or degree attainment through partnerships with institutions of higher education (Lindsey, Martinez, & Lindsey, 2007; National Child Care Information and Technical Assistance Center, 2010; Rush & Shelden, 2005). Mentoring and coaching, as part of a wider professional development plan, holds the promise of encouraging a teacher to achieve individual career goals as well.

Ground Rules or Policies to Structure a Learning Relationship

Vagueness in the mentoring process often causes conflict because the mentor and the teacher may make very different assumptions about the nature of their learning expectations. Modeling the process that is intended to engage members of a mentor–teacher learning relationship or learning community begins with brainstorming the ground rules.

REFLECTION

Complete this sentence: If I am part of a learning relationship (mentor–teacher) or participating in a group course or learning community, then supporting other learners and my own learning means that I hope we will . . .

Now, compare the list that follows to your initial thoughts as a way to further reflect on what conditions need to be present for a safe and supportive learning context. Add or delete items from the following ideas to create a *learning partnership agreement*.

Learning Partnership Agreement Guidelines

- Be present and participate.
- Give respect to others.
- Recognize power differences.
- Be open to learning about differences.
- Be confidential.
- Listen, pause, and allow others to speak.
- Have information in languages other than English.
- Encourage others.
- Avoid turning concerns into gossip.
- Understand that mentoring requires feeling safe to share.
- Consider a new point of view.
- Support inclusive learning conditions.
- Acknowledge that misunderstandings require opening up to another's perspective.
- Stay for the agreed period.

These ideas may be considered *ground rules*, or guidelines, for successful learning partnerships.

- **Be present and participate**. There are many ways to engage in learning, including listening and discussing. Join in the learning by participating. This usually means finding a place for discussion that is safe from distractions which pull you away from dialogue and reflection.
- **Give respect to others.** Allow others to express their points of view. Be open to hearing the observation that you may have stopped others from participating or did not understand cultural expectations or other protocol.
- **Recognize power differences.** If you are a supervisor, are an instructor, or have professional power over another person in the learning relationship, recognize that your position of power involves a responsibility to be sensitive to a protégé's occasional reluctance to participate. Taking the risk to try something new may result in a variety of feelings and consequences. Identify the intent, purpose, and nature of your relationship. Will this mentoring process result in an impact on an employment evaluation, a grade in a course, licensing of a program, and/or an inquiry into a topic area? Be clear about all of the professional hats you are wearing, and be open to negotiating the goals of the mentoring relationship. Try to understand and remember the risks that a protégé takes on when entering into a mentoring relationship. Avoid having hidden agendas.

- **Be open to learning about differences.** Wonder about practices or perspectives that are new to you. Remember, reflection and discussion before action are central to the learning process in a mentoring relationship.
- **Be confidential.** What is shared should not be discussed in other places. Information and issues about children, families, staff, and programs are confidential. Review and refer to the *NAEYC Code of Ethical Conduct and Statement of Commitment* (2011).
- **Listen, pause, and allow others to speak**. Turn off cell phones and other technological devices, and be present when engaged in dialogue with another person. Discuss whether serving food or finding other ways to make participants feel comfortable will facilitate or impede your work. Be sensitive and aware of cultural expectations. Ask, for example, whether eating while another person is speaking or otherwise presenting his or her concerns is appropriate. Is "talking over" someone rude or the way to brainstorm ideas? Notice and ask others what has been problematic for them in the past, and request that they tell you if a communication barrier begins to develop.
- **Arrive on time, and stay for the agreed period.** Communicate if you are going to be late or cannot meet. Know how to contact each other in case of emergency.
- **Understand and support the need for participants to have information in languages other than English.** Mentors need to represent the languages and cultures of the community of children and families in any area. This means that future adult mentors should represent the diversity of the community. Recognize that a diverse mentoring and learning community is an asset for everyone's learning. This may require simultaneous translation or other ways of allowing all participants to use their dominant language.
- **Avoid turning concerns into negative gossip.** Use constructive comments or make suggestions directed at the source of your concern. This means directing concerns to an individual or to the professional development group rather than to persons outside of your mentoring or learning community. When concerns are about persons outside of the group, focus on seeking suggestions for examining the problem (e.g., an issue of supervisors who seem unsupportive) rather than naming specific persons. Harming an individual's reputation is not the focus of professional development. Seeking solutions to familiar and common workplace and professional problem scenarios should be the goal.
- **Consider a new point of view** as something to challenge your usual ways of thinking and doing.
- **Encourage others.**
- **Support inclusive learning conditions.**
- **When misunderstandings occur, open yourself to another's perspective and try to repair your relationship**. If you have a strong emotional response to a conversation, communicate to others that you need time to become calm before rejoining the discussion. Recognize that it takes time for trust and understanding to be built.
- **Remember that the mentoring process begins only when participants feel safe to learn.** Take responsibility for your part of establishing a comfortable learning climate.

The Learning Community Agreements in *Soy Bilingue: Adult Dual Language Model* (Cronin, 2008) include more specific ground rules that identify inclusive practices which are especially supportive in diverse and multilingual learning groups (pp. 28, 29).

REFLECTION

Which of the previous ground rules do you find very important? Why? Do you have a list of other ground rules from past learning experiences that you want to share? What made them effective? How were they used? Have you ever had to backtrack and develop new ground rules after conflict or confusion occurred?

Be present and participate. Arrive and stay for the agreed period.	Give respect to others.	Recognize power differences. Remember the mentoring process begins only when participants feel safe to learn.	Consider a new point of view as something to challenge your usual ways of thinking and doing.
Listen, pause, and allow others to speak.	Be confidential.	Be open to learning about differences.	Encourage others.
When misunderstandings occur, open yourself to another's perspective and try to repair your relationship.	Avoid turning concerns into negative gossip.	Understand and support the need for participants to communicate and have information in languages other than English.	Draw on others' experiences to inspire your ground rules to support inclusive learning conditions.

Qualities and Characteristics of Mentors

As you read the list that follows, consider the teaching–learning relationship strengths that you have. Use the list to support your thinking. Add strengths not listed. How do the personal characteristics and skills associated with successful learning partnerships support you in the role of mentor? In which areas do you need to grow? What qualities do you share with any persons who mentored you?

REFLECTION

Learning partnerships are more successful when mentors have a growing capacity for the characteristics shown in italic in the boxes that follow. What specific strengths do you have? Underline your strengths, and add any others not listed after each description.

Caring and accepting. Engages with others in caring and accepting ways. Is humble and establishes a warm and positive climate needed to help others feel safe to teach and learn. Promotes supportive working relationships. Accepts himself or herself and is comfortable stating what he or she does and does not know. Enjoys the success of others.

Responsiveness. Joins with others to discover what and how they prefer to learn. Is able to plan, organize, and manage work in response to the needs of others. Honestly acknowledges the feelings, challenges, and frustrations of being a teacher or a learner. Is persistent and is able to model ways to overcome challenges to achieve jointly agreed-upon goals.

Reliability. Is willing to commit to work collaboratively with others over time to solve problems of teaching practice. Uses the time of others well by meeting commitments and being prepared. Honestly states what participation or support is possible and what resources are available.

Establishing equal partnerships. Has a vision of exemplary teaching practice that embraces diversity and promotes social justice. Recognizes that how he or she thinks is influenced by his or her experiences and cultural, gender, race, ethnicity, and social-class background. Connects and networks with others. Understands that the role of the mentor is to support others in achieving their goals.

Curiosity. Is able to reflect with integrity and insight upon decisions and actions. Has a passion for pursuing connections, implications, and relationships among ideas and how they relate to practices. Has skills or interest in learning how to facilitate a process of inquiry, observation, and reflection.

Changing strategies as needed. Helps others to engage in changing practices by understanding the many ways that adults learn. Conveys high expectations with encouragement for achieving them. Knows that conflicts may sometimes occur and that relationships can be repaired. Understands the process of change and the possible consequences of change in group and program settings.

Communicating in many ways. Is able to explain purposes, intentions, plans, and goals. Gives instructive feedback sandwiched with positive and reflective comments. Speaks the language and understands the culture(s) of the local community, or partners with others who do.

Respected and respectful. Displays high integrity and is worthy of the role of professional mentor, as identified by many members in the local early childhood community. Understands professional confidentiality. Has clear professional boundaries.

Professional. Follows professional codes of ethics. Demonstrates knowledge of codes and standards and is competent in specific areas of professional content. Partners with others who have expertise and experience that the mentor does not have. Knows community resources. Models having balance in his or her professional life and personal life.

Qualities needed may be found in one mentor, a peer mentor, or in groups of mentors and teachers. Mentor–teacher interactions should facilitate teaching–learning environments that foster the use of both the emotional resources and the intellectual capacities of the participants. The application of both the feeling and thinking sides of individuals to the overall goals of collaborative problem-solving is at the heart of the power of mentoring.

Mandated Professional Development

Sometimes, the ideal start to a mentoring or coaching relationship does not occur. When a teacher is identified as struggling or is employed in a program that has been evaluated as deficient, required professional development may begin in an atmosphere that feels strained at best. Teachers may be defensive as they wrestle with reconciling their image of themselves as caring and capable with an outside evaluation that challenges that long-held positive view of their capacity. What is the role of the professional providing targeted coaching in such a situation? The qualities of being caring, accepting, responsive, respectful, confidential, and acting as a professional (among other characteristics) are needed even more in such a context. Consider this scenario:

Silence falls over the group of 10 teachers at the monthly staff meeting as they see the early childhood education coach enter the room.

Coach: Hi, everyone. As you know, your director invited me here today to discuss some issues identified during your program's annual performance review. I know these are not the conditions that you wanted to see me about. In the past, you have chosen the professional development areas to focus on.

Tonight, we are required to examine the topics of medication management and child health records. However, the process that I propose we use is the same as in the past when you have chosen the topics.

Let's problem-solve which one of several choices that I will present to you is the best way to comply with specific health guidelines. The end result is mandated, but the way we get there needs to fit this program. Also remember—all programs have deficiencies, and your willingness to examine your practices really says a lot about all of you as professionals who care deeply about the children in your care.

The goal for our meeting tonight and for the follow-up coaching sessions in the next several weeks is to create and then implement a written plan with these sections:

1. Description of the practices we need to address.
2. Proposed timeline to meet all health and safety requirements.
3. Identification of responsibility for specific staff to take leadership on correcting past practices and establishing new ones.
4. Documentation plan to address the changes that will put the program in compliance with health and safety standards.

But before we get started, does anyone have any comments or suggestions?

Mary: Yes. I think they are way too picky about these things, but I am willing to learn.

Sue: I agree, but since I want the parents to know that we are doing everything we should, I think this will be helpful. You can never be too safe when young children are involved.

Lonnie: I have questions about our playground. Will we have time to talk about other safety areas?

Coach: How about if I pass out these blank cards, and you jot down anything that you are wondering about? I promise that we will examine all of the areas which you want to discuss by the end of our several weeks of group coaching sessions. Does that sound like a good way to start?

REFLECTION

How did this coach set the boundaries on planned learning while still respecting these teachers as adult learners? Do you have any additional suggestions for this coach? Have you ever been in a situation like this, as a supervisor, as a professional-development provider, or as a teacher? How did you feel? What helped and what did not help you to participate effectively in a mandated professional development experience?

Backward Planning: Consider Where You Have Been in Order to Plan for Where You Want to Be

1. Review the list of positive mentor interaction descriptors that follows. The descriptors fall into one of three categories: feelings (attitudes, dispositions), thinking (knowledge), or applying (skills, actions).

   As you read this list, consider to which category each descriptor relates, and write each of them into a box. A sample item has been inserted. Why did you make these choices? Which ones are your strengths? Which ones are areas that you want to grow in? Do some descriptors belong in more than one column? Do you have other ways of categorizing these descriptors that better reflect a local set of values for a particular community? Identify a few descriptors that you want to explore more in the coming chapters.

Feelings: Using my heart (attitudes, dispositions)	**Thinking:** Using my head (knowledge)	**Applying** it to my setting: Using my hands (skills/actions)
• Empathic	• Able to plan, organize, and manage	• Interested in problem-solving

Characteristics of Effective Mentors: Put descriptors into the feeling, thinking, or applying boxes.

• Drive to make a difference	• Persistence and energy	• Knowing what you know and what you don't know	• Respectful, open, caring
• Aware of own values and beliefs	• Able to plan, organize, and manage	• Interested in getting to know, listening, and building trust with others	• Speaks the language and shares cultural and other knowledge and skills of a local community
• Flexible	• Positive attitude and self-concept	• Has specific professional content knowledge, experience, and expertise	• Ethical
• Makes learning engaging	• Empathic	• Reflective	• Analytical

• Knowledgeable	• Disciplined	• Shares power with others	• Curious
• Humble	• Accepting and fair	• Interested in problem solving	• Willing to work with others
• Experienced in making programs work	• Repairs relationships when conflict occurs	• Able to bridge theory or content ideas into daily practices	• Enjoys facilitating others' growth and development

2. Think of an instance in which a mentor and supervisor is the same person. How is that person in his or her supervisory role able to support a staff's professional growth? Describe a situation in which a person's holding both roles might cause conflict in multiple areas. What considerations does a supervisor need to have to also act as a mentor? If you are the protégé, what do you want from a mentor who is also your supervisor?

3. Jot down what comes to mind when you consider completing these statements:
   • People who know me tell me that I am good at . . .
   • I realize that my strengths are . . .
   • Areas that I want to learn more about are . . .
   • Areas that I struggle with are . . .

4.   Mentors and protégés bring past experiences, professional qualifications, skills, and knowledge to learning relationships. Briefly jot down skills or knowledge that relate to the areas in the list that follows. Note what comes to mind first, and complete the sentences.
   • My strength in promoting child development and learning is . . .
   • My strength in observing and documenting child learning is . . .
   • My strength in facilitating or designing teaching and learning experiences for young children in specific content is (math, literacy, creative arts, social or physical development, etc.) . . .
   • My strength in working with families and my local community is . . .

Jot down responses to questions 2, 3, and 4 in the provided space.

Understanding What Matters in Relationship-Based Professional Development Competencies

Participants representing all parts of the early childhood education field identified, in focus groups in 2009 and 2010, the need for core competencies in those who provide professional development (PD) as one of the most urgent PD issues today (NAEYC, 2011, p. 18). Although this text shares in every chapter specific research-based mentoring and related relationship-based practices, no nationally accepted, single set of mentoring or related competencies exists to date. To begin the conversation of *what matters most* for these professionals would require an examination of perhaps the most frequently used set of existing relationship-based competencies. The Minnesota Center for Professional Development (2009a), updating and expanding on the work of MN SMART (Minnesota Sharehouse, Mentoring, Assistance, Resources, Training, 2005), adopted core competencies for mentoring, coaching, consultation, and technical assistance (i.e., relationship-based professional development practices, or RBPD).

These general RBPD core competencies, along with guidelines for professionalism, address the general skills, knowledge, attitudes, and behaviors that lay the foundation for developing a professional relationship. The five areas are adult learning, building relationships, assessment and planning, communication, and change. The guiding principles include professional development and responsibility areas. The original MN SMART work (2005) involved the review of effective curricula and current research conducted to identify and align competencies for RBPD with childcare and youth-care staff. The competencies were field tested by enlisting 97 mentors, coaches, and/or consultants to complete a survey about the relevance of the competencies and their usefulness for practitioners.

The area of cultural competency, embedded in the *building relationships* area, is described as "integrating cross-cultural awareness and divergent points of view" and using "an individualized, culturally competent approach." However, this is an area in which indigenous and diverse conceptualizations of mentoring and coaching have greatly expanded on these basic notions. After working with three major early childhood mentoring and leadership programs from 1997 to 2003, Cecelia Alvarado identified a major lesson learned as the need to "reflect the experiences, models, values, behavioral norms, and aspirations of the particular community that is engaged . . . (in mentoring and leadership development)" (2004, p. 38). Lindsey, Martinez, & Lindsey's (2007) notion of *culturally proficient coaching* suggests the expansion of these competencies to include being educationally responsive to diverse populations by reflecting on necessary values, beliefs, and behaviors that foster cross-cultural interaction in unbiased environments. Nabobo-Baba & Tiko caution that "when it comes to understanding mentoring, there is a need for cultural analysis to examine how mentoring is perceived, theorized, and experienced in . . . specific indigenous context(s). . ." (2009, p. 76). Chapter 2 continues to explore concepts of cultural competence with application to the role of the mentor.

As you read the competencies in Figure 1.1, remember that these are knowledge and skills that will be developed over an entire career. Professionals are always in the process of growing and learning and never fully achieve them. Relationship-based professionals continually seek to grow their own abilities as well as those of others. The awareness that we are all involved in a dynamic, shifting, and ever-changing process of learning may help mentors to model acceptance of their own strengths and struggles in order to fill in their gaps in understanding, thereby supporting the same in others.

Figure 1.1 General Core Competencies for Relationship-Based Professional Development (RBPD)
....

General Knowledge and Skills
Content Area I: Adult Learning
Competency

- Demonstrates ability to apply motivational strategies in relationship-based (RB) settings
- Demonstrates a partnership model when planning and designing goals and improvement plans
- Acknowledges and builds on the experience and knowledge that *adults** bring to the RB setting
- Facilitates opportunities for adult to practice new learning before integrating new knowledge into daily activities
- Provides opportunities for adult to integrate new learning into his or her current setting, experience, and knowledge base
- Lays the groundwork for transfer of learning by providing materials and activities that promote ongoing learning and the development of learning communities
- Demonstrates a commitment to shared learning *and co-inquiry* by utilizing a feedback *and dialogue* process that is strength focused**
- Facilitates a comfortable learning environment that acknowledges all contributions
- Provides adult interactions that are tailored to individual learning styles and preferences
- Incorporates a process of goal setting and ongoing review of goals

Content Area II: Building Relationships
Competency

- Uses positive *and culturally relevant* "people skills" to develop a respectful and responsive relationship with adults***
- Demonstrates respect for and interest in the individual abilities of others
- Partners with adult to identify learning and communicating styles and preferences
- Demonstrates feelings of care and empathy that are strength based and focused on positive change when working with adult
- Provides support as needed by adult while maintaining professional boundaries in the RBPD relationship
- Demonstrates a commitment to the concept of shared learning by utilizing strategies that encourage sharing, joint problem-solving, and developing partnerships

- Demonstrates an individualized, culturally competent approach to the relationship
- Demonstrates cultural proficiency in integrating cross-cultural awareness and divergent points of view

Content Area III: Assessment and Planning
Competency
- Uses strategies and appropriate tools to objectively observe the adult and the program
- Provides reliable *evidence-based* data to adult****
- Uses multiple strategies and tools to assess the adult's and the program's improvement needs and to develop measurable goals
- Provides adult with the skills and tools necessary to self-evaluate and the opportunity to discuss and analyze findings
- Supports adult in using relevant data to prioritize needs and develop personal and professional goals
- Provides assistance and tools for continuously evaluating adult's personal progress and the progress of the program toward goals
- Provides guidance in making *mid-course adjustments* to goals
- Uses reflective practices to reexamine actions and feelings expressed by adult

Content Area IV: Communication
Competency
- Demonstrates active and responsive listening techniques with adult
- Utilizes a range of effective communication techniques designed to address both verbal and nonverbal communication with adult
- Asks *what, where, when, who,* and *how* questions to clarify beliefs, thoughts, and actions
- Demonstrates ability to facilitate the RBPD process of timely goal-focused meetings and conversations
- Strategically identifies possible conflicts and addresses them through positive conflict-management strategies

Content Area V: Change
Competency
- Demonstrates ability to respond effectively to adult's ever-changing needs through planning for and managing change
- Identifies and utilizes a variety of tools based on the adult's stage of development and approach to change
- Demonstrates understanding that improvement is continuous and not static
- Understands the impact that learning has on the dynamics of the change process
- Demonstrates the ability to manage and facilitate change
- Understands conflict management and demonstrates resolution strategies

Guidelines for Conduct and Professional Responsibilities
Content Area I: Professional Development
Competency
- Demonstrates knowledge and competence in specific content area, quality standards, and best practices in field related to specific discipline
- Advocates, supports, and works towards implementation of industry standards of quality
- Demonstrates personal leadership in the field through ongoing education and field building
- Demonstrates knowledge of codes and licensing regulations

Content Area II: Professional Relationships
Competency
- Articulates and follows a code of ethics for making personal and professional decisions
- Maintains confidentiality in all areas, especially when discussing issues and solving problems

- Demonstrates ethical and professional behavior that includes trustworthiness and individual integrity
- Addresses needs of adult without personal bias of values, beliefs, prejudices, and past experiences
- Uses reflective practices to reexamine actions and feelings expressed by adult

---

Note: The MN SMART competencies were reviewed by 20 Washington State community college administrators of an early childhood mentoring and college course program known as *Bridges to Higher Education* (Chu, 2008). This group suggested the following changes:
*The term *client* is replaced by *adult* throughout the competencies.
**The terms *co-inquiry* and *dialogue* are added.
***The term *culturally relevant* is added.
****The term *evidence-based* is added.
The competencies do not identify the education and experience needed in specific early childhood education content areas (e.g., child development). The purpose of these competencies is to identify the relationship-based adult teaching and learning knowledge and skills required by an effective mentor, coach, or consultant.
Adapted with permission of the Minnesota Center for Professional Development. (2009a). *General core competencies for relationship-based professional development.* St. Paul, MN: Metropolitan State University. Retrieve at http://www.mncpd.org under the tab "Relationship Based Professional Development" and scroll down to "General Core Competencies."

REFLECTION

Save your responses to the following questions, and use them as a needs assessment to support your learning as you read this book. Reread the RBPD core competencies. Put a check next to the competencies that you feel you understand and are able to demonstrate.

1. Now, go back to the checked competencies, and ask yourself the following questions:
   - How deeply do I understand these competencies? Jot down one response for each: (w) well, (sw) somewhat, or (?) not sure.
   - How frequently am I able to demonstrate related skills and behaviors when working with adults in a professional learning relationship? Jot down one response for each: (c) consistently, (st) sometimes, or (r) rarely.
2. Consider the competencies that you did not check. Which ones do you feel that you do not understand? Which ones do you understand, but you have little or no experience in doing? Does your assessment of your skills and knowledge vary from setting to setting or with different individuals? Jot down in each of the six boxes that follow several competency content area activities that you want to understand or to be able to demonstrate more consistently.

I want to learn more about:	
Adult Learning	**Building Relationships**
Change	**Communication**

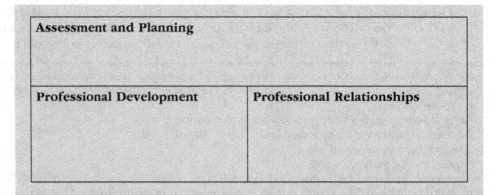

3. Do you think that education and experiences aligned with these competencies would support more responsive relationship-based practices for individuals acting as mentors, coaches, or consultants in early childhood-education fields?

4. Professional organizations, researchers, practitioners, and individuals in other professional systems are involved in developing and revising competencies for various roles as new evidence and awareness of the needs of the field arise. What would you add to or change in these RBPD competencies to include more areas of cultural competence, evidence-based practices, and inquiry-focused learning?

Plan to Demonstrate Relationship-Based PD Competencies* for Mentors or Coaches

How might a mentor or a coach demonstrate competence or identify areas for improvement? One way is to gather evidence that demonstrates relationship-based PD competencies in action. The evidence can then be examined for the promotion of change over time in teacher practices and organizational supports for those practices. Begin by writing a competency goal statement. Identify one competency and ways to gather evidence that link mentoring or coaching activities and behaviors to the competency goal. An example of a goal statement is as follows:

The mentor is able to demonstrate the ability to build relationships *(competency area) through* goal setting *(specific activity) by* taking anecdotal notes *(way to gather evidence) of the* weekly dialogue with the teacher and director *(observable behaviors).*

Create and document a goal that is observable or measurable by going through the next steps.

1. *Choose a competency area, a specific mentoring activity, and a way to gather evidence of change over time in that competency.* Multiple sources of evidence should be used to document mentor or coach behaviors and link them to the relationship-based PD competencies when working with teachers and/ or organizations. Evidence of competency could be gathered across different

mentoring and coaching projects and compiled into a showcase portfolio to document a range of abilities, skills, and knowledge demonstrated across competency areas. Choices include

✓ on-site anecdotal notes or other written observations of a mentor or coach;

✓ video documentation;

✓ narrative summary of coaching activities and processes with related outcomes;

✓ satisfaction surveys completed by teachers and program participants;

✓ interviews of teachers, administrators, and others;

✓ self-assessment by mentor or coach;

✓ identifying specific behaviors to highlight competency and document outcomes of work with teachers; and

✓ other ways to document work with teachers and organizations that demonstrate mentoring and coaching abilities, skills, and knowledge over time.

2. *Choose a relationship-based PD competency area, and document a specific activity.*

Adult Learning	Building Relationships
✓ uses motivational strategies ✓ partners to plan, design goals, and improve plans ✓ builds on experience and knowledge ✓ integrates new learning into setting, experience, and knowledge base ✓ promotes ongoing learning ✓ develops learning communities ✓ uses co-inquiry process ✓ utilizes a strength-based dialogue process ✓ facilitates comfortable learning environment ✓ acknowledges all contributions ✓ individualizes interactions to meet needs ✓ engages in ongoing review of goals	✓ uses positive and culturally relevant skills ✓ demonstrates respect and interest ✓ learns communication styles and preferences ✓ offers strength-based care and empathy ✓ maintains professional boundaries ✓ encourages joint problem-solving ✓ offers individualized, culturally competent approaches ✓ respects divergent points of view

Change Process	Communication
✓ supports planning/managing change ✓ engages in improvement cycles ✓ manages and facilitates change ✓ understands conflict management	✓ applies active, responsive listening techniques ✓ employs effective communication techniques ✓ clarifies beliefs, thoughts, and actions ✓ engages in timely goal-focused conversations ✓ applies positive conflict-management strategies

Assessment and Planning
✓ uses appropriate tools to objectively observe teacher and program ✓ uses reliable evidence-based data

✓ assesses adult and program improvement needs and develops measurable goals
✓ uses skills and tools to self-evaluate
✓ discusses and analyzes findings
✓ uses relevant data to prioritize needs
✓ develops personal and professional goals
✓ continuously evaluates personal and program progress toward goals
✓ supports adjustments to goals
✓ uses reflective practices to reexamine actions and feelings

Professional Development	Professional Relationships
✓ knows specific content areas, quality standards, and evidence-based practices ✓ knows standards of quality ✓ links to ongoing PD and resources for program improvement ✓ has knowledge of codes and licensing regulations ✓ facilitates both teacher and program improvement	✓ understands and uses a code of ethics ✓ abides by confidentiality requirements ✓ avoids bias in language/beliefs ✓ uses reflective practices to reexamine actions and feelings ✓ has a written agreement clarifying role, responsibilities, and processes

*Adapted with permission of the Minnesota Center for Professional Development. (2009a). *General core competencies for relationship based professional development*. St. Paul, MN: Metropolitan State University. Retrieve at http://www.mncpd.org under the tab "Relationship Based Professional Development" and scroll down to "General Core Competencies."

3. *Write a goal statement in the following format:*
   The mentor or coach is able to demonstrate the ability to _____ (competency area) _____ (specific activity) by _____ (way to gather evidence) of _____ _____ (observable behaviors).
4. *Create an action plan, and document evidence.*
   How will you specifically implement the goal and record evidence of working toward it? Create basic questions to answer when you visit and dialogue with a teacher. Examples are as follows:
   • What occurred during the visit?
   • What did the teacher and children say and do?

If your goal is related to communication strategies, for example, then document those used with the teacher. Choices might include paraphrasing, clarifying, problem-solving, and demonstrating. Recording progress toward goals should include noting short- or long-term changes in the teacher or children's behaviors. Finally, think about the overall impact of your involvement by reflecting on what seemed to work well and what you want to do differently next time. Having evidence of mentoring or coaching competencies demonstrates that the PD professional has the tools to help other adults to implement interventions supporting early childhood education quality.

Summary

This first chapter encourages the reader to experience the power of reflection by actively writing about or discussing with others what it means to foster a relationship based on teacher learning and professional development. Understanding mentoring terms and purposes, clarifying roles and functions, identifying goals and ground rules, and valuing the qualities and characteristics related to fostering effective learning relationships is foundational to beginning a mentoring relationship.

Finally, it is important to also consider what matters most in relationship-based professional-development competencies. Continue to explore and reflect on the nature of the adult professional learning relationship, and revisit what you have learned in Chapter 1 by examining Figure 1.2. What are some challenges and ways to strengthen mentoring relationships through attention to these key concepts?

Figure 1.2   Summary of Concepts Explored in Chapter 1

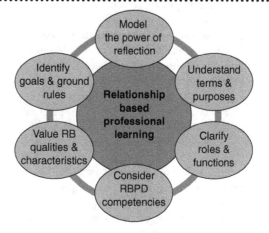

References

Administration for Children and Families (ACF), Office of Head Start (OHS), & National Center on Quality Teaching and Learning (NCQTL). (2012a, May). *What do we know about coaching?* Retrieved from http://eclkc.ohs.acf.hhs.gov/hslc/tta-system/teaching/docs/What-Do-We-Know-About-Coaching.pdf

Alvarado, C. (2004). Authentic leadership: Lessons learned on the journey to equity. *Zero to Three, 25,* 32–39.

Barnett, W. S., Epstein, D. J., Friedman, A. H., Sansanelli, R., & Hustedt, J. T. (2009). *The state of preschool 2009: State preschool yearbook.* New Brunswick, NJ: National Institute for Early Education Research, Rutgers University.

Building Bridges to Higher Education. (2008). Washington State Department of Early Learning (WA. State D.E.L.). Unpublished Curriculum. Contact WA State D.E.L. at P.O. Box 40970, Olympia, WA. 98504-0970 or 1-866-482-4325 or communications@del.wa.gov

Buyssee, V., & Wesley, P. (2005). *Consultation in Early Childhood Settings.* Baltimore, MD: Paul H. Brookes Publishing Co.

California Early Childhood Mentor Program. San Francisco, CA: City College. Retrieved from http://www.ecementor.org

Chu, M. (2008). *Bridges with Higher Education* (2007–2008): Grantees' annual report survey to the Washington Department of Early Learning. Unpublished data for program. Contact: M. Chu, Western Washington University, 501 High Street, Bellingham, WA 98225.

Cronin, S. (Ed.). (2008). *Soy Bilinuge: Adult dual language model for early childhood and elementary teacher education.* Seattle, WA: Center for Linguistic and Cultural Democracy.

Darling-Hammond, L., Hammerness, K., Grossman, P., Rust, F., & Shulman, L. (2005). The design of teacher education programs. In L. Darling-Hammond & H. Bransford (Eds.), *Preparing teachers for a changing world: What teachers should learn and be able to do* (pp. 390–441). San Francisco, CA: Jossey-Bass.

Elliott, K., Farris, M., Alvarado, C., Peters, C., Surr, W., Genser, A., & Chin, E. (2000). *The power of mentoring. Taking the lead: Investing in early childhood leadership for the 21st century.* Report of the Center for Development in Early Care and Education, Wheelock College, Boston, MA.

Goe, L. (2007). *The link between teacher quality and student outcomes: A research synthesis.* Washington, DC: National Comprehensive Center for Teacher Quality.

Hamre, B., Pianta, R., Burchinal, M., Field, S., Locasale-Crouch, J., Downer, J., et al. (2012). A course on effective teacher-child interactions: Effects on teacher beliefs, knowledge, and observed practice. *American Education Research Journal, 49,* 88–123.

Lindsey, D. B., Martinez, R. S., & Lindsey, R. B. (2007). *Culturally proficient coaching: Supporting educators to create equitable schools.* Thousand Oaks, CA: Corwin Press.

Lutton, A. (Ed.). (2012). *Advancing the profession: NAEYC standards and guidelines for professional development.* Washington, DC: NAEYC.

Minnesota Center for Professional Development. (2009a). *General core competencies for relationship based professional development.* St. Paul, MN: Metropolitan State University. Retrieve at http://www.mncpd.org under the tab "Relationship Based Professional Development" and scroll down to "General Core Competencies."

Minnesota Center for Professional Development. (2009b). *Guidelines for conduct and professional responsibilities.* St. Paul, MN: Metropolitan State University. Retrieve at http://www.mncpd.org under the tab "Relationship Based Professional Development" and scroll down to "Guidelines for Conduct and Professional Responsibilities."

MN SMART (Sharehouse, Mentoring, Assistance, Resources, Training), Minnesota Department of Human Services. (2005, June). *Growing smarter: Understanding and planning for relationship-based professional development among child and youth care providers in Minnesota.* Retrieved from http://mnsmart.metrostate.edu/docs/MNSMART_Final_Report.swf

Nabobo-Baba, U., & Tiko, L. (2009). Indigenous Fijian cultural conceptions of mentoring and related capacity building: Implications for teacher education. In A. Gibbons & C. Gibbs (Eds.), *Conversations on early childhood teacher education: Voices from the working forum for teacher education* (pp. 73–81). Redmond, WA: World Forum Foundation and New Zealand Tertiary College.

National Association for the Education of Young Children (NAEYC). (2012). *Advancing the early childhood profession: NAEYC Standards and Guidelines for Professional Development.* A. Lutton, (Ed.). Washington, DC: NAEYC.

National Association for the Education of Young Children (NAEYC). (2011). *NAEYC Code of Ethical Conduct and Statement of Commitment.* A position statement of the National Association for the Education of Young Children. Revised April 2005. Reaffirmed and updated May 2011. Retrieved from http://www.naeyc.org/files/naeyc/file/positions/Ethics%20Position%20Statement2011.pdf

National Association for the Education of Young Children (NAEYC) and National Association of Child Care Resource and Referral Agencies (NACCRRA). (2011). *Early childhood education professional development: Training and technical assistance glossary.* Washington, DC: National Association for the Education of Young Children. Retrieved from http://www.naeyc.org/GlossaryTraining_TA.pdf

National Child Care Information and Technical Assistance Center. (2010). *RBPD: Models, qualifications, training, and supports.* Retrieved from http://nccic.acf.hhs.gov/poptopics/rbpd.html

New Teacher Center. (2011). *High quality mentoring and induction practices.* Santa Cruz, CA: Author. Retrieved from: http://www.newteachercenter.org/sites/default/files/ntc/main/resources/BRF_HighQualitymentoring%26InductionPractices.pdf

Opfer, V. D., & Pedder, D. (2011). Conceptualizing teacher professional development. *Review of Educational Research, 81*(3), 376–407.

Ramey, S. L., & Ramey, C. T. (2005). *Creating and sustaining a high-quality workforce in child care, early intervention, and school readiness programs.* In M. Zaslow & I. Martinez-Beck (Eds.), *Critical issues in early childhood professional development.* Baltimore, MD: Paul H. Brookes Publishing Co.

Rush, D. D., & Shelden, M. L. (2005). *Evidence-based definitions of coaching practices.* CASEinPoint, *1*(6).

Rush, D. D., Shelden, M. L., & Hanft, B. E. (2003). Coaching families and colleagues: A process for collaboration in natural settings. *Infants and Young Children, 16*(1), 33–47.

Scott Heller, S., & Gilkerson, L. (Eds.). (2009). *A practical guide to reflective supervision.* Washington, DC: ZERO TO THREE.

Strickland, D., & Riley-Ayers, S. (2007). *Literacy leadership in early childhood: The essential guide.* New York: Teachers College Press.

Sullivan, D. (2010). *Learning to lead: Effective leadership skills for teachers of young children.* St. Paul, MN: Redleaf Press.

U.S. Department of Health and Human Services, Administration for Children and Families, Office of Head Start. (2012). *Head Start relationship-based competencies for staff and supervisors who work with families.* Retrieved from: http://eclkc.ohs.acf.hhs.gov/hslc/standards/IMs/2012/resour_ime_005_060612.html Web link to document on this page.

Villani, S. (2009). *Comprehensive mentoring programs for new teachers: Models of induction and support.* Thousand Oaks, CA: Corwin.

Web Resources

American Association of Colleges for Teacher Education (AACTE)
http://www.aacte.org

American Associate Degree Early Childhood Educators (ACCESS)
http://www.accessece.org

Association for Childhood Education International (ACEI)
http://www.acei.org

California Early Childhood Mentor Program
http://www.ecementor.org

Center for Child Care Workforce
http://www.ccw.org/

Center for Children and Families (CC&F), Education Development Center, Inc.
http://ccf.edc.org

The Center for Early Childhood Leadership
http://cecl.nl.edu

Center for Mentoring and Induction at Mankato State University (CMI)
http://ed.mnsu.edu/cmi

Child Development Policy Institute
https://www.cdpi.net/cs/cdpi/print/htdocs/home.htm

Child Development Training Consortium
http://www.childdevelopment.org/cs/cdtc/print/htdocs/home.htm

Children Now
http://www.childrennow.org/index.php

Coaching Competencies for Colorado Early Childhood Education
http://cocoaches.net/uploads/Coaching_competencies_Oct_2010.pdf

Early Childhood Research & Practice (ECRP), University of Illinois
http://www.ecrp.uiuc.edu

The Education Commission of the States (ECS)
http://www.ecs.org

The Future of Children
http://www.futureofchildren.org

Head Start Bureau–*Steps to Success*
http://www.step-net.org

Head Start Information & Publication Center (HSIPC)
http://www.headstartinfo.org

High/Scope Educational Research Foundation
http://www.highscope.org

McCormick Center for Early Childhood Leadership
http://cecl.nl.edu

Minnesota Center for Professional Development
http://www.mncpd.org/rbpd.html

National Association of Child Care Resource and Referral Agencies
http://www.naccrra.org

National Association for the Education of Young Children (NAEYC)
http://www.naeyc.org

National Black Child Development Institute
http://nbcdi.org

National Child Care Association
http://www.nccanet.org

National Institute for Early Childhood Research
nieer.org

National Mentoring Institute
http://www.mentoring.org

North American Reggio Emilio Alliance (NAREA)
http://www.reggioalliance.org

Program for Infant/Toddler Care
http://www.pitc.org

U.S. National Committee of the World Organization for Early Childhood Education (OMEP-USNC)
http://omep-usnc.org

●●●●●●●●●●●●●●●●●●●●●●●●●●●●●●●●●●●●●

CHAPTER 2

Building Professional Development Relationships With Adults

The chapter supports your growing capacity to

- partner with others for learning;
- join and plan for a learning partnership;
- begin a cycle of strategies by establishing expectations;
- understand and apply concepts influencing cultural competence and equity; and
- evaluate progress in a mentoring relationship.

Exploring effective ways that mentors initially join and plan for professional learning relationships with early childhood teachers is the focus of this chapter. Increasing responsiveness to and awareness of the whole teacher (as mentee, or protégé) through an examination of concepts that influence cultural competence and sustain or weaken engagement in learning is embedded in this discussion. The ideas are applied as foundational strategies associated with general mentoring guidance or specific coaching skills to support reflective relationship-based practices.

How you are is as important as what you do.

Jere Pawl & Maria St. John, discussing working
with young children and their families (1998).

In learning and teaching, manner, deportment, and tone are just as important, if not more important, than what is said.

Unaisi Nabobo-Baba & Lavinia Tiko, discussing
Fijian cultural conceptions of mentoring, 2009.

An emphasis on mentoring for professional development includes the assumption that teachers learn best in a positive climate based on trust and respect. Teachers joining with a professional guide need a mentor who empathically connects to their concerns and experiences. This concept asserts that the power or the failure of a professional-development relationship lies first in the *way of being* of the professional working with an early childhood teacher (Johnson & Brinamen, 2006). A focus on relationships also implies that mentoring requires the involvement of a consistent, predictable adult who understands a process for individualizing learning by asking questions, listening, and remaining emotionally present. In *Promoting First Relationships,* the authors (Kelly, Zuckerman, Sandoval, & Buehlman, 2003, p. 22) refer to supporting the learning of caregivers or families of young children as first requiring "forming mutuality" (p. 22). Johnson and Brinamen (2006) also identify *mutuality of endeavor* as one of the keys to an effective *consultative stance*. Current professional definitions (NAEYC & NACCRRA, 2011) would add mentoring and coaching stances or dispositions as needing the same qualities. Wenger applies the concept of *mutuality* to the establishment of *mutuality of engagement*, or committing to participate together, to make sense of ideas and experiences (Wenger, 1998, p. 137).

A mentor must remember that an initial focus on building a relationship for learning is much more than establishing a comfortable climate. It is the dynamic interaction of teachers—needing to feel safe to think out loud and plan for gathering information about their questions—with a professional or group, designed to both support and challenge their thinking. Connecting a teacher to others who have an ongoing and collective commitment to learning may result in fostering collaboration for a learning community, or a *community of practice* (Wenger, 1998), within a program or between teachers from different programs in one community (Elliott, Farris, Alvarado, Peters, Surr, Genser, & Chin, 2000, p. 12). A powerful outcome of relationship-based mentoring is seen when an individual teacher's feeling of isolation is replaced with a new willingness to join a community of practice or with "groups of people who share a concern, a set of problems, a passion about a topic, and who deepen their knowledge and expertise in this area by interacting on an ongoing basis." (Wenger, McDermott, & Snyder, 2002, p. 4).

It is ironic that, after a mentor successfully builds trust and safety, the next step is to encourage a teacher to wrestle with dilemmas of practice, which often cause feelings of unease, disequilibrium, or confusion. Comparing the differences between beliefs and practices, values and reality, and suggested practices may stimulate a teacher's wondering about what might be possible. It is these gaps and discrepancies associated with a teacher's values, beliefs, approaches, and thinking that may be motivators for change (Woolfolk Hoy, Hoy, & Davis, 2009). However, if the gaps between the everyday practices and the new strategies being explored are too great, a teacher may dismiss any new ideas as not fitting his or her situation (Coburn, 2001). Overwhelming a teacher with new information does not tend to produce change, because time is needed to develop, absorb, and apply new knowledge to practice (Garet, Porter, Andrew, & Desimone, 2001; Guskey, 2002). The more common experience reported by preschool teachers is one of being isolated in classrooms or in roles with too little collaboration with others and little or no support for reflecting on practices (Barnett, Epstein, Friedman, Sansanelli, & Hustedt, 2009). Reversing the isolation of experienced teachers through a cycle of observation, practice, reflection, and expert feedback about their own practices has been shown to lead to more supportive teaching interactions (Pianta, Mashburn, Downer, Hamre, & Justice, 2008) and the implementation of effective curricula (Strickland & Riley-Ayers, 2007).

REFLECTION

Make a list of ways in which partnering with another adult for the purpose of increasing and applying professional skills and knowledge is different from simply building a friendship with a colleague. Compare your list with strategies in Table 2.1 that either weaken or promote learning partnerships.

Table 2.1 Conditions for Learning Partnerships

Conditions for Learning	Effective Strategies	Disruptive Strategies
A mentor creates conditions for learning partnerships with teachers when he or she	Examples of effective mentor professional relationship-building strategies	Examples of mentor choices that may weaken professional learning relationships
Builds trust and demonstrates respect	Is fully attentive and a good listener; is willing to focus on emergent issues	Switches the subject abruptly to a prearranged topic without responding to an emergent dilemma
Maintains openness and flexibility	Encourages practice when needed or tries out new strategies relating to interests	Reduces support before teacher is comfortable with new skills or knowledge
Shows interest in goals, points of view, and interests of teacher	Shifts perspective or plans in order to better match interests of teacher	Uses technical language that intimidates a teacher into silence
Has clear professional boundaries	Reviews and negotiates a learning agreement; arrives at an arranged time and is organized and prepared	Has no clear agreement on roles and expectations for mentor or teacher meetings
Focuses on learning needs	Uses mentoring strategies that are preferred by the teacher	Does not individualize or differentiate mentoring strategies to fit teacher's preferences
Celebrates reaching short-term goals	Notices progress toward a larger goal and makes connections	Suggests dropping a goal for one that is "easier," expresses frustration, or unfavorably compares the teacher with others who have reached goals faster

Read the left-hand column in Table 2.1 for ways in which mentors create positive learning partnership conditions. Then, read across from left to right to see associated mentor strategies that either strengthen or disrupt learning.

Partnering With Others for Learning: A Continuum of Choices and a Network of Relationships

Engaging in understanding the thoughts, feelings, hopes, and dreams of another person is foundational to the role of the mentor. Projecting an attitude that might be described as simultaneously interested and uncritical is a requirement. The mentor's level of expertise and knowledge about a topic is irrelevant if empathy and insight are not present. The ability to respond sensitively to the thoughts and feelings of others over time through a sustained, intensive, and job-embedded professional-development collaboration (including a significant number of contact hours) is associated with teacher effectiveness (Guskey, 2002). A mentor probably will find it impossible to establish an emotional or an intellectual connection through brief and sporadic meetings. Consider the following, If *relationship*, defined as a learning partnership, is truly at the center of any mentoring process, what is a continuum of effective options for how this relationship would look in practice? How can programs avoid the "one size fits all" pitfall of the isolated workshop, yet take into account the complexities of available resources in a community and the specific program needs? How does mentoring or other individualized learning fit into an overall professional-development context? What piece of the professional-development puzzle does mentoring fit in?

REFLECTION

Consider and discuss the examples in Table 2.2 of different learning needs, resources, and mentoring strategies that keep a teacher's learning going.

- Read the three "Teacher Learning Needs Scenarios."
- Match the specific mentoring learning needs identified for each scenario with the corresponding number in the center column labeled "Mentor as Resource Responses."
- Finally, read the "Mentoring Strategies for Learning" column for each matching number. Discuss or journal about Table 2.2 by considering the importance of applying the right resources and mentoring strategies to meet a teacher's specific learning needs.

Often, the same mentor is asked to fill all of the different professional needs identified in these scenarios. Using the prompts *ask—connect—expand* may serve to remind a mentor to consider a teacher's needs first and to respond by thoughtfully choosing the type of mentoring partner that is the best fit for a teacher's situation.

Table 2.2 Learning Needs, Resources, and Strategies to Keep the Learning Going

Teacher Learning Needs Scenarios	Mentor as Resource Responses	Mentoring Strategies for Learning
1. *New teacher* needs induction into the profession in many areas.	1. *Peers and experts* are needed who are currently in the same role or who have had experience in similar roles.	1. *Ask:* What teacher on-site or in a similar role or program might act as a peer mentor? Does the mentor understand the cultural context of the program?
2. *Teacher wants to be more effective* and is curious about many program areas.	2. *Mentors have the content, skills, and knowledge*—or they partner with others—to meet learner needs.	2. *Connect:* How will this mentor be supported from a wider *community of practice* to share the mentoring?
3. *Experienced teacher* needs support for a new role and new responsibilities.	3. *Mentors from outside* the early childhood field with specialized abilities, knowledge, or relationships can offer needed personal and/or professional guidance.	3. *Expand:* What in-depth coaching is needed in an area in which the mentor is not knowledgeable or is uncomfortable teaching? Is this situation shared by other teachers? Would a related study group, course, or group field trip be needed along with individualized mentoring?

Regardless of the diversity in focus of different professional-development partners, all must interact in a learning context that takes into account a teacher's prior knowledge, beliefs, practices, and experiences. Practices may not change—or conversely, may not be maintained—if the underlying beliefs and values of the teacher are not discussed. Consequently, even changing an unsafe behavior, such as drinking hot coffee while playing with toddlers, may be more complex than it would initially seem. An invited expert on safety must usually do more than simply inform program participants in order to effect the avoidance of having hot liquids near children. Digging deeper into the context of the school would include the consultant asking, *What policies might prevent teachers from meeting their own needs? Are teachers receiving their required breaks? What other factors are contributing to a lack of compliance with commonly understood safety practices?*

To add to the complexity, change must occur in multiple areas of influence (e.g., among peers, at the program level, at systems levels) for teacher growth to occur and be sustained (Clarke & Hollingsworth, 2002). Mentors, coaches, and consultants need to consider the existence of different levels of influence (Johnson & Brinamen, 2006) in a teacher's network of professional relationships. Although mentors cannot directly influence all of the variables that a teacher's role involves, they can make the teacher more aware of them and recommend bridging and connecting to them by fostering the development of needed professional skills and dispositions.

REFLECTION

Read Table 2.3, and discuss how choosing a coach with specialized expertise or using an outside consultant during a time of crisis might be better choices than involving only a well-known mentor with more general early childhood knowledge. Could you imagine a scenario in which a longstanding mentor bridged the needs of an early childhood program or teacher by bringing in and working with another coach or consultant? Why is fitting the learning need to the learning response so important?

REFLECTION

As you read the scenarios that follow, Table 2.3 ask yourself these questions: *What are possible issues for the mentors, coaches, and consultants to consider while building their relationships with the teachers in these scenarios? What connections might the teachers need to keep the learning going with a wider network of other professional relationships?*

Table 2.3   Matching the Learning Need to the Strategy for Learning
....

Knowledge/Skill Needed	Coach* Needed (person with specific expertise or skill who helps to identify and achieve skill development in another)	Strategies for Learning: Ask—Connect—Expand
Scenario: Teachers want to implement dual-language plans with effective strategies and improve their daily interactions with children. *Specific observational and assessment skills needed* to use a specific tool or research-based strategy.	*Coaches:* May serve in a different professional role from the learners and have specialized knowledge and skills.	*Ask:* What specialist or person with this specific expertise is able to model, teach, and support the concepts, skills, and behaviors needed? *Connect:* How will this specific goal be linked to broader goals and mentoring for overall quality improvements? *Expand:* What *community of practice* will support the learners to maintain what has begun?

Teacher Knowledge/Skill Required	Consultant* Required (facilitates the resolution of specific work-related issues)	Strategies for Learning in a Crisis: Ask—Connect—Expand
Scenario: Child Care Licensing or Head Start reviewers require health and safety policy and practice changes after a series of child accidents occurs over several months.	*Consultants* (usually from outside of a program) have broad experience with specific types of problem-based issues in the work setting. Collaborative and problem-solving processes involving *supervisors and administrators* often occur in collaboration with consultants during times of crisis.	*Ask:* How will this crisis, needing immediate technical information and action, be put into perspective for staff? *Connect:* Who will support the PD needed for the new policies to be implemented and maintained over time? *Expand:* Who might follow up with longer-term mentoring to uncover other issues needing examination?

*Role descriptions based on Lutton, A. (Ed.). (2012). *Advancing the profession: NAEYC standards and guidelines for professional development.* Washington, DC: NAEYC. pp. 84–86.

Mentor scenario (see REFLECTION questions before Table 2.3): General guidance needed for overall professional growth

As Rosemary (mentor) and Jane (teacher) talked, Jane mentioned that she was feeling worried about her ability to take on the new duties of supervising the afternoon preschool program. Jane said, "If I am still making mistakes as a preschool teacher myself, how can I supervise other teachers?" Rosemary helped Jane to explore whether she thought the pressure she was feeling might have played a part in several other problems that she had shared that day. As they continued to talk, Jane decided to relieve some of the pressure by talking to her director about her worries.

Coaching scenario: Performance-based outcomes requested

Sam, the director, shared with Maria, the visiting literacy coach, as follows: "I used to go to workshops and get frustrated with myself and the other teachers because we didn't seem to use the information after the sessions. So, we started a monthly teacher study group this year. We look at one topic in depth for at least several months. We all decided that we needed even more than this. We are so excited that we signed up for some on-site coaching from you in the literacy strategies that we read about. I think this is going to be the 'magic bullet' for meeting our language and literacy outcome goals!"

Consultation scenario: Specific concerns need to be resolved

The five staff members had their arms folded and looked uncomfortable as Lucy, the local public health nurse, started a discussion about appropriate practices with hot liquids in an infant or toddler room. Finally, Mary, one of the infant caregivers, said with tears in her eyes, "You know, we are horrified that the coffee was spilled on the toddler. This is not that kind of a place. It will never happen again, and no one feels worse about this than every one of us." Lucy stopped handing out her safety checklists and said, "I know. We have known each other a long time, and I know how much you care for the children. I should have started out by saying that."

Joining and Planning for a Learning Partnership

We know intuitively and from attachment research on early relationships that young children must receive warm, consistent, nurturing, and responsive care in order to grow and learn well (Ainsworth, Blehar, Waters, & Wall, 1978). The way that children learn to think and feel about who they are and about others is formed in the earliest interactions with the important adults in their lives (Bowlby, 1973). There is agreement among childcare researchers and practitioners that quality programs involve warm "interactions with adults in a safe, healthy, and stimulating environment, where early education and trusting relationships combine to support individual children's physical, emotional, social, and intellectual development" (Scarr, 1998, p. 100). What does this research suggest about what the adult teachers working with young children need for themselves? It would seem that if adults are to nurture children, they also must experience nurturing. Adults working in early care and education settings benefit from the power of consistent and supportive relationships guiding their professional growth. Virmani and Ontai (2010) found that childcare providers who had supervisors who used a more reflective mentoring style, which they called *reflective supervision*, were more insightful, open, accepting, and able to consider the complexities of a problem when compared with childcare providers who had traditional supervision. This suggests that the provider's capacity to be open to learning is enhanced by a supportive adult guide.

Siegel (1999, 2010) refers to a process called *mindsight*, which combines insight and empathy and names the way that two minds connect with the experiences of each other. Patterns of shared communication and information exchange develop through this process. In a mentor–teacher learning partnership, joining together requires some tried-and-true ingredients. Consider in Table 2.4 the requirements and sensitive responses of a positive learning relationship (the left and middle columns), and then contrast those with the consequences of not being sensitive to these learning needs (right column).

Table 2.4   Building a Learning Relationship

Building a learning relationship requires:	Mentors might respond by:	Notice and consider the consequences of a mentoring process that is:
taking time to build trust, comfort, and a positive climate.	having a planned first meeting and conveying interest in what is shared.	trying to quickly solve problems and offer help without first understanding the issues or contexts.
acting as a safe haven for the teacher to share frustrations and successes.	avoiding the role of the expert at first and doing a lot of listening and questioning.	assuming that everyone is initially excited to have your expertise and support.
establishing a clear purpose or negotiating to be able to answer the simple question, *Why are we doing this?*	stating what is not the purpose (i.e., evaluation review) and taking the time to come to shared agreements about the focus and process.	assuming that all involved understand the purpose and the process and agree with it; having fuzzy professional boundaries and veering into areas better left to a supervisor.
demonstrating that the teacher is valued as a colearner through willingness to explore a work-based dilemma.	wondering, brainstorming, listening to different points of view, and questioning in order to understand perspectives.	getting most information from one person (i.e., lacking multiple perspectives) or suggesting strategies that have worked well in different contexts before understanding the current issues.
creating the opportunity to think about both observations and the feelings that they cause, without being judged.	paraphrasing back what a teacher says and questioning what that causes her to think about.	sticking only to the facts or only exploring feeling and not integrating how a teacher thinks, feels, and acts in a situation.
considering influences of program, culture, community, and other contexts as assets.	drawing out what the teacher is sharing to illustrate the circles of influences on a situation or program.	ignoring the influences of culture and community or speaking of them only when problems occur (i.e., using a deficit approach).

REFLECTION

What comes to mind after reading the following quote?

When individuals are allowed to continue thinking about and exploring their own ideas without interference from another or the imposition of another agenda, the knowledge gained is their own. It comes from within. It is implicitly rather than explicitly derived. This is the same kind of active learning we so advocate for in young children.

(Wightman, Whitaker, Traylor, Yeider, Hyden, & Weigand, 2007, p. 32, quoting B. Weigand).

When has this happened for your learning, or when have you facilitated it for others? Which idea from Table 2.4 might support what this quote describes?

Use Figure 2.1 to consider the assets present in any mentoring relationship or how a specific mentor–teacher learning partnership is functioning.

Figure 2.1 Learning Partnership Asset Checklist

After reading each row, evaluate the following by checking, bulleting, or circling assets that are:

✓ *Consistently* present
■ *Sometimes* present
○ *Not yet* part of the mentor's repertoire of practices

Big Ideas	Questions for the Mentor	✓ Consistently ■ Sometimes ○ Not Yet
First, be curious	Have I tried to avoid the attitude, stance, and position of the expert at the very beginning of the partnership? This does not mean denying content expertise, but it indicates the need for a curious and open stance of first supporting a teacher's need to generate questions before I give answers. An exception is when health, safety, or other critical information is requested by a teacher or indicated by observed workplace conditions.	
Listen and learn	Do I listen and gather information from the teacher?	
Observe and engage in dialogue	Do I observe and engage in dialogue and resist trying to immediately save others with my knowledge?	
Focus on interests, and adapt to readiness	Do I keep in mind the need to link the appropriate content information to the teacher's interests, readiness to use it, and preferred style of learning?	
Build on knowledge, and guide	Do I build on what a teacher already knows and is able to do? In what ways do I increase the teacher's sense of expertise and act as a guide?	
Problem-solve the immediate crisis	When being asked about crisis situations, such as instances of health and safety concerns, do I help put needed information in context in order to keep the learning going?	
Strive to understand context	Do I understand or do I work to understand the unique characteristics, as well as the cultural and community context, of the teacher's work?	
Remain humble	Do I remain humble and admit what I do not know?	

Refer for a better fit between mentor and teacher needs	Do I recognize when I am not the best match (e.g., lack needed content knowledge, don't have insights into the context, lack language skills or cultural expertise) for a particular teacher, program, or setting, and do I then work to bring in another professional or partner with others to meet the needs of teachers?	
Connect to keep the learning going	Do I partner with others to connect teachers to people in their professional networks of relationships to keep the learning going?	
Maintain a goal-focused partnership	Have we negotiated a goal or focus? Have I redirected focus back to the goal when we stray too far into unrelated areas? Do I notice progress over time and celebrate it? Do I know when to suggest that we set a new goal or narrow our focus to a smaller objective?	

REFLECTION

After reading Figure 2.1, journal about general successes and challenges in a specific mentoring relationship. Consider patterns that you have observed in any learning partnerships with which you have been involved or that you have observed. Ask other mentors, a supervisor, or a confidential colleague about ways to increase effective learning partnership assets in areas that you have noticed need to be made more consistently supportive.

A Cycle of Strategies Beginning With Establishing Expectations

Starting off well means that some questions should already have been answered before the first mentor and teacher meeting takes place. Both partners of a teaching–learning relationship should work together by already having taken time to consider—or receive formal orientation to—the overall purpose and goals of the mentoring process. Ideally, everyone involved should be aware of any special focus (e.g., literacy practices) and other parameters of the process (e.g., required amount of participation), as well as who is sponsoring these efforts (i.e., a nonprofit foundation, state agency, professional organization, or federal grant). Participants who have had to complete an application form or respond to a reflective question such as "Why do I want to be involved in a mentoring relationship?" will be more likely to come to a first meeting ready to join a learning partnership. Business matters, such as completing any necessary parent permission forms or other agreements for confidentiality (or human subject requirements for research), should occur before mentoring begins. Hanft, Rush, and Sheldon (2004) refer to this phase as the *initiation process*. Head Start has published procedures on beginning well when implementing mentoring and coaching programs in *Steps to Success—Decision Makers Guide* (U.S. Dept. of Health and Human Services, 2005).

Before the First Meeting Between Mentors and Protégés

Those sponsoring early childhood mentoring should consider and be prepared to answer the questions in Table 2.5. Mentors should also be well prepared to answer these questions for themselves, sharing relevant information with the protégé, as needed. Mentors need to be able to convey, in a matter-of-fact way that is informational and inviting, the broad vision and features of a specific mentoring process. Broad mentoring goals may be communicated, for example, through a group orientation to a mentoring program, in written descriptions posted on a website, in face-to-face gatherings, via phone and email, or all of the above. When a mentor shares his or her rationale for expected outcomes, along with specific examples from past mentoring, it is helpful to teachers considering being involved. Conducting individual and/or program needs assessments before meeting is another way to inform and take the pulse of an early childhood program setting before mentoring begins.

Table 2.5 Before Mentoring Begins—Why are we doing this?

Mentors should understand and be able to share with the teacher, as needed:	Teachers (as protégés) should have the opportunity to ask their supervisor, program, and the mentoring program:
1. Why are we doing this? What is our purpose? How will I be matched to teachers or programs? Am I able to request other resources if I can't meet specific requests for support?	1. Why should I do this? What am I committing to do? How will I be matched with a mentor? What if I prefer a different mentor?
2. What are the vision, mission, and general goals of this mentoring process?	2. What do the mentor and my supervisor or program participants see as the purpose of my involvement in this mentoring process?
3. How are mentors selected? What are the mentors' roles and expectations? Who supervises the mentors?	3. What are the expectations of me? How much input will I have into the process?
4. What type of observation, assessment, or feedback will take place?	4. What type of observation, assessment, or feedback will take place?
5. What are our expectations for possible learning outcomes of this work together?	5. What are possible learning outcomes of this work together?
6. What barriers might we encounter?	6. What challenges might I encounter?
7. How might change impact involved programs?	7. How will my supervisor and program participants feel about my participating? Will I have release time from my work to meet the goals of the mentoring process?
8. How will we resolve differences that might occur?	
9. How will we evaluate this mentoring process?	

Not exploring the questions in Table 2.5 can make the mentoring process vulnerable to common pitfalls such as program policies that do not release teachers from their duties to meet or mentors' not knowing what is expected of them. All of these beginning issues are important to solve before anything else is attempted. Having expectations of the mentor, teacher, and program participants in writing and signed by all involved is one common way to facilitate a shared understanding of a relationship-based professional-development process.

REFLECTION

Discuss the ideas from Table 2.5 in small groups comprising colleagues who have facilitated professional development. If you have experienced the role only of the teacher, examine how not having the answers to these questions affects your willingness to participate.

Is this list of questions complete? What is missing? What is a helpful and appropriate way to share information and answer common questions that a teacher, supervisor, or program participant might want to know before mentoring begins?

First Visit: Learning About Each Other

Once a mentor and a teacher are matched, they need to arrange to meet. Now that both the mentor and the teacher understand the general purpose of their professional-development relationship, gathering and exchanging information is the next step.

Commitment to the Mentoring Process

Choose a way to meet. Find the time and the space. Arranging for the time and finding a space to meet and talk is a hurdle that some mentoring pairs have great difficulty in achieving.

Mentors sometimes try to meet with teachers while the teachers are caring for groups of children. This rarely works.

Arranging to meet.   Where and when should we meet?

- *Would meeting in a coffee shop or place away from the work site work best? If we do that, how can we remain confidential about program issues? Is meeting during the children's nap time a possibility? Will program policy allow the teacher to be released from work for the period needed for dialogue with a mentor?*

The first visit sets the tone for a professional learning relationship. Although learning basic information to plan for future meetings is needed, this first contact especially requires a mentor to respond sensitively and show empathy by listening nonjudgmentally and by encouraging the teacher to share what he or she expects and needs. The mentor's wondering out loud and modeling curiosity rather than sharing any answers to urgent dilemmas can facilitate this sharing. The mentor should also consider giving the teacher a sense of what the mentor values and will bring to the process. For example, a mentor might say, "I believe that setting aside this time to hear your stories of your teaching experiences will allow us to examine the children's perspectives that you said you are interested in exploring. I think I can support you with some more resources and ideas for learning." Notes from this first meeting (which should be copied and shared with the teacher) should include responses to the questions and prompts in Figure 2.2.

Figure 2.2   Information Needed Before the Mentoring Process Begins
• •

Beginning the Mentoring Process   Date _____   Name _____

What are the strengths and resources of the teacher (protégé)?

What are the needs, interests, and suggested focus for our mentoring time?

What questions still need to be answered to identify possible challenges?

Additional information includes the following:
- Mentoring contact information: _____
- Purpose of visit, phone call, or online communication: _____
- Focus of inquiry or discussion: _____
- Strategies discussed and next steps: _____

REFLECTION

If you are in a group, form pairs. Have one person play the role of early childhood teacher and the other play the role of visiting mentor. If you are using this book for self-study, take turns imagining yourself in the mentor and teacher roles in the scenario. Use the questions that follow, and adjust them to fit what seems most effective.

The goal of the conversation is for the mentor to put the teacher at ease and begin to establish a working relationship. Sensitivity to individual, cultural, and other preferences will change how this initial *interpersonal dance* proceeds. Connecting the goal of getting to know each other with establishing and understanding the purpose of the learning relationship is key. Trying out being responsive to individual styles and needs is the purpose of this role-play.

Role-Play—Part I.   The mentor will initiate the interaction by

- greeting the teacher;
- explaining the purpose of the mentoring visit and what the mentor can offer;
- identifying or negotiating with the teacher what might be expected from him or her; and
- and arranging for a second visit.

The teacher's responses should be improvised on the basis of what the mentor says. The mentor's portion of the conversation might go something like this:

"This is when we arranged to meet. Is this still a good time?"

"I am here to see whether there is any way that I can help you to use some of the ideas from class here in your program. I am not here to evaluate anything. My job is not like that of a childcare licensor, director, principal, or supervisor. My role is to support you with resources in the area of _____" (i.e., infant care, child guidance, etc.).

"When I come is flexible, and we can plan to make it fit both of our schedules. But I do have only a total of ____ hours to support and visit you this quarter."

"First, I was wondering whether you had any questions or concerns. Okay, if you think of something later, here is how you can contact me:_____."

"It would help me if I could learn a little about your work."

"Would it be okay if I just observed the class for a while to get to know your program better? I might take a few notes to remember what I want to ask you about."

Based on Kelly, et al. (2003). *Promoting first relationships: A curriculum for service providers to help parents and other caregivers meet young children's social and emotional needs.* Seattle, WA: NCAST-AVENUW Publications (pp. 31–32).

Role-Play—Part II.   Switch roles, and continue the conversation by using the questions that follow. Adjust them to fit what feels most natural and effective. The goal of this part of the conversation is for the mentor to continue to promote a positive climate while also beginning to learn what the teacher needs and is interested in, and to explore what the teacher wants to learn with the support of the mentor.

- What do you enjoy most about being a teacher (childcare provider, etc.)?
- Could you describe your program? (How many children are in your care, etc.?)
- I was wondering what you think children need most from you.
- What are the most challenging parts of the day in caring for children?
- Can you describe a current challenge?
- How would you like to get support for your role here?

REFLECTION

Discuss the role-play and consider the following:

When you were the teacher as protégé: What suggestions do you have for the mentor to make that first meeting feel more comfortable? Did you feel that you understood the purpose of the learning relationship? Were you able to ask questions, share, or negotiate how you wanted to meet in the future? Did you begin to think about or share what your interests or teaching dilemmas were?

When you were the mentor: Did you have to change the scenario script to make the conversation flow better? What seemed to work, and what did not seem comfortable? Did you share what you saw as the purpose of the learning relationship? Were you able to ask questions, listen, share, or negotiate how you wanted to meet in the future? Did you begin to have some sense of what interests or teaching dilemmas might exist for this teacher?

Both roles: Do you have any other considerations for how to listen and ask questions to promote a positive relationship? Are there different or more effective ways to start a mentoring relationship?

Next Visits: Agreeing on a Focus and a Question to Investigate

Ideally, the teacher will identify some area of practice, an intense interest, or a problem that he or she wants the mentor to help explore. Even if the mentoring program dictates a specific focus (e.g., infant and toddler care) or has a specific homework assignment associated with a linked college course, the teacher should still be encouraged to identify an interest within those topic or assignment boundaries. Choice is a key ingredient in the mentoring relationship. Individualizing and supporting in areas that the teacher chooses are foundational to this relationship. An important role of the mentor is to listen, ask questions, and observe in order to be able to put the teacher's interest into the form of a research question.

Mentors also need to clarify what they cannot do—expertise that they do not have—and link the teacher to resources that are outside the mentor's areas of knowledge, time, skill, or focus. Often, teachers do not immediately open up about what they want to discuss. This could be because they have not reflected on it or because they don't feel comfortable enough to share their thoughts at the early stage. A mentor may request an observation first and have a conversation second to better facilitate the choice of a focus. In other cases, a specific focus might be agreed upon before the mentor's first observation. Gradually asking, not interrogating, before and after observing the teacher is helpful to the mentor's work. The questions in Figure 2.3 can help the mentor gain initial insight into the teacher's needs.

Figure 2.3 Learning a Teacher's Mentoring Needs

* Would a one-on-one mentoring relationship be helpful to you?
* Do you currently have anyone whom you see as a professional mentor to you?
* What do you enjoy most about being a teacher (childcare provider, etc.)?
* Could you describe your program? (How many children are in care, etc.?)
* What do you think children need most from you?
* What are the most challenging parts of the day in caring for children?
* Can you describe a current challenge?
* How would you like to get support for your role here?

Observe and Discuss

Choosing to observe a teacher's program allows a mentor to better understand the area of interest that the mentor and teacher may have decided to explore in the first conversation. Some mentoring programs are funded to use a specific tool, such as the *Infant-Toddler Environment Rating Scale* (Harms, et al., 1990), as a baseline for checking on quality and fostering a beginning dialogue for goal setting. If observation or other evaluation tools are a part of a mentoring program, they must be discussed and understood. Program and teacher consent for use of all evaluation or assessment tools should be obtained. Consent involves making sure that everyone not only understands the tool, but also agrees on its purpose and use in the mentoring process. The best way to torpedo a mentoring relationship is to surprise the teacher with an unexpected evaluation or assessment agenda of their skills. The teacher needs to give informed consent to all evaluations if the relationship is going to start and remain on a foundation of trust.

Review: The mentor should take narrative, descriptive notes of his or her observation of the teacher or program. This may or may not include use of a specific observation tool. To establish a partnership relationship, the mentor could suggest that the teacher keep a journal about his or her intense interests, concerns, or questions. The teacher's journal and the mentor's observational notes will then foster a dialogue or become the basis for a *conference*.

The First Conference or Debriefing of an Observation

This should occur as soon as possible after the first observation. The mentor and teacher need time to discuss the observation and then determine a focus and a goal. If a teacher is worried about how children are pushing on the playground, a research question to investigate might be reframed by the mentor as "How do children use the outdoor play area?" The teacher's journal is also a source of conversation and may spark the development of a teacher question to investigate. The mentor should check to be sure that the teacher is interested in the focus that they have identified, by asking again, "What do you want to accomplish?" Finally, the intention to answer these questions will move the process to planning for gathering information. A mentor could give suggestions and ask, "How could you gather information on that research question?" Be sure to identify what you have agreed will happen between mentoring visits.

Making Meaning From Information and Moving to Action Steps

Subsequent visits require time to check on the process of gathering information, reviewing observations, and discussing the possible meanings of the data. Next, it is time to plan for action steps based on observations and information gathered. As additional observations take place, the mentor might suggest that he or she observe the teacher's interacting with children or observe an environment after changes have been made. Discussion and feedback after the mentor observes the teacher in action or after they both view a video of teacher and children interacting together provide powerful feedback for making positive changes in practices (Pianta, et al, 2008). Mentors can ask, "What have you tried? How could you do it differently? Sounds like you have decided to implement . . . . Let's talk about how that worked next time we see each other." This cycle includes

1. **joining together:** and creating a clear plan with the understanding of what the teacher and mentor, or coach, will each do (e.g., teacher observes children, mentor observes teacher and children);

2. **observing children and teacher's interactions** and other information gathering;
3. **discussing/giving feedback** throughout the process;
4. **reflecting/interpreting** the information gathered; and
5. planning for **action** and implementing ideas or practicing skills.

The process is then repeated as many times as needed (Rush & Shelden, 2005). The power of this process is that it is dynamic and sometimes transformational because it includes reflection on action (Osterman & Kottkamp, 2004). Beliefs about, for example, how children learn are explored though practicing new strategies based on actual information about real children. Infused into the teacher's exploration is expert (or experienced) feedback about a specific focus. The attention to a research question or a *focus* (e.g., *How do children learn to make friends?*) limits the discussions so that teachers do not get overwhelmed or confused. Ideas for inquiry into new questions can be put in a *parking lot of ideas* for future cycles. See Section II for a more in-depth discussion of this process.

Mentors need to be flexible to support teachers in achieving their goals. The amount of time allocated for each step of the cycle, the number of meetings, and the way the conversations occur (face-to-face or via phone or online) in moving through these stages will depend on the mentoring program and the needs of the teacher. The important idea is to move through a full cycle to allow the teacher to experience all of the components of inquiry and support for expanding an understanding of effective teaching practices.

Changes in the Mentor–Teacher Relationship Over Time

As the cycle repeats itself for the first time, a mentor may find that he or she needs to initiate, assist in, or model skills before teachers are ready to try a new practice. Mentors may need to initiate offering feedback at first; but as the meetings continue, the teacher may have a better understanding of the questions he or she wants to ask and may begin to direct the learning more. Finally, performing by the teacher during all phases of the mentoring cycle becomes more consistent. The mentor can slow down a teacher's learning if the mentor does not recognize or observe the point at which the teacher wants to take more of a lead in the process. Mentors need to be responsive to a teacher's hints or direct requests for a new learning focus and understand when it is time for the process to conclude. Connecting a teacher to another form of professional development such as a college course, a teacher learning community, or involvement in a professional organization may keep the learning going.

Repairing Relationships When Conflict Arises

Mentors must recognize and be explicit about the fact that they honor differing views and ways to achieve identified goals. If conflict or a withdrawal of teacher interest or participation occurs, mentors should consider what factors might be contributing to a challenging learning climate. Reflecting on reasons for differing views is one place to begin, and it involves first looking at oneself. Openness to hearing concerns and changing styles to better fit the needs of a teacher is required in the mentoring role. Sometimes, finding another mentor who is a better fit for a teacher (involving a greater understanding of an individual, program, or cultural context) is the best choice. Withdrawal of support by a program to allow for teacher release time, personal issues, or any number of other influences may affect the learning relationship. In other situations, a period of disruption can signal learning and growth as a teacher tries to hint to a mentor that the teacher needs to control the pace, focus, and content of the learning. What is going on? A mentor needs to consider all levels of influences on the teacher rather than focus on his or her own feelings of being a mentoring success or failure.

If a mentoring relationship was mandated by a quality-improvement initiative, for example, or if a supervisor required a teacher to participate in a mentoring partnership, resistance to participation may bubble up at any time. Going back and revisiting the purpose and intent of the mentoring process is needed to allow the teacher to share concerns and worries before a plan to address the teacher's learning goals and needs can begin effectively. Reassurance that confidentiality and trust are central values and requirements may also be needed if a teacher has had a negative experience in past professional-development interactions.

Mentors must be sensitive to signs of conflict and be interested in figuring out how to work with varied reactions to the disequilibrium that learning may create. Mentors, just like teachers of young children, cannot ignore conflict while they strive to foster collaborative dialogue. In fact, disequilibrium is expected as teachers develop and grow. Mentor development involves becoming increasingly proactive in problem solving as part of the everyday process of working with adult learners.

REFLECTION

Consider the two scenarios that follow involving conflict and changes in one mentor–teacher relationship over time. Discuss possible issues in the scenarios, and consider the teacher's and mentor's different perspectives. What might be the mentor's responses in order to repair the mentoring relationship?

1. Marlene is a well-respected family childcare owner who has participated for over six months in a mentoring program through her local childcare resource and referral agency. She was excited to begin the program and to focus on learning about new literacy strategies for her toddler and pre-school-age children. Recently, she has canceled the last two visits. Marlene did not tell the mentor, but she is upset and disagrees with changes in her childcare environment that her mentor wants her to make. Marlene made excuses that she was busy, but she is actually feeling that perhaps she needs a break from mentoring.

2. Sally is a mentor with an early childhood literacy and childcare-center professional background. She has been working with Marlene once a month for six months. Previously, she was a teacher in several well-respected local childcare centers. She is puzzled and frustrated that Marlene has canceled their last two scheduled visits. In talking to colleagues, Sally has begun to consider that her lack of experience in a family childcare setting may be problematic. She wonders, "Do I need to reconsider the environmental changes that we discussed? Did Marlene agree when she didn't really want to make the changes?" Sally knows that she needs to repair the relationship. Sally wonders, "How can I turn this conflict into a problem-solving situation in which I listen to Marlene to learn more about what works in her setting?"

Concepts Influencing Cultural Competence and Equity

Understanding what a teacher knows and is able to do is the point at which mentoring and effective teaching begin. In our current accountability-based education world, some advocate that professional development should not stray too far from teaching skills based on "externally developed, research-based, and standards-aligned instruction," which teachers should learn to reproduce accurately (Bausmith & Barry, 2011, p. 176). Others suggest that teachers are much more than consumers of best practices offered in an "outside-in, top-down, teacher-deficit model" (Anderson & Herr, 2011, p. 287). The mentor or teacher-educator is entering this debate with the professional task of also encouraging awareness of families' "funds of knowledge" (Gonzalez, Moll, & Amanti, 2005), and incorporating these cultural insights into their teacher practices. Chang (2006) suggests that early childhood programs can be both culturally competent and of high quality if skilled teachers operate in programs with low teacher–child ratios, appropriate group sizes, age-appropriate curriculum, engaged families, linkages to comprehensive services, culturally and linguistically appropriate assessment, and available bilingual education (p. 10). The inquiry, or teacher-researcher strategies described in this text, is a method supported in part by research on coaching effectiveness (Rush & Shelden, 2005) and teacher study, action research, and inquiry groups (Stremmel, 2007; Somekh, 2010; Wilson, 2008) for helping teachers who are not only striving to be culturally competent, but are also wrestling with how to appropriately adapt research-based practices to their setting.

A mentor's role in relation to cultural competency may range from encouraging greater insight in a teacher lacking in knowledge to learning from—or even simply *not disrupting*—a teacher who is already skilled in culturally relevant practices. Elliott, et al., suggest that when mentoring programs begin, the designers should wonder and ask, "Are there trusted 'grassroots' leaders who are ready to mentor others, but have never been asked?" and "Have we recruited mentors with the language abilities and culturally preferred qualities of interaction and knowledge of a local community?" (2000, p. 32). Mentors have the opportunity to both educate and empower a diversity of teachers. All mentors and early childhood practitioners should, at a minimum, understand their own culture, acknowledge differences, engage in self-assessment, strive to acquire cultural knowledge and skills, and view adult and child behavior within a cultural context (Cross et al., 1989). Copple and Bredekamp give a rationale for the importance of embedding cultural competence in teaching practices by stating the following:

> When young children are in a group setting outside the home, what makes sense to them, how they use language to interact, and how they experience this new world depends on the social and cultural contexts to which they are accustomed. A skilled teacher takes such contextual factors into account, along with the children's ages and their individual differences, in shaping all aspects of the learning environment (2009, p. 10).

Building relationships occurs in a specific context. In order to be competent, the mentor's understanding of the concept of culture is essential. *Culture* is defined as follows:

> an integrated pattern of human behavior, which includes but is not limited to—thought, communication, languages, beliefs, values, practices, customs, courtesies, rituals, manners of interacting, roles, relationships, and expected behaviors of a racial, ethnic, religious, social, or political group; the ability to transmit the above to succeeding generations; dynamic in nature.

(National Center for Cultural Competence, 2004, p. 4).

Quality Benchmarks for Cultural Competence Project (QBCCP) has developed concepts of *cultural competence*, which many state Quality Rating Improvement Systems (QRIS) systems are choosing to embed in their early childhood programs and related standards (NAEYC, 2009, pp. 3–4). The QBCCP concepts are summarized in Figure 2.4.

Figure 2.4   Cultural Competence Concepts

Concept 1: Children are nested in families.

Concept 2: Identify shared goals among families and staff.

Concept 3: Authentically incorporate cultural traditions and history in the classroom.

Concept 4: Acknowledge child development as a culturally driven, ongoing process that should be supported across contexts in a child's life (e.g., school and home).

Concept 5: Individuals' and institutions' practices are embedded in culture.

Concept 6: Ensure that decisions and policies embrace home languages and dialects.

Concept 7: Ensure that policies and practices embrace and respect families' cultural values, attitudes, and beliefs toward learning.

Connections

After reading Figure 2.5, imagine that you are a mentor working with a Head Start teacher who is interested in investigating the question *How can we increase family involvement in our program?* How could you connect one or two QBCCP concepts to related evidence and the beginning of actions to implement these ideas? Begin by brainstorming a few ideas for each blank box in Figure 2.5. How could this process support embedding cultural competency concepts into the mentoring process? What other ways could this happen?

Figure 2.5   Embedding Cultural Competence Concepts in Your Planning

Teacher Question: *How can we increase family involvement in our program?*		
Identify a related QBCCP concept(s):		
Identify a standard that requires family involvement. (See NAEYC accreditation, Head Start Performance Standard, State licensing, etc.)	**Choose some evidence** to collect or documentation to gather and people to interview.	State some **beginning ideas for implementing or taking action** to increase family involvement (after evidence is collected).
Example (Head Start Performance Standard): *Making programs open to parents at any time, involving parents in the development of program curriculum, and providing parents opportunities to volunteer or become staff.*		

Evaluating Progress in a Mentoring Relationship

One way to be more proactive and prevent conflict, as well as check for learning in a mentoring relationship, is to embed evaluation throughout the process. Different levels of evaluation can occur. The broadest level might be a mentor and teacher's reflection on the question *Do I see specific evidence that the mentoring process has supported a teacher's ability to . . . ?*

- Work with mentors, peers, and colleagues to commit to participating together to discuss ideas about effective practices and to reflect on actual experiences.
- Compare current practices to stated values and beliefs about teaching.
- Recognize the accountability required in the teacher's role, and be able to connect actual practices to a professional vision of supporting the overall development of children and families.
- Develop a variety of teaching practices, and use them with growing flexibility and intentionality (Carroll, 2007).

A more concrete and specific evaluation is found in the list of questions that follows.

Mentors should ask themselves, *In what ways did I work to*

- get to know and build trust with the teacher (as protégé)?
- orient the teacher to the mentoring process, including the time frame and possible schedule?
- learn about the teacher and his or her early childhood program?
- explore with the teacher what he or she wanted to learn, to change, or to have happen?
- encourage the documentation of a problem or gather information on a teacher's area of interest?
- be flexible during implementation?
- problem-solve through dialogue and reflective feedback?
- encourage and challenge the teacher through use of open-ended and probing questions?
- evaluate our work together (How did you know that you accomplished your goals?) and leave with ideas for next steps?
- infuse cultural competence concepts into our discussions?

Do any of these areas bring up questions for you? What are you still wondering about?

Based on Buyssee, V., & Wesley, P. (2005). *Consultation in early childhood settings.* Baltimore, MD: Paul H. Brookes Publishing Co.

Summary

Building professional relationships with adults is not the same as getting along with a colleague. This work is based on planning for a goal-focused learning partnership that requires cultural competence. The professional-learning relationship is sustained (or weakened) by a mentor's ability (or inability) to establish or negotiate expectations and engage a teacher in reflection and application of his or her learning.

Figure 2.6   Summary of Building PD Relationships With Adults
....

Documenting learning over time is key to this process and allows a teacher to be able to evaluate his or her own progress. Review Figure 2.6 and the key concepts for building PD relationships with early childhood teachers.

Writing a reflective journal on one or more of the four ideas that follow will allow you to process and plan for ways to bring the ideas alive in your work with teachers. As you journal, ask yourself the following questions:

What am I still wondering about? What do I find confusing? Does something seem hard to achieve in my context? What barriers and challenges, as well as successes, can I think of from my past work supporting teachers or other colleagues?

Revisit your readings and past reflective journal writing for inspiration and evidence to support your summary reflections. As you reflect, especially consider how you do the following things:

1. **Establish a mutual understanding of the purpose of the mentoring visit.**
   - It takes time to build trust and comfort.
   - Be a safe haven to allow a teacher to share frustrations and successes.
   - The purpose of mentoring may be established by a program, or it may be negotiated by the mentor and teacher themselves.

2. **Recognize the need for understanding and respecting the teacher as protégé.**
   - Learn over time (or come to the mentoring visit understanding) the unique characteristics, as well as the cultural and community context, of the teacher's work.
   - Promote respect and safety while still challenging the teacher to consider areas in practices that may cause some discomfort.

3. **Respond sensitively, and show empathy.**
   - Listen nonjudgmentally.
   - Encourage the teacher to share what he or she expects and needs.
   - Set aside time to share stories, feelings, and histories.

4. **Repair relationships when conflict arises.**
   - Be open to hearing concerns and to changing your style to better fit the needs of the teacher.

References

Administration for Children and Families, Office of Head Start, National Center on Quality Teaching and Learning. (2012, May). *Practice based coaching.* Retrieved from http://eclkc.ohs.acf.hhs.gov/hslc/tta-system/teaching/docs/practice-based-coaching.pdf

Administration for Children and Families, Office of Head Start, National Center on Quality Teaching and Learning. (2012, May). *What do we know about coaching?* Retrieved from http://eclkc.ohs.acf.hhs.gov/hslc/tta-system/teaching/docs/What-Do-We-Know-About-Coaching.pdf

Ainsworth, M. D., Blehar, M., Waters, E., & Wall, S. (1978). *Patterns of attachment: A psychological study of the strange situation.* Hillsdale, NJ: Erlbaum Associates.

Anderson, G. L., & Herr, K. (2011). Scaling up "evidenced-based" practices for teachers is a profitable but discredited paradigm. *Educational Researcher, 40*(6), 287–289.

Barnett, W. S., Epstein, D. J., Friedman, A. H., Sansanelli, R., & Hustedt, J. T. (2009). *The state of preschool 2009: State preschool yearbook.* New Brunswick, NJ: National Institute for Early Education Research, Rutgers University.

Bausmith, J., & Barry, C. (2011). Revisiting professional learning communities to increase college readiness: The importance of pedagogical content knowledge. *Educational Researcher, 40*(4), 175–178.

Bowlby, J. (1973). *Attachment and loss* (Vol. 2): *Separation: Anxiety and anger.* New York: Basic Books.

Buyssee, V., & Wesley, P. (2005). *Consultation in early childhood settings.* Baltimore, MD: Paul H. Brookes Publishing Co.

Carroll, D. (Summer, 2007). Developing dispositions for ambitious teaching. *Journal of Educational Controversy, 2*(2). Retrieved from http://www.wce.wwu.edu/Resources/CEP/eJournal/v002n002/a010.shtml

Carter, M. (2004). *Side by side: Mentoring teachers for reflective practice.* [Video]. Seattle, WA: Harvest Resources.

Chang, H. (2006). *Getting ready for quality: The critical importance of developing and supporting a skilled, ethnically and linguistically diverse early childhood workforce.* Oakland, CA: California Tomorrow.

Clarke, D., & Hollingsworth, H. (2002). Elaborating a model of teacher professional growth. *Teaching and Teacher Education, 18,* 947–967.

Coburn, C. (2001). Collective sense making about reading: How teachers mediate reading policy in their professional communities. *Educational Evaluation and Policy Analysis, 23,* 145–170.

Copple, C., & Bredekamp, S. (Eds). (2009). *Developmentally appropriate practices in early childhood programs serving children from birth through age 8.* (3rd ed). Washington, DC: National Association for the Education of Young Children.

Cross, T., Bazron, B., Dennis, K., & Isaacs, M. (1989). *Toward a culturally competent system of care* (Vol. 1). Washington, DC: Georgetown University Child Development Center, CASSP Technical Assistance Center.

Darling-Hammond, L., Wei, R. C., Andree, A., Richardson, N., & Orphanos, S. (2009). *Professional learning in the learning profession: A status report on teacher development in the United States and abroad.* Dallas, TX: National Staff Development Council.

Elliott, K., Farris, M., Alvarado, C., Peters, C., Surr, W., Genser, A., & Chin, E. (2000). *The power of mentoring. Taking the lead: Investing in early childhood leadership for the 21st century.* Report of the Center for Development in Early Care and Education, Report, Wheelock College, Boston.

Garet, M., Porter, S., Andrew, C., & Desimone, L. (2001). What makes professional development effective? Results from a national sample of teachers. *American Educational Research Journal, 38*(4), 915–945.

Gonzalez, N., Moll, L. C., & Amanti, C. (2005). *Funds of knowledge: Theorizing practices in households, communities, and classrooms.* Hillsdale, NJ: Erlbaum Associates.

Guskey, T. R. (2002). Professional development and teacher change. *Teachers and Teaching, 8,* 381–391.

Hanft, B., Rush, D., & Sheldon, M. (2004). *Coaching Families and Colleagues in Early Childhood.* Baltimore: Paul H. Brookes Publishing Co.

Harms, T., Cryer, D., & Clifford, R. (1990). *Infant-toddler environment rating scale.* New York: Teachers College Press.

Johnston, K., & Brinamen, C. (2006). *Mental health consultation in child care: Transforming relationships among directors, staff and families.* Washington, DC: ZERO TO THREE.

Kelly, J., Zuckerman, T., Sandoval, D., & Buehlman, K. (2003). *Promoting first relationships: A curriculum for service providers to help parents and other caregivers meet young children's social and emotional needs.* Seattle, WA: NCAST-AVENUW Publications.

Lutton, A. (Ed.). (2012). *Advancing the profession: NAEYC standards and guidelines for professional development.* Washington, DC: National Association for the Education of Young Children.

Michigan Association for Infant Mental Health. (2002). *Michigan Association for Infant Mental Health training guidelines.* East Lansing, MI: Author.

Nabobo-Baba, U., & Tiko, L. (2009). Indigenous Fijian cultural conceptions of mentoring and related capacity building: Implications for teacher education. In A. Gibbons & C. Gibbs (Eds.), *Conversations on early childhood teacher education: Voices from the working forum for teacher education* (pp. 73–81). Redmond, WA: World Forum Foundation and New Zealand Tertiary College.

National Association for the Education of Young Children (NAEYC). (2009). Quality Benchmarks for Cultural Competence Project. Retrieve from: http://www.naeyc.org/files/naeyc/file/policy/state/QBCC_Tool.pdf

National Association for the Education of Young Children and National Association of Child Care Resource and Referral Agencies. (2011). *Early childhood education professional development: Training and technical assistance glossary.* Washington, DC: National Association for the Education of Young Children. Retrieved from http://www.naeyc.org/GlossaryTraining_TA.pdf

National Center for Cultural Competence. (2004). *Planning for cultural and linguistic competence in systems of care . . . for children & youth with social-emotional and behavioral disorders and their families.* Washington, DC: National Center for Cultural Competence, Georgetown University Center for Child and Human Development. Retrieved from http://www11.georgetown.edu/research/gucchd/NCCC/documents/SOC_Checklist.pdf

Osterman, K., & Kottkamp, R. (2004). *Reflective practice for educators.* Thousand Oaks, CA: Corwin Press.

Pawl, J. H., & St. John, M. (1998). How you are is as important as what you do . . . in making a positive difference for infants, toddlers and their families. ZERO TO THREE: National Center for Infants, Toddlers and Families, Washington, DC.

Pawl, J. H. (1990). *Infants in day care. Reflections on experiences, expectations, and relationships. Zero to Three, 10*(3), 1–6.

Pianta, R. C., Mashburn, A. J., Downer, J. T., Hamre, B. K., & Justice, L. (2008). Effects of web-mediated professional development resources on teacher–child interaction in pre-kindergarten classrooms. *Early Childhood Research Quarterly, 23*(4), 431–451.

Ramey, S. L., & Ramey, C. T. (2008). Establishing a science of professional development for early education programs: The Knowledge Application Information Systems theory of professional development. In L. M. Justice & C. Vukelich (Eds.), *Achieving excellence in preschool literacy instruction* (pp. 41–63). New York: Guilford Press.

Rush, D. D., & Shelden, M. L. (2005). *Evidence-based definitions of coaching practices.* CASEinPoint, *1*(6). Retrieved from http://www.fippcase.org/caseinpoint/caseinpoint_vol1_no6.pdf

Scarr, S. (1998). American child care today. *American Psychologist, 53,* 95–108.

Siegel, D. J. (1999). *The developing mind: How relationships and the brain interact to shape who we are.* New York: Guilford Press.

Siegel, D. J. (2010). *Mindsight: The new science of personal transformation.* New York: Bantam.

Snyder, P., Hemmeter, M. L., Artman, K., Kinder, K., Pasia, C., & McLaughlin, T. (2012). *Early childhood professional development: Categorical framework and systematic review of the literature.* Manuscript submitted for publication.

Somekh, B. (2010). The collaborative action research network: 30 years of agency in developing educational action research. *Educational Action Research, 18*(1), 103–121.

Stremmel, A. (2007). Teacher research: Nurturing professional and personal growth through inquiry. *Voices of practitioners.* National Association for the Education of Young Children. Retrieved from http://journal.naeyc.org/btj/vp/pdf/Voices-Stremmel.pdf

Strickland, D., & Riley-Ayers, S. (2007). *Literacy leadership in early childhood: The essential guide.* New York: Teachers College Press.

Trivette, C., Dunst, C., Hamby, D., & O'Herin, C. (2009). *Characteristics and consequences of adult learning methods and strategies.* (Winterberry Research Synthesis, Vol. 2, No. 2). Asheville, NC: Winterberry Press.

U.S. Department of Health and Human Services, Administration for Children and Families. (2005). Steps to success: Decision maker guide. In *Steps to success: An instructional design for early literacy mentor-coaches in Head Start and Early Head Start.* Washington, DC: Author. Retrieved from http://eclkc.ohs.acf.hhs.gov/hslc/resources/ECLKC_Bookstore/PDFs/2CB1B8CB26CDE21894032EE5FF136829.pdf

Virmani, E. A., & Ontai, L. (2010). Supervision and training in child care: Does reflective supervision foster caregiver insightfulness? *Infant Mental Health Journal, 31*(1), 16–32.

Wenger, E. (1998). *Communities of practice: Learning, meaning, and identity.* Cambridge, UK: Cambridge University Press.

Wenger, E., McDermott, R., & Snyder, W. M. (2002). *Cultivating communities of practice: A guide to managing knowledge.* Boston: Harvard Business School Press.

Wightman, B., Whitaker, K., Traylor, D., Yeider, S., Hyden, V., & Weigand, B. (2007). Reflective practice and supervision in child abuse prevention. *Zero to Three, 28*(2), 29–33.

Wilson, N. (2008). Teachers expanding pedagogical content knowledge: Learning about formative assessment together. *Journal of In-Service Education, 34*(3), 283–298.

Woolfolk Hoy, A., Hoy, W. K., & Davis, H. A. (2009). Teacher's self-efficacy beliefs. In K. W. Wentzel & A. Wigfield (Eds.), *Handbook of motivation in school* (pp. 627–655). Mahwah, NJ: Erlbaum Associates.

●●●

CHAPTER 3

Communicating to Support Teacher Awareness

The chapter supports your growing capacity to

- mentor through dialogue;
- communicate for understanding and build common ground;
- pay attention to communication basics;
- listen with attention and acknowledgment;
- give and receive feedback for reflective thinking;
- engage in a cycle of mentoring communication strategies;
- understand asynchronous communication basics—online, virtual, and written feedback;
- reflect on conflict and repair relationships;
- recognize and support effective teacher dispositions; and
- practice culturally responsive mentoring.

Communication to increase a teacher's awareness of his or her practices and interactions is the focus of this chapter. Increasing effective listening and reflective feedback, and exploring ways to resolve conflict and increase cultural competence, are central to the development of the mentoring process. A mentor's effective communication skills include joining with a teacher to nurture a growing capacity for responsiveness, curiosity, persistence, and questioning of their own perspective. The mentoring process has the potential to affirm to a teacher with promising dispositions that he or she has the potential to be a professional with a repertoire of effective practices.

> *I sometimes read a poem by Langston Hughes about life not being "no crystal stair" to my daughter. For me, the poem is about poverty and persevering through it. A mother explains to her son about how life is like a rickety, falling apart staircase with missing steps. If you cannot keep moving up, then stay on the step you are at. The goal is not to go backwards; and somehow, a way will be shown to you that will enable you to keep climbing. . . . I am strong. I know how to ask questions to find the right people to talk to. I know how not to get frustrated when filling out one form after another and how to retain my dignity when I am treated disrespectfully. There have been times that I have doubted myself; but, my early childhood mentor has gone out of her way to let me know that she believed in me. She has helped me to keep climbing.*
>
> Reflective writing by a participant in a mentor–teacher preschool practicum

Mentoring Through Dialogue

●●

Consider this scenario. Mariyanna is a teacher in a community childcare program. She is working on using questions more effectively with the children in her care and has been asked by her mentor to document some of her conversations with children. She recorded and then examined this vignette:

> *Amanda (age 4):* "I wish I was a bird."
>
> *Teacher:* "You wish you were a bird. Why?"
>
> *Amanda:* "I wouldn't have to go to school."
>
> *Teacher:* "Where would you go, Amanda?"
>
> *Amanda:* "South Dakota."
>
> *Teacher:* "How do you know that you would like South Dakota?"
>
> *Amanda:* "I want to see what it looks like."

Mariyanna then recorded in her journal the following thoughts:

I was delighted by Amanda's and my conversation about her imagining to be a bird and flying to South Dakota. . . . I wondered, "Why does Amanda express longing to escape school? Did she see a passing bird overhead that caught her fancy? Does she have a longing for freedom but not the language skills to express that concept yet? Do I read too much into the remarks of a four year old?"

The mentor, who in this case was a college instructor, recalled Mariyanna's previous journal comment before her child observation:

I feel I am not doing as good a job of using language to promote thinking as I could do. I find myself being aware of trying to find a balance between asking too many and not enough questions. I don't want to distract her and end her interest in what she is discussing and drawing.

At the next conference, the teacher shared her observations and reflections. Sparks of interest were now flying for both the mentor and the young teacher. They now had a common experience to explore with curiosity. They wondered together, *What did Amanda's comments mean?* They decided that without more conversations with this child, they could not know. Her words might mean anything from wanting to get away from school because of conflicts with her friends to planning for a magical play adventure, taking on the persona of a bird.

The mentor could see that this teacher was now receptive to applying what had previously been discussed about conversation strategies that promote cognitive development. How had feelings of fear and confusion changed to being "delighted" by the possibilities of trying out new conversation strategies? The mentor had first listened to the teacher and learned the issue that the teacher wanted to discuss (e.g., conversation strategies), thus learning of her feelings and fears. Then, the mentor suggested that the teacher observe and gather information about this child and her preschool experiences. Now was the time for the mentor (who had established trust and facilitated turning the feeling of fear into a sense of curiosity and ongoing research) to use mentoring communication strategies to spark more teacher awareness. Open-ended questions began their reflective conference: *What did you notice? Why did that work? What might you do differently?* Now, a return to a discussion of language development strategies was helpful rather than overwhelming for the teacher.

Individual and small-group dialogues are an effective way to promote a teacher's thinking about his or her practices. Mentors who resist giving an initial evaluation and instead provide descriptive feedback or stimulate a teacher's thinking with open-ended questions enable teachers to problem-solve to improve their practices (Gallacher, 1997). By first sharing concerns, worries, and teaching stories, educators may begin to dream of a new way of working in early childhood classrooms. Only then is the teacher ready to effectively use the assistance of a knowledgeable mentor.

Communicate for Understanding and Building Common Ground

Often, finding the best ways to promote understanding of concepts that will help a teacher to be more effective is what initially preoccupies a mentor's thoughts. Mentors may forget that verbal communication involves both sending (speaking) and receiving (listening) information and that they should first *listen* before focusing on *being heard*. Teachers, however, may be preoccupied with wondering whether it is safe for them to share concerns, what impact power differences might have on their comfort level in sharing, and whether enough time will be allowed for them to explain their point of view. Teachers may be doing all of this thinking while simultaneously, quietly noticing culturally influenced communication patterns involving eye contact, physical space differences, changes in tone of voice, and subtle facial expressions and body movements, all of which can send nonverbal messages of interest or disinterest (Sockalingham & Waetzig, 2012, p. 118). With all of this mental activity going on, it is easy to understand how mentors and teachers may initially misunderstand each other. Because the mentor has the obligation to set the tone of the professional learning relationship, the mentor's primary communication goal should first be to *listen for understanding*. This listening may come in the form of quietly observing or asking open-ended questions that encourage a teacher to share while a mentor takes notes. The initial goal for the mentor is not to solve the teacher's problem but to understand the teacher's perspective. Mentors should work hard to put themselves in the shoes of the teacher. The goal of understanding first means that communication should be used to check for understanding.

Pay Attention to Communication Basics

Even experienced mentors who use a variety of methods to monitor communication flow can sometimes feel as if they are trying to view the invisible. Just as a pilot has a checklist to review before taking off, a mentor should have a mental checklist of communication basics. Begin by recognizing how critical communication is to the establishment of a social and emotional climate that will support professional problem solving. Mentors try to help others find solutions that fit their specific situation. Dialogue, rather than trying to convince someone of a specific position, is usually the best way to begin. This is much more difficult than merely having good intentions and professional knowledge about best practices in an area of expertise such as child development. Navigating communication means recognizing that even short phone or e-mail encounters send important messages about what a mentor values. Asking for explicit feedback to learn whether a concern was met or a question answered is one way to check the pulse of a learning relationship. Silently watching a videotaped classroom interaction with a teacher and waiting for him or her to comment on what he or she is wondering is another way.

Communication involves a complex interplay between people who are both expressing and receiving messages. In a mentoring or other professional-development relationship, the goal is to intentionally work to establish a trusting and collaborative working style at every opportunity to interact. In contrast, beginning with inflexible rules or legal jargon that communicates a high-stakes atmosphere of win/lose outcomes will establish a competitive and low-trust climate. Mentors need to consider the importance of taking the time to care about ways in which all forms of communication (e.g., by direct verbal conversation, in writing, and through nonverbal cues or verbal hints) affect other people in learning relationships. The first goal of the mentor is to learn how a teacher learns best and how the mentor can promote the teacher's thinking, rather than to create a climate of evaluation and accountability. Mentoring should be centered on teachers and the problems or issues that they identify. If teachers perceive the process to be strength-based and "no-fault," they will more easily engage with the mentoring process (Knight, 2011).

Listen With Attention and Acknowledgment First

Understanding the teacher's point of view through effective listening encourages the teacher to share information. Mentors may use what they have heard to facilitate examination of what the teacher is doing and saying. New ways of teaching can then develop. However, the opposite may also result when the mentor is not listening well and is primarily focused on an external agenda. Many educators have had the experience of a supervisor or colleague mechanically parroting back their words to them in an attempt to make them feel heard and understood.

When repeating back phrases by stating, "I am hearing you say . . .," it is essential that the speaker convey not only the words that they heard but also a feeling of respect, acceptance, and undivided attention. Doing so requires skills that are often referred to as *active listening* (Rogers & Farson, 1957). Otherwise, the teacher may feel that this communication style is like a false front, or a veneer, of caring, whereas in reality the mentor has no intention of understanding or exerting the effort to search for deeper meaning.

Mentors, instead, should probe for an understanding of teachers by listening with empathy (Covey, 2004). The overall style of listening that is most effective in mentoring emphasizes acceptance first. It involves putting aside judgment in order to focus on learning what the teacher is communicating. Even if mentors are not always correct in their understanding, teachers greatly appreciate the effort it takes on the part of the mentors to listen to their experiences and to strive to learn how they feel before offering solutions. Specific skills involved in effective listening are paying attention, acknowledging, paraphrasing, and summarizing.

Listening and Responding

Includes paying attention, acknowledging, paraphrasing, and summarizing

- *Paraphrasing:* I am hearing that you tried to limit the materials in the house area. In other words . . .
- *Acknowledging:* So, you are feeling . . .
- *Clarifying:* You are noticing . . . What do you mean by . . .? Would this be like . . .?
- *Check for understanding:* Do I make sense? . . . Let me see whether I heard you right. . . . Okay, I am understanding . . . Can you give me an example of . . .?
- *Encouraging:* Yes . . . . Please go on. . . . That's interesting.
- *Elaborating:* Tell me more about . . .
- *Avoiding premature problem solving:* I'd rather listen more before suggesting . . .
- *Affirmation:* I like listening and learning about your observations.
- *Summarizing:* There seem to be several ideas here to try next week.

The communication basics required in mentoring are often lacking in other forms of professional development. If our goal is measurable changes in children's learning and in teachers' practices, then the communication skills outlined next should be used in an ongoing, individualized, and intensive way that helps a teacher apply evidence-based practices in an educational setting (Darling-Hammond & Richardson, 2009; Knight, 2009).

Noticing and Supporting

Be aware of nonverbal cues or body language that convey interest. *Example: Leaning slightly toward the speaker with a relaxed, open manner, and maintaining good eye contact.* Note: Body language conveying interest may vary in different contexts and cultures, and with different individual styles.

- *Supporting:* I know you can do it!
- *Telling your story:* I struggled with that situation when I was a toddler teacher.
- *Demonstrating:* Watch how I put in one puzzle piece while he watched.
- *Informing:* That rash could be contagious. He needs to see a doctor.
- *Drawing inferences:* Timmy may need more encouragement to use the toilet.
- *Evaluating:* The strategy that you used to encourage participation worked well.

Bellm, Whitebook, and Hnatiuk (1997) found that "thinking about examining experiences, activities, and human interactions and events" requires mentors to use effective ways of communicating. Adapted from their documented and tried-and-true strategies are the following communication basics:

Seeking Information

- *Questioning:* How many toddlers are usually in this room?
- *Silence:* (Pause. Wait attentively while the other person thinks.)
- *Organizing:* Listing the several themes I am hearing . . .
- *Shifting Focus:* So, a value, a belief, or an assumption is . . .
- *Building:* Yes, and that's a great place to start the conversation about . . .
- *Finding Consensus:* Would you say that focusing on early literacy strategies is . . .? How can we bring these ideas together? It seems to boil down to . . . How does that connect to . . .?

Open-ended questions to promote thinking lower the teacher's risk that he or she will feel uncomfortable and stay silent in a dialogue, because these questions are framed to generate conversation without right or wrong answers. Teachers engaging in professional development will assess the risk of a response to any question posed by an "expert." They will wonder, "Are different views valued?" The mentor who brings out what teachers know, feel, and believe, while also respecting the varied responses, is allowing for a conversation to continue long enough for new information or strategies to be considered. Teachers will mull over the question "What do I think?" before considering the question "Do I want to try this?" Open-ended questions promote thinking and serve as a provocation or catalyst for engaging with new content.

Open-ended questions

Promoting thinking and more conversation involves practice in using questions that invite many responses, such as the following:

- How do you feel about it?
- How will you use it? How do you see this working?
- What do you think about it?

- How can we make sense of this?
- Can you tell me more about . . . ?
- Why do you think that is important?
- What do you think this means?
- What else could support your idea?
- On the other hand . . . What do you think is another way to think about it?

REFLECTION

Consider the previous examples of mentor feedback to a teacher, and think of times that you have used these same strategies. Why do you think that these communication basics are so effective? Try to use them in the next few days in interactions with friends, family, and coworkers. What felt comfortable to you? In what areas do you need to practice more? How does timing influence what you choose to say after listening?

Give and Receive Feedback That Supports Reflective Thinking

Initially, a mentor and teacher must find time to talk, observe, and set goals. The beginning of a new mentoring relationship is a delicate time. Mentoring goals usually involve fostering new practices or trying old ideas in new ways. This means that the challenging of some current practices will usually occur. How can the mentor meet such challenges while fostering trust and respect? Ongoing, specific feedback from someone respected by the teacher (Oja & Reiman, 2007) is a primary technique used by successful mentors, coaches, and consultants.

The content of this feedback should use the teacher's experience in meaningful ways. The mentor may have just observed or viewed a videotape of the teacher's interactions with children. Mentor and teacher may have toured the teaching environment and discussed how well it is functioning. Then, after the mentor listens, notices, and seeks information (see previous discussion in this chapter), subsequent meetings should include feedback that supports the teacher's reflection on practice. A mentor's feedback is more effective after a teacher has shared his or her own views and insights into a teaching dilemma or situation (Hanft, Rush, & Shelden, 2004). Now, questions are needed that promote reflective thinking and that prompt recognition of current practices and support connections to values, goals, and research.

Verbal feedback is most effective when it is specific and relates to something in which the teacher seems interested or that the mentor observed. It should connect teachers back to what they say that they value. Begin with positive comments that are specific, descriptive, and strengths-based. Everyone has strengths. A mentor must discover them and share what is seen and heard. Consider the following example:

- She looks up at you often. I can see that you have a great time together.
- Your circle time stopped when the children were ready to move on. You noticed their interests and needs.

When mentors move to reflective comments, they must feel that the teacher is now ready for an analysis of his or her actions and choices. The purpose of reflection is to facilitate discussion of what a teacher already knows or does, wants to know or do, or is considering doing in the future.

....

Reflective comments are open and nonjudgmental. These comments help a teacher to see from the child's, parents' or another teacher's perspective. Questions to promote reflection and find meaning in everyday events include the following:

- Can you talk more about that?
- What have you tried before?
- What evidence do you have about that?
- What do you want to happen?
- Tell me about a time when you saw this . . .
- How does the child look at it?
- What patterns are you noticing?
- What gaps do you see in the plan?
- Do you know how the family views this?
- How would you connect this choice to your program goals?
- What does it mean when . . .?
- If this happens again, what do you think you will say or do?

....

These questions support what Schon (1983) referred to as the professional development need for both *reflection on action* (looking back) and *reflection in action*, or reshaping actions during teaching. The goal is also for the teacher to establish a general habit of *reflection for practice* for the purpose of establishing future choices that are based on being aware of what previously were unexamined assumptions (Killion & Todnem, 1991). This last form of reflection involves the teacher in both reviewing what happened and being able to identify future choices.

Finally, the time for sharing technical information or instructive feedback has arrived. This is what most mentors have wanted to do from the moment they met the teacher. This is also what they may have been asked for repeatedly but have put off until after a period of listening and observing, noticing, seeking information, giving positive feedback, and facilitating teacher reflection. Mentors have told this author that it feels counterintuitive to wait so long to share their knowledge, skills, and resources. Yet, they later report greater effectiveness when they offer new ideas formulated on the basis of sensitivity to their mentoring role. This role requires offering new ways of seeing a problem only after taking the time to facilitate thoughtful reflection that is reciprocal and builds on the mentor's knowledge of a teacher's needs and readiness for specific instructional strategies (Flaherty, 1999).

....

Instructive feedback is very time dependent.

- Add a few ideas after positive and reflective feedback. Include an empathetic point of view. Mentor comments may also reinforce what is already happening.
- A mentor should not start with instructive feedback, even if the teacher is asking the mentor to give advice immediately. If a mentor gives instructive feedback too early, it may make the teacher feel judged or confused, or react defensively. Instructive comments offered before the mentor knows the teacher could feel condescending to the teacher if the teacher is already applying the suggested strategy, or it could make the teacher feel stressed that he or she isn't doing it yet.

A mentor's instructive comments might be as follows:

I noticed that Mary, the child you wanted me to observe, stayed close to you at breakfast. Let's discuss ways that you might change the environment to encourage exploration. Mary needs to practice her social skills with her friends. Maybe we can talk more about that this afternoon.

It can be hard to get 10 preschool children outside at one time. Have you tried dividing the class up into smaller groups and asking another teacher to help with that transition?

When you greeted Juanita and showed her where to put her coat, she seemed relieved and happy. She is new to the school, so that made her feel as if she belongs.

Mentors try to get teachers to slow down long enough to reflect and think about what they are doing. Using the communication strategies outlined here will support productive mentor–teacher conversations. Now, reflect on how to keep these conversations going by considering the purpose of mentor–teacher conversations. Choose to engage a teacher in thinking about his or her practices by collaborating together.

Encourage Thoughtful Review of Practices by

- **informing and sharing the advantages** of using movement activities to engage preschoolers at gathering time;
- **comparing and describing two opposing views** on how to guide children to take turns;
- **classifying and referring to different categories** of children's literature;
- **analyzing cause and effect or associations by reviewing research** on different hand-washing techniques for preventing the spread of infectious disease;
- **problem solving** by describing a specific problem, raising questions, observing, and analyzing gathered information and trying a new strategy or plan of action;
- **persuading** by supporting a teacher to go on a field trip to another program environment to see ideas that you have been discussing in action;
- **using nonverbal modeling** of effective listening by sitting in close proximity to children; and
- **communicating without words** by exchanging curriculum ideas through art, music, or drama.

When concluding a mentoring conversation, share how much you enjoyed having the opportunity to observe the teacher and get to know his or her program a little. Then, affirm for the teacher that he or she can do it. Bellm, Whitebook, and Hnatiuk (1997) suggest concluding with affirmations to keep the ongoing mentoring relationship strong.

Conclude with affirmations to support ongoing reflection

- You can find your own way to do this.
- I liked talking to you about . . .
- It was very interesting to look at that issue today.

- You can experiment and explore ideas about . . .
- Meeting your needs and finding a way to support the children is important.
- You can do this at your own pace.
- You can ask me for help.
- You can figure out how to do this. I know that you can find a way that works best for you.

••

By varying the ways in which mentors communicate to support a teacher to think and reflect differently, mentors may facilitate understanding, learning, and growth in teaching. These strategies, when used in a spirit of co-inquiry, or mentor–teacher collaborative inquiry, enhance professional development in a variety of settings (Bray, Lee, Smith, & Yorks, 2000).

••
Connections
••

Practicing verbal feedback strategies requires finding other adults willing to be mentors or teachers in a role play. Practice the communication strategies outlined in this chapter.

1. **Pair and share:** Role-play as either a mentor or a teacher who are having a conversation. Imagine that this conversation is occurring after the mentor has observed the teacher's facilitating an outside gardening activity with young children. Practice using each type of feedback if you are playing the mentor. Then, switch roles.
2. **Form four groups:** Form listening, positive, reflective, and instructive-feedback small groups. Reflect in each group on times that you have used each type of feedback, and discuss how and when it seems to work best. Share comments with the large group.
3. **Form groups of three:** Each of the three persons should choose to take on the role of teacher, mentor, or observer.
   - Imagine that you are a teacher. Identify the type of setting in which you work (e.g., childcare center, family childcare home, Head Start, early primary school, etc.), one need or desire that you have for learning about something specific (e.g., increasing skill in child guidance), and at least one challenge that concerns you (e.g., finding time to meet).
   - Pretend that you are the mentor. Create a few facts about your background, your mentoring program affiliation, and anything else that you want to share.
   - Be the observer of the other two, and watch the conversation. Prompt the mentor to use positive, reflective, instructive, and affirmative feedback at least once in the conversation.
4. **Resource to promote your reflection:** View one scenario from the DVD *Learning Through Observation* (Zbar & Lerner, 2003), or use a videotaped interaction of a teacher and mentor that occurred while they were discussing experiences of the teacher. What types of feedback did you observe? How did they work? What would you change? How would you connect what you saw with the ideas from this chapter? Use this graphic to help you recall effective mentoring communication strategies.
5. If you are currently working with a teacher or early childhood professional, ask for permission to videotape a mentoring conversation for

the purpose of reviewing your communication strategies. Review the video and ask yourself, "What strategies are effective, and what do I want to do more or less of?" Consider asking the teacher what he or she felt worked and what communication strategies did not facilitate his or her learning.

Cycle of Mentoring Communication Strategies

The implications of increasing the depth of thinking and critical analysis of teachers through building on existing curiosity are that the quality of adult teaching and learning experiences are improved. There is an art to communication that is intuitive and hard to teach. It is honed over a lifetime of observing others and noticing nonverbal cues. Yet, professionals who act as mentors can become more intentional and effective by completing a cycle of communication strategies, outlined in Figure 3.1, that support a cycle of teacher research or inquiry. The three main stages involve communication to (1) observe, notice, and respond; (2) reflect and analyze evidence; and (3) apply, plan, model, and modify by clarifying what you hope will happen.

1. **Jigsaw:** Form three teams, and have each take strategies from the *Observe*, *Reflect*, and *Apply* sections of the graphic. Teach these ideas to the other two teams, and check your understanding by acting out scenarios in which these strategies are used. Ask the other teams to call out or write down which strategy you were using and why it is effective.

Figure 3.1 Cycle of Communication Strategies: Observe, Reflect, and Apply

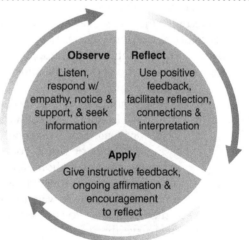

Asynchronous Communication Basics: Online, Virtual, and Written Feedback

Professional development cannot be assumed to occur in a face-to-face environment only. High-quality adult learning that meets the research-based criteria of being (a) content focused, (b) coherent, (c) collaborative, (d) ongoing, (e) intensive, and (f) linked to hands-on learning, with (g) opportunities for reflection (Darling-Hammond & Richardson, 2009), may also occur in a variety of virtual-learning contexts.

Mentors may combine phone-call consultations, e-mail correspondence, online course discussions, and video exchanges along with face-to-face contact. The first skill required for mentors' communicating in an online or a distance-learning context is to learn whether any barriers exist for teacher participation. Ask yourself these questions:

- Who will facilitate the skills, technology tools, and any technical support needed?
- Does everyone understand how and when to participate and the expectations of involvement?
- Is sufficient time built into the mentoring plan to allow for teachers to become comfortable in participating in an online or virtual environment?
- How will confidentiality be maintained for the teacher and any children or families regarding program issues discussed?
- Who will mentor the mentor or adult educator when unexpected problems occur?

The benefit of asynchronous communication for the teacher is the flexibility to write comments, ask questions, post video, or communicate within a specified period. The challenge for some teachers, according to current research, is that adults are more successful in online learning environments if they are organized and motivated when working independently (MacMillan, 2008). This means that mentors must be sensitive to blending many forms of communication in order to individualize the mentoring strategies and meet the needs of teachers. However, adult educators are often surprised at how comfortable some teachers feel in online discussions. The teachers may find that this medium allows more time for reflection and is less threatening than a face-to-face or group-discussion setting. Ironically, virtual conversations may also break the isolation of teaching by allowing teachers to share concerns and solutions at any time of day or night. Having mentors who write and speak more than one language offers more teachers the opportunity to participate online.

The adult educator, or mentor, is responsible for creating the same relevant, interesting, and individualized conversations online as would occur face-to-face (Torrance & Donahue, 2007). The same sequence of communication basics that have been discussed in this chapter applies online. However, some special considerations for the mentor who is communicating asynchronously include the following:

- Is our communication interactive and responsive?
- Do I reply frequently enough to foster a positive learning relationship?
- Do I individualize my comments online just as I would in a face-to-face setting?
- In a group class or virtual community, am I modeling how to share differing points of view without dominating, unintentionally insulting others with blunt comments, or avoiding wresting with complex ideas?
- Am I blending multiple ways to communicate that seem the best mix for this person or group (face-to-face, video, discussion board, phone conversations, etc.)?
- Do I have the disposition to be a colearner alongside some teachers who may have much greater expertise in technology than I do?

Conflict and Problem-Solving

When problems or disagreements occur, consider these communication skills and strategies:

1. *Assertion skills:* Sometimes, conflict occurs due to small details that are vague or unresolved. Clarify the details of the mentoring relationship in order to avoid problems.

- I know you prefer to meet on Mondays, but I am not able to meet then because I am required to be at another meeting. Can we find a day that works for both of us?

2. *Awareness of ourselves as mentors:* When frustrations build, first consider whether there is an understanding of what values, beliefs, and cultural assumptions or biases might be involved in a mentoring interaction. Mentors should ask themselves these questions:
   - Is my suggestion the only way to do it, or are there many right ways?
   - Is this best practice, or is it simply how my family did it?
   - Do I understand the teacher's point of view?
   - Who could help me gain more awareness of a point of view with which I am unfamiliar?
   - Do I have high expectations for this teacher, or am I assuming that he or she can't perform well?
   - Am I aware of the power dynamics in our teaching–learning relationship that might be getting in the way? If I am a supervisor and a mentor, is this preventing a true partnership from developing?
   - Would someone else be a better mentor for this person?

   Mentors need others in similar roles to help them sort out patterns that they may be seeing in their interactions with teachers. Consider who is available to support digging deeper into experiences that may influence views on race, culture, class, ethnicity, sex roles, sexual preference, and so on. Individuals and mentoring systems should address the following question: *What ongoing professional-development conversations will the mentor have to support this essential work and to debrief his or her mentoring experiences?*

3. *Collaborative problem solving:* When you as a mentor are offering instructional feedback and ideas to solve work-based dilemmas and are feeling some resistance from a teacher, consider backing up and joining with the teacher to collaboratively solve a problem. An example of this communication strategy can be expressed as follows:

   Let's brainstorm a list of possible options for improving the play area. We could then select the options that fit your criteria and make a plan. How do you feel about it?

   Follow-up questions might include the following:
   - How do you think the children will feel about or react to this solution?
   - What do you need in order to feel that this is worth trying?

   Just as virtually every children's curriculum for teaching social skills includes the teaching of problem-solving skills (Joseph & Strain, 2004), so also should every mentoring communication tool kit include these steps. Use them either formally (review each step and record responses) or informally in the natural flow of conversation.

· ·

When **problem-solving,** remember to

- acknowledge that the problem exists;
- define the problem together;
- investigate possible solutions to try to solve the problem;
- examine the pros and cons of each possible solution;
- agree on something to try; and
- determine a time to come back and evaluate the actions taken.

· ·

4. *Notice signs of burnout, and seek referrals and help from others:* Problem solving and other strategies may not be effective if the teacher is experiencing emotional or physical exhaustion and general dissatisfaction with his or her position. Doubt, blame, and irritability may creep into the conversation of anyone feeling very worn out. Although there are many reasons for teacher exhaustion, one commonly overlooked association is what Figley (1995) and Wolpow et al. (2009) have referred to as "compassion fatigue." Mentors need to know when communication skills are not enough to reach teachers who need significant support to take care of themselves before they can continue to care for children. In other situations, teachers may simply need support from a mentor to become more aware of their overloaded feelings that arise from their experiences of working with children and families undergoing trauma. Changes and increased support from supervisors and a program may involve encouraging or facilitating discussion, for example, between the teacher and a program director. Mentors, of course, are mandated reporters if their concerns reach the level of child abuse and neglect of the children in a teacher's care.

In such circumstances as those just described, recognize signs that teachers need to take care of themselves, and encourage them to seek support, including professional help. Early care and education as a profession carries a high risk for fatigue, exhaustion, and eventual burnout. Sometimes, mentors are invited to "educate" a teacher, whereas these symptoms must be examined before new professional growth may occur. Listen carefully when a teacher reports or exhibits more than one of the following conditions:

- *Health:* Change in appetite, low energy, fatigue, upset stomach, backache, or loss of sleep
- *Feelings:* Irritability, anxiety, guilt, anger, sadness, lack of empathy, or a general feeling of being exhausted
- *Routine behaviors:* Changes in routine; absent-mindedness; losing things; being accident-prone; or sleep disturbances such as nightmares, impatience, irritability, or moodiness
- *Thinking:* Reduced concentration, lack of focus, confusion, rigidity, self-doubt, perfectionism, difficulty in making decisions, or fuzzy thinking
- *Social Relationships:* Mistrust, intolerance, loneliness, change in interest, or being emotionally unavailable

(Based on Wolpow et al., 2009, p. 42)

REFLECTION

Both mentors and teachers gain satisfaction from working with others to facilitate learning and growth. Honing communication skills to maximize the facilitation of a teacher's professional growth is a primary focus of the mentor's development. After reflecting on the "Notice signs of burnout" section, ask yourself whether you have at times recognized that teachers or colleagues needed to take care of themselves rather than learn something new. What did you do? Where did you find support and resources or find a way to encourage them to take care of themselves?

Recognize and Support Effective Teaching Dispositions

How are some teachers able to stay in the profession despite experiencing challenges, and how do they retain their belief that they can make a difference for young children and their families? One of the factors may be the reflective, professional disposition of the teacher. Specifically, Wadlington and Wadlington (2011) found an association between teachers' being able to reflect on their decisions without becoming overly anxious and the tendency of teachers to stay in the profession. These teachers were able to hold high expectations for themselves, collaborate more with others, and believe that they could make a difference. Teachers who suppressed emotions and discussions about their challenges were more likely to feel stress and burnout. The researchers found a strong desire to improve teaching and a willingness to engage in examination of their teaching as being associated with less reported teacher burnout. Mentors can strengthen reflective professional dispositions for teaching by raising a teacher's awareness of his or her own strengths and areas for growth.

First, mentors need to notice when a teacher shows caring, sensitivity, and responsiveness (Noddings, 1984). Previous chapters have discussed the importance of nurturing relationships and responsive interactions with children and families. A mentor needs to also foster a "repertoire of practice" (Chu & Carroll, 2011) that includes

> the ability to make connections with others, entertain their perspectives, appreciate their unique background and knowledge, and recognize gaps in their own knowledge and experience that may make it difficult for them to understand and appreciate the experience of others. (p. 24)

Beginning this task implies that the mentor has skills that encourage the teacher to persist in the face of challenges and remain curious when faced with frustrations. To engage in wondering about what they need to understand or implement requires teachers to have the "capacity for critical reflection to test and challenge their own perceptions, decisions, and actions" (p. 24).

Recognizing the dispositional strengths of a teacher and building on them to develop professional practices requires mentors to support connections through conversations and interactions. See Figure 3.2, which illustrates how a mentoring

Figure 3.2   Dispositions for Teaching

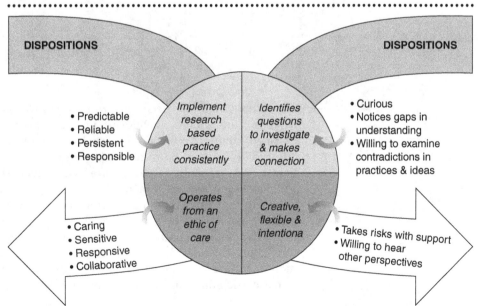

process has the potential to move a teacher with promising disposition (outside the circle) to become a professional with a repertoire of teaching practices (in the circle).

REFLECTION

Connect behaviors in the following four scenarios with the effective teaching dispositions associated with each. (See Figure 3.1.) Discuss times when you have noticed personal strengths in teachers that align well with effective professional teaching practices. If you were a mentor working with the teachers in these scenarios, how might you comment on their strengths and connect these strengths to their teaching goals in order to begin your mentoring process?

1.

2.

3.

4.

1. *Predictable, reliable, persistent, and responsible—one family childcare teacher:* Mary is a family childcare teacher who has a reputation with her enrolled families for beginning each day with a renewed enthusiasm. She can be counted on to remember things that parents told her the day before and pleasantly requests information needed, without judgment or irritation. One mother remarked, "Mary, I gain so much strength from watching you each morning. I often remember what you told me, that children need us to be present, to show up, and to really listen to them every day. I just recently realized that that is what you do for the adults, too." Mary thanked the parent. Later that day, she would meet with a mentor from a local agency to support her to implement a social–emotional curriculum with her toddlers. She was excited but worried about

whether she would be able to work with what was referred to as a *research-based curriculum.*

2. *Caring, sensitive, responsive, and collaborative:* Rebecca is a preschool teacher who is known for her ability to teach social skills. When 5-year-old Hattie pushed her best friend down on the playground, Rebecca skillfully comforted the victim and helped Hattie problem-solve ways to take turns, using a wagon that was the center of their dispute. Later, Rebecca was asked by her director, "What is most important to your vision for the program?" Rebecca replied, without hesitation, "My goal is always to foster a caring community of learners." The director was thrilled and said, "Rebecca, can you share how we do this with the new mentor coming to help us with our focus on social and emotional development?" Rebecca felt overwhelmed at that request and was unsure whether she was capable of explaining her practices.

3. *Curious, notices gaps in understanding, and willing to examine contra- dictions in practices and ideas* Victor is a student intern from the local community college's early childhood-education program. He comes to a Head Start preschool classroom every Thursday morning to observe the children and document their interactions during "science time." Next week, he needs to identify a question of interest to explore with the children. His supervisor or mentor–teacher tells him that it should be easy because he is a curious and observant person who asks lots of questions of her each week. "What do you notice that the children are wondering about?" asks the Head Start teacher. "Well, I have many pages about their explorations at the worm bin. Wow . . . that's it. I guess I just answered my own question." The Head Start teacher was excited and said, "Review your notes. What do the children know, and what do they want to know? You can get started as a colearner and fellow scientist with them next week!"

4. *Takes risks with support and willing to hear other perspectives:* At the weekly teacher's meeting, Brenda reads her anecdotal notes about an accident that happened in her toddler room. Her question for her fellow teachers is about how to stay open to toddler ideas while keeping the space safe for them. She reads her notes:

   Liam, Jordan, and Chiara have been sliding down the indoor toddler ramp for 15 minutes. They play together by imitating each other's actions. Chiara brings little carpet squares out so that they can "ski" down the ramp. She places both feet on the small carpet squares and braces as she pushes her body down the ramp. Boom! Chiara is now crying and rubbing her head as she lies at the bottom of the slide on the gym mat. "I okay," says Chiara.

   Another teacher notes that Brenda is one of the most creative teachers at the center, but she wonders about the safety of this situation. "I think there must be a way to both keep safe and be creative! Let's talk about it."

Mentors need the ability to promote teacher self-awareness in routine conversations. Effective mentors don't underestimate the power of using conversation to set a comfortable climate that encourages a teacher to share his or her thoughts. Knight (2011) has found, after decades of working with instructional coaches and teachers, that productive dialogue occurs only when teachers feel that they are valued for who they are. He views teacher-guided partnerships that promote considering, evaluating, exploring, and learning to be at the heart of improving educational settings.

REFLECTION

1. Recall a time when you have experienced or you have facilitated engaging an adult's brain to think in new ways by asking questions or by making observations in a conversation. What was said? What connection was made?

2. Effective conversations clarify ideas and support learning through talking and listening. Perhaps this second-grade child put it best when she said, "*When we talk to each other, we put our brains together and we become one big smart!*" (Zwiers & Crawford, 2011, p. 209). What are your strengths in facilitating conversations with either children or adults that probe and support others to reflect on their experiences and become "one big smart"?

Culturally Responsive Mentoring Practices

Culture influences communication style, ways of working with others, and preferred ways of learning. It is a guide for how to act, and it influences our activities, beliefs, and values. It may be hard for anyone to describe his or her culture. However, we clearly feel when we are made to feel comfortable or disrespected for our deep values or ways of being. Increasing skills in cultural competence is a lifelong goal and process. Being effective in the mentoring process requires an intense interest in learning to understand another's perspective and how that perspective is similar to or very different from one's own. Cultural competence includes the ability to alter mentoring approaches to match the specific cultural and community context. Debra Sullivan (2010) notes in *Learning to Lead*, ". . . if you suggest solutions that only make sense to you, you will be telling others that their perceptions are wrong" (p. 52). We need to allow room for adults to learn in the ways that they prefer.

What are some strategies to increase the chances that a mentoring process will be culturally sensitive and responsive? *The Power of Mentoring* (Elliott et al., 2000), in discussing the *Taking the Lead* study of mentoring projects at the Center for Career Development in Early Care and Education at Wheelock College, summarized what the study found from diverse communities that established early childhood adult-mentoring programs. Strategies included

- matching the teacher with a mentor who is very knowledgeable about the teacher's cultural and community context. This includes a mentor who speaks the language or languages used by many of the teachers and families in the program setting;
- forming mentoring teams made up of early childhood professionals from more than one cultural group who support a diverse cohort of protégés in a group-discussion setting;
- partnering with elders or other members of a cultural community to establish early childhood educational support.

The *Taking the Lead* project (Elliott et al., 2000) findings suggest the importance of recruiting emerging or grassroots early childhood leaders as mentors who represent and/or understand the community. Required early childhood-education and experience qualifications must also include an understanding of the community context and a possession of cultural competency skills. As noted earlier, in some settings that may mean that no one person will have all of the qualities, education, or experience needed, and mentoring teams or partnerships working with small groups of teachers may be more effective than one-on-one mentoring relationships.

REFLECTION

Consider the questions that follow, and reflect upon a time when you were involved in or you knew of a local early childhood professional-development or mentoring program. Answer the questions to consider whether the planning process took into account the importance of preparing for culturally responsive mentoring. If you have never been involved with or observed a mentoring program, interview a professional who has had this experience and ask for subjective answers for these questions.

- Is the planning group for a mentoring program made up of members of the local community and cultural groups?
- Does the mentoring program take into account cultural values or standards that should affect the nature or design of the program?
- What languages should mentors be able to speak?
- Should teachers choose their own mentors?
- What qualities do local early childhood teachers seek in a mentor?
- Do potential mentors understand the socioeconomic issues in the community?
- If mentors are qualified to support learning in a specific early childhood content area, do they understand the program context (e.g., family childcare, center care, for-profit or nonprofit organization, federally or state-funded preschools, etc.) of their protégés?

Areas of Cultural Sensitivity

All mentors can benefit from considering their professional-development needs in the area of respect for and understanding of diversity. Gonzalez-Mena (2008, pp. 32–39) identifies common areas that are often misunderstood between people of different backgrounds. They are as follows:

- *Personal space:* How close do you feel comfortable sitting or standing next to someone when you are talking?

- *Smiling, touching, and eye contact:* Do you smile frequently to be polite, or only when you are extremely happy? Do you avert your eyes to show respect, or look directly into someone's eyes to be respectful? What do you know about differences in cultural rules regarding touching?
- *Silence:* Is it okay to interrupt? Is it best to wait? Does it make a difference when and with whom?
- *Time concepts:* Do you feel the need to get right to the point, or socialize first? What does it mean to be late for something?

Communication, Culture, and Sustaining Learning Relationships

Understanding and using skills for effective communication are fundamental to any learning relationship. Professional colleagues who understand a specific school or program or who have cultural or social insights into a mentoring context are important *mentors for a mentor.* Working to strengthen and sustain responsiveness to teachers who may belong to or identify with groups (e.g., gender, ethnicity, religion, language) very different from those of the mentor involves collaborating with colleagues who will offer honest feedback on observed or shared mentoring interactions. Knowledge of communication tools in this chapter will always need to be adapted to fit a specific cultural or community context. Mistakes and misunderstandings are inevitable, but learning relationships will be sustained and will grow when mentors increase their capacity for critically examining their interactions on the basis of their hearts (attitudes of responsiveness) and their heads (communication knowledge), and then use their hands (their actions) to promote respect for the diversity of different of ways to achieve high-quality early childhood programs.

REFLECTION

What are some ways for mentors to support teachers to explore how bias in practices may affect their work with each other? Infusing conversations about cultural relevancy into any mentoring focus topic is the job of the mentor. What knowledge or skills does the mentor need in this area?

Summary

Supporting teachers' awareness of their interactions with children requires a mentor to understand how to use a cycle of communication basics effectively. (See Figure 3.3.) Communication choices that build upon common and culturally responsive understanding are at the heart of the process of mentoring. These choices include facilitating observation, reflection, and application of new ideas to a setting. Small transformations may be facilitated, one conversation at a time, by noticing effective

Figure 3.3 Summary of a Cycle of Mentoring Communication Strategies

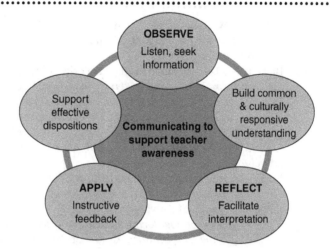

teaching dispositions and making teachers aware of how they can build upon their existing assets to become the teachers they want to be.

Review the big ideas from this chapter, represented in Figure 3.3. Then, consider videotaping yourself as you practice some of the communication strategies in the chapter by dialoging with a teacher. Videotape yourself up to three times to practice the cycle of mentoring strategies associated with *observing, reflecting,* and *applying.* (See Figure 3.1.) If you have less time, videotape only one of the three suggested conversations that follow:

1. First, find a teacher who will allow you to observe him or her, to take notes on his or her teaching, and to share something that you have observed for the purpose of improving an aspect of his or her teaching practices. (For example, observe a circle time and focus on child-guidance strategies.) Ask the teacher what focus he or she is interested in your observing for later discussion. Videotape your conversation with the teacher. Review it later, and *notice how well you listened, responded with empathy, and sought information* sensitively from the teacher.

2. Next, videotape yourself in dialogue with this same teacher to give him or her support to understand the meaning of your observational notes. Focus on an area of interest to the teacher. View the video for evidence of your use of *positive feedback and facilitation for reflection* (for example, your use of open-ended questions) to support the teacher to interpret what the observation meant for him or her.

3. Finally, videotape a third conversation in which you give *instructive feedback* to the teacher about questions that he or she has regarding ways to continue growing in and learning about an area of interest. End with an affirmation or encouragement. Analyze the videotape for effective communication strategies that were specific, descriptive, and strength-based.

Taking the risk to apply these communication strategies, analyzing them, and trying out some more strategies will model for the teachers with whom you work the value of your reflection on your own learning.

References

Bellm, D., Whitebook, M., & Hnatiuk, P. (1997). *Early childhood mentoring curriculum: A handbook for mentors.* Washington, DC: The National Center for the Early Childhood Work Force.

Bray, J. N., Lee, J., Smith, L. L., & Yorks, L. (2000). *Collaborative inquiry in practice: Action, reflection and making meaning.* Thousand Oaks, CA: Sage.

Chu, M., & Carroll, D. (2011). Linking the achievement gap with the recruitment and education of future teachers for Washington State. *Washington State Kappan, 5*(1), 23–26.

Covey, S. (2004). *Seven habits of highly effective people: Powerful lessons in personal change.* New York: Free Press.

Darling-Hammond, L., & Richardson, N. (2009). Teacher learning: What matters? *Educational Leadership, 66*(5), 46–53.

Elliott, K., Farris, M., Alvarado, C., Peters, C., Surr, W., Genser, A., & Chin, E. (2000). *The power of mentoring. Taking the lead: Investing in early childhood leadership for the 21st century.* Report of the Center for Development in Early Care and Education, Wheelock College, Boston.

Figley, C. R. (1995). *Compassion fatigue: Coping with secondary traumatic stress disorder in those that treat the traumatized.* New York: Brunner-Routledge.

Flaherty, J. (1999). *Coaching: Evoking excellence in others.* Boston: Butterworth-Heinemann.

Gallacher, K. (1997). Supervision, mentoring and coaching. In W. P. J. McCollum & C. Catlett (Eds.), *Reforming personnel in early intervention* (pp. 191–214). Baltimore: Paul H. Brookes Publishing Co.

Gonzalez-Mena, J. (2008). *Diversity in early care and education: Honoring differences.* New York: McGraw-Hill.

Hanft, B., Rush, D., & Sheldon, M. (2004). *Coaching families and colleagues in early childhood.* Baltimore: Paul H. Brookes Publishing Co.

Joseph, G., & Strain, P. (2004). Building positive relationships with young children. *Young Exceptional Children, 7*(4), 21–29.

Killion, J., & Todnem, G. (1991). A process for personal theory building. *Educational Leadership, 48*(7), 14–16.

Knight, J. (2009). Coaching: The key to translating research into practices lies in continuous, job-embedded learning with ongoing support. *Journal of Staff Development, 30*(1), 18–22.

Knight, J. (2011). What good coaches do. *Educational Leadership, 69*(2), 18–22.

MacMillan, M. (2008). Online learning: A professional growth opportunity for early childhood teachers. *Teaching Young Children, 1*(3), 8–9.

Noddings, N. (1984). *Caring: A feminist approach to ethics and morals education.* Berkeley: University of California Press.

Oja, S. N., & Reiman, A. J. (2007). A constructivist developmental perspective. In M. E. Diez & J. Raths (Eds.), *Dispositions in teacher education* (pp. 93–117). Charlotte, NC: Information Age Publishing.

Rogers, C., & Farson, R. E. (1957). *Active listening.* Chicago: University of Chicago Industrial Relations Center.

Schon, D. (1983). *The reflective practitioner: How professionals think in action.* New York: Basic Books.

Snyder, P., Hemmeter, M. L., Artman, K., Kinder, K., Pasia, C., & McLaughlin, T. (2012). *Early childhood professional development: Categorical framework and systematic review of the literature.* Manuscript submitted for publication.

Snyder, P., & Wolfe, B. (2008). The big three process components of effective professional development: Needs assessment, evaluation, and follow-up. In P. J. Winton, J. A. McCollum, & C. Catlett (Eds.), *Practical approaches to early childhood professional development: Evidence, strategies, and resources* (pp. 13–51). Washington, DC: ZERO TO THREE.

Sockalingham, S., & Waetzig, E. Z. (2012). Building common ground. In G. M Blau & P. R. Magrab (Eds.), *The leadership equation: Strategies for individuals who are champions for children, youth and families* (pp.107–140). Baltimore: Paul H. Brookes Publishing Co.

Sullivan, D. (2010). *Learning to lead: Effective leadership skills for teachers of young children* (2nd ed.). St. Paul, MN: Redleaf Press.

Torrance, D., & Donahue, C. (2007). *EC E-learning: A national review of early childhood education distance learning programs*. Washington, DC: Center for the Child Care Workforce.

Wadlington, E., & Wadlington, P. (2011). Teacher dispositions: Implications for teacher education. *Childhood Education, 87*(5), 323–326.

Wolpow, R., Johnson, M., Hertel, R., & Kincaid, S. (2009). *The heart of learning and teaching: Compassion, resiliency and academic success*. Olympia, WA: Washington Office of Superintendent of Public Instruction (OSPI) Compassionate Schools. Retrieved from http://www.k12.wa.us/compassionateschools/pubdocs/TheHeartofLearningandTeaching.pdf

Zbar, L., & Lerner, C. (2003). *Learning through observation: 5 video vignettes to spark reflection and discussion*. Washington, DC: ZERO TO THREE.

Zwiers, J., & Crawford, M. (2011). *Academic conversations: Classroom talk that fosters critical thinking across disciplines*. Portland, ME: Stenhouse.

CHAPTER 4

Adult Learning and Planning for Teacher Development

The chapter supports your growing capacity to

- identify effective professional development features of mentoring;
- understand adult development and learning theories;
- uncover mentor assumptions and images of the adult learner; and
- plan with a teacher for an individualized professional development plan.

This chapter examines effective ways to support adult development and learning. Stages of teacher development and how they relate to the practice of mentoring are explored. Ways to assist the early childhood mentor to join with a teacher to recognize what the teacher already knows and does and to plan for continued professional development (PD) are examined. The chapter emphasizes the mentor's role in discovering the adult learner's capacity to connect rigorous and relevant content to ongoing, active learning experiences. Mentoring adults is suggested as a way to combine both teaching and learning into one effective adult-education experience. Individualized and practice-focused education holds the promise of meeting the adult's need for high-interest, relevant content connected to applied learning. Mentoring should combine both rigor and active learning into a relevant and engaging form of professional development.

A successful mentor listens, takes the time to have clear understanding of the protégé, poses questions for reflection, values the protégé's experience, and does not overwhelm the protégé with information.

The Power of Mentoring
(Elliott et al., 2000, p. 35)

Mentoring as Effective Professional Development

Although much more research is needed into the effectiveness of mentoring as a professional-development strategy for early childhood teachers, it is clear that when mentoring aligns with the identified components of effective professional development, it positively influences both teachers and children. Zaslow, Tout, Halle, Whittaker, and Lavelle (2010) reviewed the literature on individualized practice-focused approaches to professional development and found that most approaches showed evidence of positive effects on teachers' practices with children, or on child outcomes. They caution that more work needs to be done to distinguish between the specific practices that are the most effective in improving child outcomes. Until more research on *practice-focused*, or mentoring interactions is conducted, those involved in mentoring programs should examine the processes and overall structure of the programs to see whether the teacher as mentee is experiencing the powerful learning associated with effective professional development (see Figure 4.1), as identified by the National Staff Development Council (Darling-Hammond, Wei, Andree, Richardson, & Orphanos, 2009) and by Trivette, Dunst, Hamby, and O'Herin (2009).

Figure 4.1 Effective Professional Development

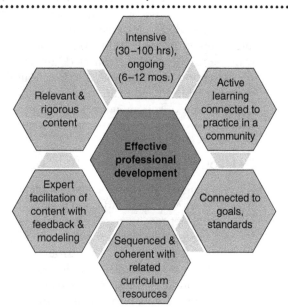

Including Research-Based PD Characteristics in the Mentoring Process

Effective mentoring should be aligned or combined with related professional-development and system improvements to include the characteristics shown in Figure 4.1.

Research points to the need for professional development to be ongoing or renewed periodically, or else it may never be applied (Norris, 2001; Burchinal et al., 2002). Additionally, more intensive and sequenced professional development, rather than a practice of stand-alone trainings, is more closely associated with observed quality (Raikes et al., 2006). Donovan, Bransford, and Pellegrino note that aligning teacher education with the research on how people learn indicates the need for learning over time:

> For teachers to change their practice, they need professional development opportunities that are in-depth and sustained. In the words of one workshop participant, a one-shot workshop simplifies complex ideas until they become "meaningless mantras sold as snake oil." Many of the learning opportunities provided for teachers and other professionals violate the principles for optimizing learning. Teachers need opportunities to be involved in sustained learning. (1999, p. 27).

The National Staff Development Council's extensive review of professional development approaches found that a mentoring program that lasted from 30 to 100 hours, conducted over 6 to 12 months, boosted teaching effectiveness, especially when it was based on individualized understanding of a teacher's practices

(Darling-Hammond et al., 2009). High-quality mentoring aligns with the best practices of effective teacher education. In addition, when mentoring is combined with group seminars, peer networks, or other forms of professional-learning-community activities, it results in even greater increases in teacher knowledge and enhanced child learning (Grace, Bordelon, Cooper, Kazelskis, Reeves, & Thames, 2008; Neuman & Cunnigham, 2009). This research supports the notion that it takes time for a teacher to understand and accept a new concept because a teacher must consider how to apply the concept with specific students in a particular program setting.

Grace et al. (2008) also emphasize that effective mentoring must be responsive to a teacher's concerns, as well as address issues identified through a classroom observation by a mentor. A mentor or other provider of professional development who learns from a teacher about the program community, as well as respects the teacher's cultural knowledge, increases the chance that new research-based strategies will be implemented in a culturally compatible way and not rejected as being in conflict with the teacher's and/or enrolled families' beliefs and norms (Hall & Hord, 2006).

What does research tell us so far about the effectiveness of mentoring? Research on mentorship in early childhood education has mostly involved studies limited to specific states or communities. The following studies positively associated mentorship with increased teacher quality and effectiveness:

Did You Know?

- Teachers mentored early in their careers showed greater responsive involvement with the children in their early childhood classroom than teachers who did not receive mentoring (Howes et al., 2003).
- Fiene (2002) randomly divided a small sample of infant and toddler teachers in two groups. One group did not receive mentoring. The other group received 4 months of mentorship involving observation and collaboration to address caregiving challenges. The second group showed statistically significant improvement in the Infant and Toddler Environmental Rating Scale (Harms, Cryer, & Clifford, 1990) areas of learning activities, sensitivity, appropriate discipline, and routines.
- Children in early childhood classrooms with teachers who were mentored made greater gains on the Child Experiences Survey (FACES) and on the Child Assessment Battery than those who were not mentored (Lambert et al., 2006).
- The California Early Childhood Mentor Program (CECMP), which began in 1988, is the largest in the nation and primarily provides support for early childhood-education (ECE) teachers and administrators who are enrolled in community college courses. The mentor selection is based on the mentors' work in high-quality programs and their ability to facilitate adult learning and supervise field-based experiences of high school, community college, and university ECE students. Selection of director mentors focuses on their experience and skill in guiding other administrators.
- ECE programs with mentors have shown a lower staff turnover than is the average for the ECE field. (Retrieved from http://www.ecementor.org)
- Family childcare providers report that they feel that the isolation of their work is broken by mentoring programs in Minnesota, South Dakota, and Tennessee (Kagan, Kauerz, & Tarrant, 2008).
- Data from the multi-state Quality Interventions for Early Care and Education (QUINCE) study shows the greatest impact from on-site mentoring to be in family childcare homes. (Retrieved from http://www.fpg.unc.edu/projects/quality-interventions-early-care-and-education). See also: (Bryant, et al , 2009).

- A review of the professional development literature (ACF/OHS/NCQTL 2012a, 2012b; Snyder, 2012) involving 101 coaching studies about early childhood teachers conducted from 1995 to January 2011 (all studies included children ages 3 to 5 and reported on teacher and child outcomes) found that 76% of the studies involved practices also associated with a recent model developed at Vanderbilt University. This model, known as *Practice-Based Coaching*, involves shared teacher–coach goal planning and action steps, focused observation, the use of data to guide reflection, feedback on teaching, and the provision of general support over time.

  Studies that used components of Practice-Based Coaching lead [sic] to a range of positive outcomes for teachers including implementation of desired teaching practices, behavior support practices, or curricula; implementation of practices with fidelity; changes in teacher-child interactions; and self-reported changes in knowledge, skills, and attitudes about teaching practices. . . . [C]hild outcomes included increased participation and engagement, increased social skills and fewer challenging behaviors, increased literacy and language, and increased skills associated with the Head Start Outcomes Framework for logic and reasoning and approaches to learning (ACF/OHS/NCQTL, 2012a, pp. 2–4).

REFLECTION

1. What is your reaction to this research? Does it fit what you have experienced or what you might have expected, or are there still things that you are wondering about? How could you use this research to support your understanding of effective mentoring practices?

2. The research implies that it takes time for teachers to embrace new learning and become comfortable in applying it in their settings. When have you had the time to learn something new and practice applying it? When have you learned a new practice in a classroom setting without applying it soon afterward? Compare and contrast the two experiences.

Recognize the Stages of the Life and Teacher Development Cycle

Mentors motivate teachers to engage in learning through joining in supportive learning relationships, using effective communication skills, and developing professional-development plans based on an understanding of adult learning and development.

Lillian Katz (1995) was influenced by life cycle theories and suggested that teachers go through stages of professional development. Her experience told her that the needs of teachers change dramatically as they grow and develop professionally. A mentor must be sensitive to these stages in order to differentiate his or her interactions with teachers while also recognizing that teachers are complex people who cannot be reduced to a "stage" (Bellm et al., 1997).

Survival Stage of the Emerging Teacher or the Experienced Teacher in a New Position. The teacher in this stage is usuall y most concerned with meeting daily challenges. The realities of the early childhood program may make him or her feel inadequate and unprepared, regardless of educational background. Experienced teachers who change roles or positions may also initially demonstrate some or all of the behaviors listed next. These teachers

- may frequently seek help or advice, asking about the right or expected way to do things;
- tend to accept advice from others and distrust their own instincts;
- may remain silent in staff gatherings and not share their views and opinions;
- frequently refer challenges to director, principal, or other teachers;
- avoid taking risks and accept suggestions from experienced teachers; and
- are overly critical of themselves.

Consolidation Stage. A teacher's confidence increases as he or she is able to meet the daily needs of most children, prevent problems to which he or she once reacted, and take more time to reflect on his or her teaching goals. A teacher in this stage

- may have interest in the process of learning, how children think, and how to differentiate learning;
- may develop curriculum plans and use instructional strategies that often work as anticipated;
- has a much better sense of how to prioritize guidelines and suggestions from others;
- begins to understand the profession as a whole and where his or her role fits in;
- recognizes important learning and documents it; and
- has increased confidence and is willing to take some creative risks.

Renewal and Maturity Stages. Teachers are now looking for new ideas and practices to spark new curiosity and interest in what is becoming routine and expected. Someone in this stage is usually experienced and confident and may be observed to

- share new practices with colleagues;
- be competent in using a repertoire of practices in the moment;
- actively seek ways to grow professionally and infuse new ideas into his or her work;
- not be intimidated or defensive but show interested in receiving feedback from parents, colleagues, and others; and
- be interested in supporting others to grow professionally.

There are tensions in each teacher stage that the mentor should be aware of and recognize through his or her own observation and reflection. Consider the tensions usually present in each teacher stage described in Figure 4.2.

Figure 4.2 Stages of Teacher Development

Survival and Emerging Teacher Stage: Feelings may swing from enthusiastic and energetic to overwhelmed and lacking in confidence. Mentors need to put feelings in perspective through empathizing, noticing successful work, and immediately giving requested specific short-term information. Next, mentors should appeal to the vision of the new teacher by also discussing the teacher's long-term goals and possible long-term inquiry projects. Mentors should also link the new teacher to on-site peer mentors who are nonjudgmental and supportive. Teachers without support in this initial phase may leave their positions. Supervisory evaluations without strong professional development support usually do not motivate new teachers.

Consolidation Stage: Teachers in this stage usually know what they know and are interested in increasing their effectiveness and their satisfaction with their work. These teachers make mentors feel the most effective because the teachers are excited and grateful to learn new ideas and are usually not overwhelmed with the prospect of trying them. Teachers without professional development in this stage may become less passionate about their roles and wonder, "Is this all there is to this position?" For these teachers, considering new roles and new ways to contribute to their field is a gift.

Renewal and Maturity Stages: Facilitating, not directing learning, is needed for mature teachers. Spending time learning what this teacher knows, values, and is interested in is essential for any mentoring to be successful. This teacher has little interest in being treated like an empty vessel to be filled with knowledge. Rather, encouraging this mature teacher to mentor others in their specific areas of expertise will show respect and build a mentoring relationship. Some very experienced teachers who have not had the advantage of effective professional development and collegial support may initially resist new ideas and mentoring. For such teachers, the mentor needs to build on strengths, show authentic respect, and follow this teacher's lead to initially focus on specific areas of interest. Go slow to go fast with this teacher, and he or she may be helped to become a leader among teachers.

REFLECTION

1. Brainstorm both suggestions and questions that you have about how to best support teachers in each of the stages discussed previously. What do you need to learn about a teacher in order to mentor appropriately in each stage? What is your experience in working with or mentoring teachers in each stage?

Understanding Adult Development and Learning Theories

Mentors who are aware that adults, as well as children, are always developing and changing will be more effective in their role of supporting teacher learning.

Erickson's Adult Psychosocial Stages

Eric Erikson (1959) suggested that we go through stages over the course of our lifetime, with conflicts that must be resolved. He suggested that the *psychosocial stages of development* in the teen years involve the need to *experiment with different identities* and explore various roles, including school and career goals. The challenges of examining a *crisis of identity* are resolved through discussion with friends and mentors and an eventual development of *fidelity* to a more consistent view of oneself. Next, young adulthood (20s to 30s) involves people who are looking for partners, job satisfaction, and general social satisfaction, and are worried that they might be alone. He describes this conflict as *intimacy versus isolation.* Young teachers may have many broad life goals that are priorities in their lives. Work demands that do not allow for flexibility to meet family and life responsibilities will result in intense conflict and promote anxiety in the emerging teacher. Mentors working with teachers in their 20s and 30s should link them to resources and supports that break the isolation of their work and meet the developmental need of these adults.

In the more mature years of the 30s and 40s, Erikson describes the psychological conflict as between *being generous with life experiences and accumulated wisdom versus self-absorption.* One way to be generous is to guide the next generation. Being a teacher is valued work that meets this developmental need. In the final era (50s and onward) of our working lives, Erikson's theory implies that we are dealing with the conflict of feeling *positive about our integrity and the way that we have conducted our lives versus despair* about our choices. Choosing to mentor others is a way to give back to your profession and resolves the conflict of this mature time of life. Reorienting a mature teacher to what he or she has accomplished and contributed will be one way for the mentor to form a positive learning relationship with the teacher.

REFLECTION

1. Discuss the main concerns, tasks, or developmental challenges that you or a teacher whom you have mentored had during the teens, 20s, 30s, 40s, and 50s. Check to see whether they are similar to what Erikson predicts for these periods. Consider how these adult developmental phases might affect both the mentor and the teacher. What are other ways that both the mentoring and the teaching roles are meeting adult developmental needs?

Neuroscience and Emotional Intelligence

Understanding and learning from our emotions and the social world around us are aspects of a mentor's and a teacher's *emotional intelligence.* The concept of emotional intelligence also includes the ability to manage feelings in order to work well with others to achieve a common goal (Goleman, 2006). Persons who are using their emotional intelligence are more likely to understand messages being sent nonverbally by others in their vicinity. Mentors working with teachers who are prone to imitate others' moods without conscious awareness of their behavior may want to share recent understandings from the field of social neurobiology. Identification of specific nerve cells in our brains, called *mirror neurons*, helps to explain that we are hardwired to adopt the emotional mood and even the physical movements of those whom we perceive in our environment (Cozolino, 2006). Mentors who facilitate the combining of emotional awareness and analytical skills might choose to notice, describe, and then ask questions about observed emotionally based teacher behaviors (Bruno, 2011, p. 24) by saying something like this:

- I am noticing that your hands are clenched. What do you think that means you are feeling?
- What feelings are you sensing in this room now?
- When you feel this way, what can you do to shift your mood?
- Have you noticed that the children are imitating your body posture?

Communicating our emotional mood and sensing the feelings of others is an invisible process that mentors are able to make visible for teachers by describing and asking questions about the physical cues of others. Capable infant and toddler teachers are often acutely sensitive to subtle emotional cues and may be good mentors for helping others to increase their emotional intelligence.

REFLECTION

1. Take pictures of adult facial expressions and body postures that seem to be sending either subtle or potent messages about the adult's emotional state. Make a game of guessing the feelings of the person.

2. Take pictures of small groups of children working with an adult who seem to be imitating the teacher's emotional state. Use these pictures to discuss when such imitation has produced a positive classroom shift and when it has promoted a negative change in the classroom climate.

3. If teachers understand the CLASS assessment's (Pianta et al., 2008) dimensions of positive and negative climate, discuss how to use the behavioral indicators of these two dimensions as a way to examine teaching choices that either promote or tear down a feeling of caring in a community of learners.

Learning Theories

Adult professional development involves some aspects of learning that are constant across the life span. When mentors feel resistance from the teachers whom they are supporting, reviewing some broad characteristics of adult learning needs may highlight whether the mentor is treating the adult like a young child and consequently meeting resistance. Malcolm Knowles (1983) focused on the art and science of teaching adults, or *andragogy,* and characterized adult learners as

- extremely self-directed and not interested in being limited just to following directions to meet program goals or standards. Some self-direction is desired by most adults;
- possessing ample resources to meet their own learning needs and resentful of being seen as blank slates;
- motivated by the needs and interests of their jobs, family, and other social roles;
- interested in learning that can be applied to their life tomorrow morning; and
- focused on solving relevant and real-world problems.

Andragogy is often positioned as a binary opposite of pedagogy, or the process of teaching children. Children, in this argument, are viewed as people who have less life experience, who have their learning controlled more by adults, and who may, at least on the surface, appear to be more compliant and deferential to their teachers (Knowles, 1984). Mentors may find it more useful, however, to remember Knowles's views that the learner needs a safe place to learn, with other adults who respect their experience and ability to identify their own needs, interests, and values. This approach also emphasizes the important fact that adults are ready to learn when they have an understanding of the gaps between where they are now and where they hope to be.

Howard Gardner (1999) describes different kinds of intelligence. He notes that in most formal schooling situations, the types of intelligences that are valued are only the *mathematical* and *linguistic*. Mentors who overuse linguistic intelligence—through too much dialogue after observations, for example—should review ways to include other sensory modalities to support learning. Teachers are often encouraged to summarize, narrate, listen, and generally speak to their learning. Noticing a person's strengths or various areas of intelligence and encouraging their use gives the mentor many ways to support a teacher's learning. This theory is especially interesting for teachers because young children are experimenting with all of the intelligences.

- *Musical intelligence:* Using rhythm and the language of music to support learning
- *Spatial intelligence:* The relationships of objects to each other and using a variety of media to interest learners with this orientation
- *Kinesthetic intelligence:* Drama, dance, and other forms of movement to support understanding. Mentors use this intelligence when supporting teachers to practice actions, demonstrate strategies, and then reflect on their actions.
- *Naturalist intelligence:* Recognizing, categorizing, and using features of the environment—an emphasis in many cultures, professions, and individuals (Gardner added this to his original group of intelligences in 1999.)

The final two forms of intelligence are required for effective mentoring to occur:

- *Intrapersonal intelligence:* Individual projects and reflection are ways in which the learner comes to understand something.

- *Interpersonal intelligence:* Collaborating with others to answer questions, solve problems, and represent learning in many ways is the emphasis.

No tests exist to substantiate the validity of these ideas. However, we do know that a learner's engagement across the life span is increased as multiple teaching modalities increase (Pianta, LaParo, & Hamre, 2008). For mentors, Gardner's ideas offer the insight that once an individual has a need, helping the teacher to understand a new idea in the form that best engages him or her may allow the teacher to take the risk of considering doing something new.

Effective mentors, like skilled teachers of young children, should couple their understanding of multiple intelligences with the notion of *scaffolding* (Vygotsky, 1978) learning. This is usually thought of as a primary communication technique (e.g., open-ended questions and hints or supports to build on what is already known) to guide learning. Scaffolding by another person supports the learner to achieve more than what is possible through his or her own independent discovery. Vygotsky calls this learning area the *zone of proximal development*. The availability of the mentor to the teacher is key to the process of scaffolding. Teachers will recognize this parallel process because they are experts in using a variety of ways to scaffold children's learning.

REFLECTION

1. Malcolm Knowles helps us recognize that adults tend to demand that learning be relevant to their lives. How can using and nurturing your *interpersonal intelligence* make learning more relevant for a teacher with whom you are working?

2. Reflect on a time when you observed another person who helped you understand something in a new way through music, dance, or exploration of nature. Discuss how learning something in a different way than you expected felt or how it engaged you.

3. Recall an occasion when someone taught you something through hinting or using open-ended questions. Reflect on how scaffolding an adult's learning is key to the mentoring process.

4. Online learning is becoming more and more common. Review the five-step learning cycle of one of the free, online early childhood CONNECT instructional modules at http://community.fpg.unc.edu. How might the five-step learning cycle of (a) dilemma, (b) question, (c) evidence, (d) decision, and (e) evaluation support a mentor to reinforce face-to-face learning that meets the criteria of effective professional development described in this chapter? (See graphic of the criteria identified by Darling-Hammond, Wei, Andree, Richardson, & Orphanos, 2009.)

Facilitating Change

Is the mentor an expert, a colearner, a peer, or a combination of all? In order to facilitate change in practices and to promote positive child outcomes, a combination of all may be needed. In the expert model, an outsider or a colleague with specialized knowledge supports the assessment of a teacher's skills and knowledge, defines goals, and facilitates a plan for learning and evaluation. Mentoring practices coming out of early intervention and mental health traditions often use this sort of an approach. In this approach, the mentor is the expert who is responsible for planning and facilitating repeated skill practice until mastery is obtained by the teacher. Supporting teachers to use research-based teaching strategies in their program is sometimes used as a follow-up to teacher development workshops (Donnegan et al., 2000). New learning takes time to implement, and the teacher benefits from the expertise of a mentor who empathizes with the teacher who is challenged by infusing new ways of teaching into his or her daily routines.

Changing underlying beliefs is harder to accomplish. Transformational learning is the goal of Paulo Freire's "critical pedagogy" (1970). Freire felt that the empowerment of those who may have felt powerless to change their situations occurs only if the educator sees himself or herself as

-   equal to the learner;
-   a problem poser who partners with and facilitates the examination of issues of importance to the adult; and
-   supporting reflection plus action in a setting that may transform the learner's thinking.

When the mentoring process is applied to Freire's view of education, it begins with establishing a relationship. Both sides negotiate and discuss the expectations, purpose, goals, and strategies to be used. The mentor and the teacher join together as equal partners in learning. Investigation of a topic of interest should lead to listening, observing, and dialoguing. Reflection through dialogue then takes place. When the teacher is ready to apply and integrate relevant discoveries to his or her setting, the mentor should notice and document the teacher's learning through the solving of real problems.

Freire influenced the professional-development approaches and underlying principles of the Reggio Emilia–inspired programs. Professional-learning communities in Reggio-inspired early-learning settings view teachers as colearners and collaborators with each other (Edwards, Gandini, & Forman, 1998; Rinaldi, 2006). Teachers pose and reframe essential questions, document actions and words, and participate in co-inquiry meetings to interpret the documentation and, ultimately, plan for subsequent experiences (Gandini & Goldhaber, 2001). It is a cyclic process, making teaching and learning visible (Project Zero et al., 2003). Problem solving, critical thinking, active participation, and informed decision making are all consistent with the required skills, knowledge, and pedagogy embedded in mentor–teacher inquiry approaches.

REFLECTION

1. Think about specific mentoring situations for which either skill building or long-term investigation and reflection is the best choice. Did the age, teacher stage, or other learning conditions indicate that one choice would be better than the other? Discuss the factors in the learning context that suggest that one strategy was more appropriate than another strategy.

Uncovering Mentor Assumptions and Images of the Adult Learner

Teachers know what mentors think of them, even if it is not verbally stated. Adults who work with young children are especially sensitive and adept at reading nonverbal messages. This means that mentors must do more than *say* that they are looking for strengths in their mentees. They must authentically see the learner as having the potential to be capable, to solve problems, and to grow and learn. In order to have a positive image of the adult learner, mentors need to examine their assumptions about learning. Mentors will find that they may strongly gravitate to one adult learning theory or philosophy over others, or they may become more pragmatic and combine several.

Connection

Briefly consider your gut reactions to the questions that follow.

- Which early childhood philosophy or program approach are you able to share with teachers to support their concepts about their image of the learner?

- Which ones fit your image of the learner?

What Is Your Image of the Learner?

The learner:

- is capable, competent, interested, rich in ideas, wanting to grow. Learners' needs, interests, and experiences must be valued (Reggio Emilia, inspired by Freire, 1970; New & Cochran, 2007);
- is interested in solving problems relevant to daily life (Knowles, 1984);
- is a blank slate (Locke, 1632–1704) who needs guidance from an expert to have specific behaviors reinforced (Skinner, 1963);
- has basic needs of safety, belonging, and esteem that must be met in order to learn. All learners need to know that their mentor cares and is empathetic (Maslov, 1970; Noddings, 1984);
- is subject to changes in his or her needs, depending on the adult developmental stage that he or she is in (Erikson, 1950);
- has had diverse experiences with education in the past and has experienced unequal access to power and participation in educational settings (Freire, 1970; Darder, 1991); or
- constructs knowledge through emotional and intellectual connections within relationships (Erikson, 1950; Belenky et al., 1986; Jones, 1993; Egan, 1989).

REFLECTION

1. Of the previous comments listed, do you like one more than another, or can you see situations in which each might promote a positive image of a teacher as learner? Are there situations in which assumptions about how adults learn could damage your learning relationship? An example of an assumption that might interfere with the mentoring process is a mature teacher's being paired with a mentor who viewed her as a "blank slate."

2. What might prominent theorists who write about teaching and learning suggest that mentors consider as they engage in mentoring? Discuss your reactions to these statements and questions.

What Is the Role of the Mentor?

If well-known learning theorists were to comment on mentoring for early childhood teachers, what might be their "big ideas"? Examine the brief summaries of well-known theories that follow, and consider which ones fit your personal philosophy of learning. Do you see situations in which an approach that you generally don't like is the right choice for a particular time in a mentoring PD relationship?

The mentor is

- a facilitator and participant in the teaching–learning exchange (Knowles, 1984);
- a partner with the learner. Listens, poses problems, and facilitates observation and critical dialogue to uncover and examine issues. The goal is to empower the learner (Freire, 1970);
- an organizer and guide, providing real-life learning application (Knowles, 1984);
- an expert who sets goals and directs the learning (Skinner, 1963);
- one who demonstrates new skills and learning by observing others, combined with providing knowledgeable feedback and reinforcement about specific behaviors and practices that are effective. Over time, learners gain confidence and the ability to succeed on their own (Bandura, 1977, 2001);
- someone who understands and respects multiple forms of intelligence (Gardner, 1999);
- a facilitator of critical thinking through active, social learning that contributes to a democratic community (Dewey, 1943); or
- one who recognizes that education is never neutral and is designed to either maintain the status quo or work for social justice and change (Freire, 1970).

Diversity and Cultural Competence

This chapter has explored adult learning and development theories. Mentors must be familiar with ways that adults learn, but they must also point the mirror at themselves and ask whether they are facilitating a process that embraces a teacher's many ways of being and knowing. *Cultural competence* and related terms (e.g., *critical consciousness, multicultural awareness*) point the mentor to creating "spaces" (emotional and intellectual) where teachers are able to explore their different understandings of topics of intense interest, with full freedom of expression. If we are to develop culturally sensitive teachers who are prepared for today's early learning programs, then mentors, too, must support and engage in ongoing inquiry, reflection, and action to learn from teachers their diverse perspectives (Goto et al., 2010). This sometimes requires mentors to find their own mentors, who may have broader cultural and other diverse perspectives that they may lack, to consult with as they work with teachers.

REFLECTION

1. Think about your own professional journey. Where did you start, what are the various roles you have played, and where are you now? Reflect on any times in your career when you found yourself at a crossroads and made a change. Did you have any guides or mentors in your professional life that helped you? What did they do that was important? Have you ever been a guide to someone in the same sort of crossroads situation? What did you do?

2. Where are you in your stage of adult development? How does your life
    stage affect your goals in your role as mentor? How comfortable are you
    adjusting your style to fit a type of intelligence that is not your area of
    experience or interest? After having explored different adult-learning and
    development theories, what are you still wondering about? Who is avail-
    able to mentor you to understand a cultural or other perspective that is
    different from your own? Under what circumstances is it best to recognize
    that you are not going to be the most effective mentor for a specific teacher
    and that you should partner with another mentor to meet a teacher's needs?

Planning With a Teacher for an Individualized
Professional Development Plan

The first section of this book focused on mentoring for effective communication; relationship building; and fostering adult learning and development knowledge, skills,
and strategies. In order for the mentor to begin to put the areas explored in this first
section into practice, a mentor should find a teacher willing to engage in planning
for his or her PD. Learning to be an effective mentor, like the mentoring process
itself, requires taking what you think you have learned and what you already know
and putting them into practice. Understanding cannot be decontextualized if it is to
be understood. *Situated Learning* (Lave & Wenger, 1991) is a term used to refer to
the concept that deep learning occurs only when the learning context includes an
actual experience. It reminds the mentor that true understanding occurs when the
learner feels that he or she has the ability to put into practice what he or she knows
and has learned. First, find an early childhood teacher who is requesting mentoring to volunteer for the planning activity described next. Then, sit down with this
teacher in a specific area. Begin with a conversation to construct a teacher–mentor
professional-development plan, using the form shown in Table 4.1. Portions of this
plan could be included in an individual PD plan that many federal, state, or local
programs or school district educational systems require a teacher to have.

Plan for a minimum of one hour of uninterrupted time to complete as much of
this form as possible. However, the time needed will vary tremendously, depending
on the styles and needs of individual teacher–mentor pairs. Remember, the more you
know about the context of the teacher's work and the teacher as a whole person,
the more successful your initial plan will be. Do not force completion of the form.
Plan for a second meeting if it is clear that time for the teacher to think about your
questions would enhance his or her responses and build a more positive initiation
into the mentoring process. Go slow now to go fast later!

Complete section I, rows A–J of the form in Table 4.1. Remember that this is a
reciprocal process of both teacher and mentor exchanging what they each feel that
they will bring to the teaching–learning process. It should feel like a conversation,
and the mentor should do more listening than talking. It is the mentor's role to in-
troduce the purpose of the plan and learn from the teacher what problems he or she
wants to investigate and possible areas of learning on which to focus. In Section II
of this book, you will explore how to put this plan into action.

Table 4.1 Teacher–Mentor Professional Development Plan

Teacher–Mentor Professional-Development Plan		
I. Plan for learning about each other and creating adult learning opportunities	**Teacher/Mentee Name:**	**Mentor/Coach/Consultant Name:**
A. Strengths • Knowledge • Skills • Interests Self-assessment to discover strengths may require reviewing a relevant list of early childhood (EC) teacher competencies, standards, knowledge areas, etc.	I know . . . I can do . . . I am curious about . . .	I have experience facilitating learning in . . . I will partner with others to facilitate . . . I will also refer this teacher to . . .
B. Question(s) to investigate: Put curiosity/areas of interest into the form of a question. Identify questions of interest from everyday work with children, or review a list of EC teacher competencies, and then create a specific question or area of focus.	Prioritize specific questions to investigate (examples): 1. (Child development and learning) How does . . .? 2. (Program structure or processes) What is . . .? 3. (Teacher development areas) Why are . . .? If you do not know what your questions are, first schedule a time for a mentor to observe you in your work setting, and then come back to this section again.	
C. Short-term purpose/goals	The purpose of our PD relationship is to apply learning from (content area such as child development): _____ to (specific aspect of work responsibilities): _____ Complete this sentence: I will . . . and be able to . . . _____ Example: learn how to . . . and know more about . . ., explore ways to . . . and be able to . . ., recognize . . . and create or problem-solve . . .	

Table 4.1   (Continued)

....

D. Long-term purpose/outcomes	Mentee: My long-term professional hope and vision is to . . .	
E. Standards/knowledge area (attach relevant standards, and circle focus area)	The relevant professional standards or guidelines that I want to meet and we will refer to are . . .	
F. Strategies for investigating and learning	I believe I learn best by • reading • talking/discussing • noticing • being observed or observing others • trying out an idea • collecting information • Other	I will observe this teacher and gather information on how to support adult learning by . . . I am able to facilitate learning by . . . (listening, discussing, demonstrating, observing, etc.) Supervisors/administrators/other peer mentors who will review and support this plan:
G. Resources Needed	Educational needs: Support to participate needed: (examples: childcare, funding, computer, etc.)	Community, educational, and related needs, and other professional resources to bring information about:
H. Possible Challenges	I need support or I am concerned about . . . Considerations about my time and work setting are . . .	I am wondering about . . .

Table 4.1   (Continued)

....

I. Agreements	I am available:	I am available:
1. Review confidentiality and other requirements. Describe and negotiate other mentoring ground rules (attach).	I am not available:	I am not available:
2. Set up times to meet and a timeline.	I need you to contact me by:	I need you to contact me by:

| J. Planning for assessment/ evaluation | We will know that the goals have been met by:

Target dates for reflecting on/evaluating progress: | |

II. Documenting Progress	**Teachers and Mentors**	
Implementing: Documenting Action Steps After They Occur (example: observed, documented, reviewed information, discussed choices, put into practice, provided feedback . . .)	Observations: Review of documentation, information collected: Put into practice:	
Status: What happened? Check-in date(s):	Progress toward goals:	Facilitation of learning:
Reflection	Mentee reflects on observations, documentation, and actions chosen.	Summary of mentor feedback:
Changes Needed and Next Steps:	What was accomplished? What has changed?	Evidence of making progress or meeting goals.
	What still needs to occur? What needs to change?	What should change about the mentoring process?
	Next steps:	Next steps:

More resources for professional development planning forms:

Hanft, B., Rush, D., & Shelden, M. (2004). *Coaching families and colleagues in early childhood.* Baltimore, MD: Paul H. Brookes Publishing.

Sugarman, N. (2011). Putting yourself in action: Individual professional development plans. *Young Children, 66*(3), 27–33.

Summary

Mentoring as effective professional development requires the adult educator to understand that development continues throughout the human life span. Uncovering mentor assumptions and images of the adult learner are essential if intentional, effective, and strengths-based planning for individualized professional development is to occur. As a final chapter reflection, consider the big ideas to remember when engaging in a cycle of planning for mentoring adults as teachers.

Partnering with other adults for their ongoing learning is challenging if you don't have a plan. Use the relationship-based ideas in Figure 4.3 to jog your memory, and jot down what you want to remember and implement from this chapter.

Figure 4.3   Adult Learning and Planning for Teacher Development

Consider the following as you plan to implement ideas from this chapter:

1. *Question:* How will I plan to challenge the assumptions or reignite a passion for learning in a teacher by reframing his or her concerns or dilemmas into questions to research and learn from?

    > *To Do:* Practice this skill by having a conversation with a teacher for the purpose of identifying questions of interest from his or her everyday work with children.

2. *Observe:* What are a few ways in which I will plan with a teacher to consistently and intentionally notice what he or she is interested in learning and note progress toward his or her goals?

    > *To Do:* Turn the question from item 1 into a goal statement (see individualized learning plan).

3. *Apply:* How will I encourage experimentation and the practicing of newly identified strategies?

> *To Do:* Interview a teacher about the ways that he or she learns best—reading; talking; noticing; being observed, then given feedback; seeing something modeled; or trying out an idea. Now, practice teaching something in all of those different ways with that teacher, and compare what you both feel was most effective with what the teacher thought would be best before you tried it. For example, give an article on hand washing and infectious disease, observe hand washing for a morning in a program, give feedback on what you saw, and offer three ways to encourage children to wash their hands longer.

4. *Network:* How will I immerse teachers in rejuvenating their curiosity for learning by joining them to an adult mentor or peer mentors, or through other professional development experiences?

> *TO DO:* Take a teacher on a field trip to a program that has implemented a strategy that you are encouraging that teacher to try. Reflect on the experience. What worked? What did not?

5. *Connect:* How will I embrace the constraints present in any teacher's context and still connect him or her to research-based rigorous content and examine creative ways to apply this learning needed for their growth and development?

> *To Do:* Think of several reasons that working with a teacher in a specific program is challenging. Now try to embrace the challenge by finding a new way to connect the teacher to the content that he or she needs. For example, a teacher who cannot get release time from teaching preschoolers to discuss ways to teach problem solving might stop the learning for her. Instead, a mentor might offer to demonstrate the problem-solving process with the children during class time.

References

Administration for Children and Families, Office of Head Start, National Center on Quality Teaching and Learning. (2012a, May). *What do we know about coaching?* Retrieved from http://eclkc.ohs.acf.hhs.gov/hslc/tta-system/teaching/docs/What-Do-We-Know-About-Coaching.pdf

Administration for Children and Families, Office of Head Start, National Center on Quality Teaching and Learning. (2012b, May). *Practice based coaching.* Retrieved from http://eclkc.ohs.acf.hhs.gov/hslc/tta-system/teaching/docs/practice-based-coaching.pdf

Bandura, A. (1977). *Social learning theory.* Englewood Cliffs, NJ: Prentice-Hall.

Bandura, A. (2001). Social-cognitive theory: An agentic perspective. *Annual Review of Psychology, 52,* 1–26.

Belenky, M. F., Clinchy, B. M., Goldberger, N. R., & Tarule, J. M. (1986). *Women's ways of knowing: The development of self, voice and mind.* New York: Basic Books.

Bellm, D., Whitebook, M., & Hnatiuk, P. (1997). *Early childhood mentoring curriculum: A handbook for mentors.* Washington, DC: The National Center for the Early Childhood Work Force.

Bruno, H. (2011). The neurobiology of emotional intelligence: Using our brain to stay cool under pressure. Young Children. Retrieve from www.naeyc.org/files/yc/file/201101/BrunoOnline0111.pdf

Bryant, D., Wesley, P., Burchinal, M., Sideris, J., Taylor, K., Fenson, C., Iruka, I., Hegland, S., Hughes, K., Tout, K., Zaslow, M., Raikes, H., Torquati, J., Susman-Stillman, A., Howes, C., & Jeon, H. (2009). *The QUINCE-PFI study: An evaluation of a promising model and delivery approaches for child care provider training*. Final report. Chapel Hill, NC: University of North Carolina at Chapel Hill, Frank Porter Graham Child Development Institute.

Burchinal, M., Cryer, D., Clifford, R., Howes, C. (2002). Caregiver training and classroom quality in child care centers. *Applied Developmental Science, 6*(1), 2–11.

California Early Childhood Mentor Program. (n.d.). *California Early Childhood Mentor Program. Annual Report, 2007–2008*. Request from City College of San Francisco, 50 Phelan Avenue, San Francisco, CA 94112

Cozolino, L. (2006). *The neuroscience of human relationships*. New York: Norton.

Darder, A. (1991). Culture and power in the classroom, A critical foundation for bicultural education. Westport, CT: Bergin & Garvey

Darling-Hammond, L., Chung Wei, R., Andree, A., Richardson, N., & Orphanos, S. (2009). *Professional learning in the learning profession: A status report on teacher development in the United States and abroad*. Palo Alto, CA: Stanford University, National Staff Development Council.

Dewey, J. (1943). *The school and society*. New York: Macmillan.

Donnegan, M., Ostrosky, M., & Fowler, S. (2000). Peer coaching: Teachers supporting teachers. *Young Exceptional Children, 3*(2), 9–16.

Donovan, M. S., Bransford, J. D., & Pellegrino, J. W. (Eds.). (1999). *How people learn: Bridging research and practice*. Washington, DC: National Academy Press.

Edwards, C., Gandini, L., & Forman, G. (Eds.). (1998). *The hundred languages of children: The Reggio Emilia approach—Advanced reflections* (2nd ed.). Greenwich, CT: Ablex.

Egan, K. (1989). *Teaching as storytelling*. Chicago: University of Chicago Press.

Elliott, K., Farris, M., Alvarado, C., Peters, C., Surr, W., Genser, A., & Chin, E. (2000). *The power of mentoring. Taking the lead: Investing in early childhood leadership for the 21st century*. Report of the Center for Development in Early Care and Education, Wheelock College, Boston.

Erikson, E. (1950). *Childhood and society*. New York: Norton.

Fiene, R. (2002). Improving child care quality through an infant caregiver mentoring project. *Child and Youth Care Forum, 31*(2), 79–87.

Freire, P. (1970). *Pedagogy of the oppressed*. NewYork: Herder and Herder.

Gandini, L., & Goldhaber, J. (2001). Two reflections about documentation. In L. Gandini & Carolyn Pope Edwards (Eds.), *Bambini: The Italian approach to infant/toddler care*. New York: Teachers College Press.

Gardner, H. (1999). *Intelligence reframed: Multiple intelligences for the 21st century*. New York: Basic Books.

Goleman, D. 2006. *Social intelligence: The new science of human relationships*. New York: Bantam Dell.

Goto, S., French, K., Timmons-Flores, M., Lawrence, M., Chu, M., Cahill, S., & Sarte Prince, S. (2010). *Becoming a learning organization: A proposal for professional organizational development*. Unpublished policy paper, Western Washington University, Woodring College of Education, Bellingham, WA.

Grace, C., Bordelon, D., Cooper, P., Kazelskis, R., Reeves, C., & Thames, D. (2008). Impact of professional development on the literacy environments of preschool. *Journal of Research of Childhood Education, 23*(1), 52–74.

Hall, G. E., & Hord, S. M. (2006). *Implementing change: Patterns, principles and potholes*. Boston: Pearson.

Hanft, B., Rush, D., & Shelden, M. (2004). *Coaching families and colleagues in early childhood*. Baltimore: Paul H. Brookes Publishing Co.

Harms, T., Cryer, D., & Clifford, R. (1990). *Infant-toddler environment rating scale*. New York: Teachers College Press.

Howes, C., James, J., & Ritchie, S. (2003). Pathways to effective teaching. *Early Childhood Research Quarterly, 18*(1), 104–120.

Jones, E. (1993). Growing teachers: Partnerships in staff development. Washington, DC: National Association for the Education of Young Children.

Kagan, S. L., Kauerz, K., & Tarrant, K. (2008). *The early care and education teaching workforce at the fulcrum: An agenda for reform.* New York: Teachers College Press.

Katz, L. (1995). *Talks with teachers of young children: A collection.* Norwood, NJ: Ablex.

Knowles, M., & Associates. (1984). *Andragogy in action: Applying modern principles of adult learning.* San Francisco: Jossey-Bass.

Lambert, R., Abbott-Shim, M., & Sibley, A. (2006). Evaluating the quality of early childhood educational settings. In B. Spodek and O. Saracho (Eds.), *Handbook of research on the education of young children* (2nd ed.) (pp. 457–475). NJ: Erlbaum Associates.

Lave, J., & Wenger, E. (1991). *Situated learning: Legitimate peripheral participation.* Cambridge, UK: Cambridge University Press.

Maslow, A. (1970). *Motivation and personality.* New York: Harper.

Neuman, S., & Cunnigham, L. (2009). The impact of professional development and coaching on early language and literacy instructional practices. *American Educational Research Journal, 46*(2), 322–353.

New, R. & Cochran, M. (Eds.). (2007). *Early childhood education encyclopedia.* Westport, CT: Praeger.

Noddings, N. (1984). *Caring: A feminine approach to ethics and moral education.* Berkeley: University of California Press.

Norris, D. (2001). Quality of care offered by providers with differential patterns of workshop participation. *Child and Youth Care Forum, 30*(2), 111–121.

Palmer, P. (1988). *The courage to teach: Exploring the inner landscape of a teacher's life.* San Francisco: Jossey-Bass.

Pianta, R., LaParo, K., & Hamre, B. (2008). *Classroom assessment scoring system manual: K–3.* Baltimore: Paul H. Brookes Publishing Co.

Project Zero, Cambridgeport School, Cambridgeport Children's Center, Ezra H. Baker School, & John Simkins School. (2003). *Making teaching visible: Documenting individual and group learning as professional development.* Cambridge, MA: Harvard University Graduate School.

Raikes, H. H., Torquati, J. C., Hegland, S., Raikes, H. A., Scott, J., Messner, et al. (2006). Studying the culture of quality early education and care: A cumulative approach to measuring characteristics of the workforce and relations to quality in four Midwestern states. In M. Zaslow and I. Martinez–Beck (Eds.), *Critical issues in early childhood professional development.* Baltimore: Paul H. Brookes Publishing Co.

Rinaldi, C. (2006). *In dialogue with Reggio Emilia: Listening, researching, and learning.* New York: Routledge, Taylor & Francis Group.

Rubin, R., Sutterby, J., & Hoffman, J. (2010). Professional development in culturally diverse settings. In S. Neuman & M. Kamil (Eds.), *Preparing teachers for the early childhood classroom: Proven models and key principles.* Baltimore: Paul H. Brookes Publishing Co.

Skinner, B. F. (1963). *Science and human behavior.* New York: Free Press.

Snyder, P., Hemmeter, M. L., Artman, K., Kinder, K., Pasia, C., & McLaughlin, T. (2012). *Early childhood professional development: Categorical framework and systematic review of the literature.* Manuscript submitted for publication.

Sugarman, N. (2011). Putting yourself in action: Individual professional development plans. *Young Children, 66*(3), 27–33.

Trivette, C., Dunst, C., Hamby, D., & O'Herin, C. (2009). *Characteristics and consequences of adult learning methods and strategies* (Winterberry Research Synthesis, Vol. 2, No. 2). Asheville, NC: Winterberry Press.

Vygotsky, L. S. (1978). *Mind in society: Development of higher psychological processes.* M. Cole, V. John-Steiner, S. Scribner, E. Souberman (Eds.). Cambridge, MA: Harvard University Press.

Zaslow, M., Tout, K., Halle, T., Whittaker, J., & Lavelle, B. (2010). *Towards the identification of features of effective professional development for early childhood educators.* Prepared for Policy and Program Studies Service, Office of Planning, Evaluation and Policy Development, U.S. Department of Education, Washington, DC.

CHAPTER 5

Readiness for Change and Learning Through Inquiry

The chapter supports your growing capacity to

- understand and adapt to a teacher's readiness for change;
- match a professional-development approach to a teacher's needs;
- understand characteristics of the mentoring process to research teacher questions;
- help teachers to identify interesting questions to investigate; and
- expand the cycle of inquiry and identify areas for teacher and mentor development.

Characteristics of the mentor–teacher relationship required for the process of identifying teachers' needs, interests, and readiness for change are the focus of this chapter. Topics center on ways for mentors to match the professional-development strategy that best fits an individual teacher. Choices range from postponing mentoring when readiness to participate is not present to short-term skill-building sessions and planning for a cycle of teacher inquiry. These choices arise from the principles of action research (Perry, Henderson, and Meier, 2012; Schienfeld, Haigh, and Schienfeld, 2008; Reason and Bradbury, 2001). The chapter also explores ways for mentors to recognize how teachers think and feel about exploring new practices as an indicator for their readiness for participation in professional development (PD).

> On my first mentoring visit, the teacher told me she didn't have time to meet with me every week as the agreement said. She said she was sorry, but it just wasn't going to work now. I brought this response to my mentoring supervisor. My supervisor asked if the director had signed the agreement to give the teacher time and resources to participate. I remembered that she had and was very enthusiastic. We then looked at the "stages of change" information I had; and after looking at my visit notes, I could see the teacher seemed to be at "pre-contemplation."

> Mentor sharing her concerns at a monthly meeting, April 2012.

Sustained learning often begins with wondering, questioning, and searching for answers to existing problems. Creating a context for learning in an early childhood program means including the adults as well as the children. Ron Lally, infant and toddler program expert, shared with author Ellen Galinsky (2010) that one common characteristic of the successful Perry Preschool Project, the Abecedarian Project, and Chicago Commons Child–Parent Centers was that these programs were well-documented learning communities for teachers and parents. Lally summarized as follows:

> *[If] we're looking at really taking science seriously, [we're] saying that the teacher needs to act as a researcher—to view the child and then step back and [ask]: what is my hypothesis for what I should be doing next and [then] making the distinction between what works and what doesn't work* (Galinsky, 2010, p. 347).

Supporting a sense of wonder and rekindling a childlike curiosity, combined with needed information and skills, is essential for the emerging teacher-researcher to flourish.

Understanding and Adapting to a Teacher's Readiness for Change

Directors, principals, and higher education instructors often assume that teachers of young children not only will be ready to learn new ideas but will be excited about the professional-development opportunities that they are offered. The false assumption that early childhood teachers, who are in the business of promoting growth and development, will embrace professional development for themselves may be a factor in the failure of some early childhood quality initiatives. Effective partnering with teachers must take into account the teacher's readiness for change, identified by his or her views of existing challenges to participation.

The Transtheoretical Model of behavior change (Prochaska and DiClemente, 1982; Prochaska, DiClemente, and Norcross, 1992) offers some insight into the thinking process that many adults move through when faced with the need or opportunity to change their behavior. The model was developed originally for adults who were trying to quit smoking, and counselors discovered that they needed to adapt their support strategies to fit the different adult stages of readiness for change that each individual was in (Prochaska and Velicer, 1997). The accompanying chart is adapted from Peterson (2008), who applied the Transtheoretical Model to mentor–childcare-provider pairs who were working together in a professional-development project in Rochester, New York. Program leaders supported mentors to adjust their strategies to fit each childcare provider's stage of change. The model is adapted here and adds the term *inquiry* to refer to Peterson's terms *problem-solving* and *reflection*.

This model may not be complex enough to account for the layers of personal and program influences on any specific early childhood teacher's readiness for change and interest in professional development. These influences are many and include stressors in the areas of finances, academic readiness, emotional exhaustion from work and life responsibilities, cultural relevancy of an approach, program support of participation, and whether participation is voluntary or mandatory. However, despite complex barriers affecting how teachers feel and think about professional development, recognizing a teacher's stage of change has been found to be a valuable tool. Peterson and Valk (2010) found that an understanding of these phases helped to "reduce the mentors' anxiety and frustration level" because understanding these stages supported mentors to adjust their behavior to better match what a teacher needed (p. 59). This model helps mentors see that change is a process that takes time and may involve starts and stops before a commitment on the part of the teacher to an educational program is reached. Mentors should be sensitive to both personal and program conditions because of how they may challenge the teacher's ability to engage in professional development.

When mentors are working with teachers in the first two stages of the model (precontemplation and contemplation), they are partnering with people who have

Table 5.1   Readiness for Change

Stage of Change	Possible Adult Responses to an Invitation to Explore Changing Practices	Ways to Support in the Role of Mentor or Supportive Peer
1. Precontemplation	*Not ready to make a change.* May state he or she does not want to change or may avoid talking, learning, or analyzing his or her behavior. May become defensive and recall how past change has not worked for him or her.	Listen and learn the person's perspective. Ask how the current situation is working. Wonder what a better situation might look like, *or* simply let him or her know that you or other resources are available when he or she is ready to participate.
2. Contemplation	*Thinking about change but overwhelmed by obstacles.* May express conflicting feelings or even strong interest in participation but worry that it is not possible right now.	Learn the barriers, worries, and concerns. Paraphrase back these concerns, and encourage participation through problem solving.
3. Preparation	*Ready to change.* Expresses strong interest and may recount that he or she has been trying to figure out how to change for some time.	Work to develop a plan, including providing information and skills needed to be successful.
4. Action	*Actively engaged in change.* Has already been making changes and is interested in setting future goals and understanding the outcomes.	Ready for engaging in inquiry, including observation, interpretation, feedback, and problem solving about a question of interest.
5. Maintenance	*Maintaining change with vigilance.* Reflect on what he or she has done and needs to do to either maintain the change or continue to grow and learn.	Acknowledge the change over time that has occurred, and encourage modeling for others what has been learned. Examine how to build support through continuing involvement in professional organizations or learning communities.

Adapted with permission from Peterson (2008).

weighed the pros and cons of change and have come to the conclusion that the risks are higher than the possible rewards of professional-development activities. The lack of commitment to an educational process by a teacher is sometimes altered when social support is offered by peers who may help raise the teacher's awareness of the benefits that they received from past involvement with a mentoring process. Observing other teachers involved in professional development before committing to joining in may be helpful for teachers in these first contemplative phases. In other cases, the teacher is not ready, interested, or able to participate for any number of reasons (e.g., obligations or stressors in a current life situation, mismatch of mentoring philosophy with his or her beliefs, or plans to change careers) and needs to have his or her decision respected. This strong desire by teachers not to participate can be a catalyst for their reflection on whether teaching is the right career for them. Forcing teachers in these first stages into unwanted professional development may actually make classrooms less developmentally appropriate for the enrolled children, because for change to be sustained, it needs to be self-determined (Deci and Ryan, 1985).

Teachers in stages 3, 4, and 5 are the participants who usually make mentors feel very competent. These are the teachers who have moved out of the first two stages and decided that the rewards are much greater than the risks that come with possible change. Yet, even these teachers need support and time to make and maintain change, or else the new strategies will disappear when the support goes away (Peterson and Baker, 2011).

In addition to mentoring support for maintaining a change in practices, teachers need organizational and system supports. Mentors who work with administrators and teams of teachers may be more likely to understand ways in which organizations need to adjust to support a change in an individual teacher's practices (Metz and Bartley, 2012). Implementation science is a growing area of study that looks at stages of change in organizations and broader systems—from exploration of possible change to initial and full implementation of new practices (Fixsen, Naoom, Blase, Friedman, and Wallace, 2005; Metz and Bartley, 2012). Ways to sustain those changes are informed in a program, in part, by continuous feedback and communication about how new practices are suggesting changes in polices, and vice versa.

Making change happen in early care and education programs is complex, and it begins with increasing both individual and organizational readiness. If mentors do not find readiness for educational change present in a program for young children, then backing up and working, over a longer period, with others in in the community may be needed. Time is needed to broadly educate, gather evidence for needed practice changes, and build enthusiasm and readiness (i.e., for a PD model with a good fit for a program). Mentors should consider how working simultaneously at multiple levels of an organization (e.g., with teachers and administrators) is more likely to bring about and sustain positive changes (Metz and Bartley, 2012, p. 16) than is merely individually mentoring a teacher.

REFLECTION

1. Have you ever worked as a mentor with someone who did not seem interested in your support? How did you react? Review the *precontemplation* and *contemplation* phases described in this chapter. Share an example of a situation in which giving someone permission to drop out of a professional-development opportunity was the best choice at the time for him or her. If you have not acted in the role of mentor, answer these reflection questions from the perspective of a teacher or an adult learner.

2. In your experience, what conditions in an organization or program seem to increase the probability that a teacher will feel comfortable enough to be honest about how he or she feels about participation in professional development? Does the involvement and support of a director, principal, or other administrator help teachers fully participate in a mentoring program?

3. Under what circumstances have you changed your mentoring or teaching behaviors and increased your effectiveness on the basis of your awareness of a teacher's or another adult's readiness for change? Describe what you did and the effect on the adult.

Matching a Professional-Development Approach to a Teacher's Needs

Even when teachers are ready for and excited about professional development, the mentor should still remember that there are common phases through which mentoring pairs must move if they are to sustain their partnership. Zachary (2000) identifies these as phases of *preparation* (roles and expectations clarified), *negotiation* (goals identified), *enabling* (feedback and implementation of plans), and *closure* (evaluation and celebration). Mentors who use the communication strategies identified in Chapter 3 will move through the initial preparation period by listening with empathy and seeking information from the teacher. This delicate time when a teacher may be deciding whether he or she is ready for change is aided by a mentor who is sensitive to the point of view and questions that a teacher may have. The beginning of any mentor–teacher relationship has decision points for each member of this learning pair. Understanding the stage of change of a teacher means matching professional-development strategies to the needs of the adult. Mentoring, as an individualized approach, is based on adapting instructional behaviors to fit the teacher and situation. Examples of how mentors might differentiate their interactions with teachers according to what the teachers express or what their program conditions show include the responses shown in Table 5.2.

REFLECTION

1. Imagine how a teacher who was expressing feelings of ambivalence and of being overwhelmed (second row of Table 5.2) would react to being taught a complex *cycle of inquiry*. Have you ever overloaded anyone with more information than he or she could process? How do you check for understanding and match your approach to what a teacher needs?

2. Remember the time at which you first felt like a professional. Who supported that view that you had of yourself? What factors influenced this perception of yourself?

3. The stages of change and reactions to professional-development opportunities are not linear. Even experienced teacher veterans can lack confidence at times. How have you assisted a teacher to notice his or her strengths when he or she has temporarily lost focus and self awareness about their own needs for professional development?

Table 5.2 Matching Mentoring Strategies to the Teacher's Needs

Teacher says or shows behavior indicating:	Professional-Development Options	Mentor responds by:
✓ Disinterest ✓ Defensiveness ✓ Avoidance of information ✓ Many barriers to participation exist	No participation. Learn about other resources, and refer to supervisor for support.	Listening and learning the teacher's perspective. Forcing participation may backfire, with a teacher dropping out of a program later. Conditions may need to change in a teacher's thinking, program, or personal life to enable participation.
✓ Ambivalence ✓ Feeling overwhelmed ✓ Interest in one specific area to solve a current problem	Skill building in a specific, focused intervention. Connect to a role model on-site.	Learning what a teacher needs and matching the level of involvement to the teacher's capacity to participate. For example, demonstrate ways to read a book at circle time to engage children in conversation or five positive behavior-management strategies for the preschool teacher.
✓ A lack of confidence ✓ Is unsure about participation but is interested	Enroll "teacher buddies" or a cohort, and dialogue together.	Noticing strengths, building on them, and dialoguing about interests. Observing and commenting on effective strategies used. Taking time before teaching new skills to build a relationship. Modeling strategies.
✓ A request to connect interests into a plan of action ✓ Need for support and resources to establish goal and check for outcomes ✓ Interest in new information and new ways of interacting with children	Discuss what documentation, curriculum, and instruction are currently being used. Identify specific questions to investigate.	Presenting the "cycle of inquiry model" (described in this chapter), which includes observation, interpretation, feedback, and problem solving about a question of interest. Embedding skill building (e.g., ways to document and assess) about planning for investigating questions of interest. Celebrating accomplishments.
✓ Unsure whether permission has been granted for the teacher to take time out from teaching or direct care to meet with the mentor	Clarify with both the teacher and supervisor the roles, responsibilities, and agreements needed for participation.	Developing Memoranda of Agreement, and involving administrators in the PD process. Learning whether the program has both the willingness and the capacity to embrace participation on the part of the teacher. Considering how both the teacher's and program's readiness for change might be supported.

Characteristics of Mentoring for Teacher Inquiry

Characteristics of powerful mentoring relationships are reviewed here because these ideas are foundational to facilitating long-term changes in an individual teacher or program. Mentors should resist viewing the teacher as an empty vessel needing immediate technical information. Instead, mentors must be aware of what an individual teacher needs. When a teacher is ready for implementing new ideas and is in the action phase of his or her readiness for change, it is then time to expand the primary goal beyond specific skills acquisition. Joyce and Showers (2002) found that when instructional coaching involved a combination of *theory, demonstration, practice,* and *expert feedback* in a setting with children, a teacher's use of intended strategies rose significantly over that of teachers exposed to only one of these educational components. Helping a teacher to understand a cycle of learning, which includes identifying questions and planning for gathering and documenting information, will set the stage for the teacher to interpret the meaning of his or her data and seek more effective solutions to dilemmas. Then, at the right time, the mentor may offer the technical skill, information, or strategy needed, and the offer will be better received and more likely to be implemented. Even in situations in which teachers are asking for "quick fixes," a mini-cycle of inquiry can be demonstrated to help the teacher gain an understanding of how to identify a question and gather information before making changes to practice. Scaffolding a process of inquiry also provides a method for even an experienced mentor to move from intuitive to more intentional practices.

Principles of Mentoring: Review and Discuss Before Investigating a Cycle of Inquiry

Consider how the ideas about effective mentoring strategies presented in Figure 5.1 relate to your experience as a mentor or as one being mentored.

Figure 5.1   Effective Mentoring Characteristics

Mentoring takes time: The mentoring relationship changes as the teacher becomes a more competent, self-confident, and self-reflective practitioner.

Mentoring should fit the individual, the program, and the community: The content areas and strategies on which mentoring is based are tailored to the needs of the individual teacher, program, community, and cultural context.

Mentoring begins by the mentor's noticing strengths: Mentoring builds on the strengths of individual teachers. Mentors believe that all teachers, children, and families have strengths. The focus of mentoring evolves as new skills and knowledge are gained, trust is established, and the teacher identifies questions and areas of interest to research. Mentors view teachers as capable and interested in sharing ideas and learning.

Mentoring should be reciprocal: The mentor–teacher relationship should be a two-way street. Mentors learn as they gain insight and reflect on their own and their mentees' practices. The area of culturally relevant practices is an example of knowledge and skills that a mentor from a different cultural background, community, or area of experience may be learning from a teacher whom he or she is mentoring.

Mentoring works best when it is not part of an evaluation: Mentoring provides feedback and support for the learning and growth of an early childhood teacher. Mentors may assess teachers, but their comments are not used to influence salary, advancement, or other employment decisions. Although supervisors use some mentoring strategies (i.e., reflective supervision), a clear separation and identification of the uses and focus of the mentoring should be clarified. Directive, technical training in an area of health and safety, for example, is not usually considered mentoring. This is technical information and is an important type of professional development, but it is not the focus of a mentoring relationship. The mentoring process might identify the need for a pediatric CPR course, but teaching the CPR class is not usually considered mentoring.

Mentoring has the potential to be transformative: The mentoring relationship has the possibility of transforming a teacher from a passive recipient of information (often not applied to the work setting) into a confident teacher who has developed a way of thinking or a process for solving problems and researching teaching questions.

Shared Theory of Change: Relationship Between Stated Goals and Strategies to Achieve Them

Beginning mentoring is often more effective in program contexts in which core beliefs and values are already identified by staff and families. However, mentors don't always have the luxury of working with programs that have made an explicit link between their daily activities and program vision. In many programs, sustaining learning though the inquiry process helps a practitioner for the first time to see the connections between their activities, the outcomes, and the contexts of their change efforts. Weiss and Pasley (2006) refer to this work as creating a shared *theory of change* that has the possibility to reveal how and why a teacher, program, or other educational effort works. Part of the professional-development process facilitated by a mentor is linking foundational early childhood development ideas and program values to a teacher's specific questions.

An example of the start of this process may be seen in the following vignette, which is a compilation of several actual mentoring interactions of the author:

A toddler teacher wondered with me (her mentor) how to better explain to the family of 2-year-old Thomas what he was learning when he explored the classroom. I suggested that we plan for ways to gather information to her question, "How does Thomas learn through play?" The teacher then said that she was reading the journal Zero to Three *and liked the way an article referred to the work* From Neurons to Neighborhoods *(Shonkoff and Phillips, 2000). She pointed out the following quote: "A young child's environment is both physical and social. Its impact on development is mediated through the nature and quality of experiences that it offers and the daily transactions that transpire both inside and outside the home" (Fenichel, 2001, p. 13). She said that the quote meant a lot to her, but she needed something more specific about Thomas for the parents to understand how the play environment supported their child's learning.*

The teacher now had a research question and a purpose, and—thanks to a journal article—she also had a theory for what she believed mediated learning. She now needed support for connecting the dots between understanding *theory* (importance of the physical and social environment in learning) and explaining *practice* (facilitating learning through play). The mentoring process could now begin with support to plan for documenting, reflecting, and applying what she would learn through a cycle of inquiry. Her purpose for starting this research into how Thomas learned through play was to be better able to communicate play's importance to his family. Several weeks later, she had met with the parent and remarked that she had never been able to explain so clearly the ways that what a child did and said supported development. She was also pleased that she could share the ways that this understanding informed her efforts to plan the school environment. This very humble but insightful toddler teacher had experienced the power of taking the time to research a simple yet profound question. She and the parents had also come up with a new question about which they all wanted to gather information: *How does Thomas learn to play cooperatively with his friends?* The inquiry process began again with a more confident and engaged teacher.

Helping Teachers Identify Interesting Questions to Investigate

The cycle of inquiry begins by turning a teacher concern, dilemma, or frustration into a teacher question to investigate. If the teacher's program is already using a curriculum or specific approach for documenting and planning for children's learning, then it is best for the mentor to begin by linking to that approach and building from there. The mentor is most effective when joining with a teacher. Always ask yourself, *How can I make a teacher feel competent and excited about engaging in learning?* Beware of suggesting too much change too soon or all at once. First, invite a teacher to wonder, question, and share ideas.

Mentors begin by helping the teacher explore a question of interest. Often, the teacher does not have a question. Then, what should a mentor do? The teacher may have a problem, a worry, or a vague idea of what they are wondering. Ask the teacher to take observational notes about what he or she notices children and teachers doing and saying during a specific time of day or during specific play experiences in the classroom over time. In some situations, the mentor may have to model the documentation process for a teacher. While examining observational notes together, invite the teacher to begin the inquiry process with questions such as those posed in Table 5.3.

Table 5.3   Invite a Teacher to Wonder

What is interesting in this observation?	What does the observation tell about the child's strengths, interests, development, temperament, or learning strategies (or other area for interpretation)?	What questions does this observation generate? Turn interests, dilemmas, worries, or problems into the form of a researchable question.
After taking anecdotal or narrative notes, highlight areas of interest with the teacher.	Help the teacher choose one area that he or she wants to question and research.	Help the teacher to identify his or her concerns and frame questions.
The teacher may do this, or the mentor could model anecdotal or narrative note taking if this is new to the teacher.	Remember, effective mentors do not overwhelm teachers.	An example would be *Why is the block area a location where conflict between children occurs frequently?*

Based on concepts from Forman and Hall (2005).

Schienfeld, Haigh, and Scheinfeld (2008) found in working with teachers in the Chicago Commons Child Development Program that scaffolding teachers' development with stimulating questions and careful observation, and emphasizing thinking deeply, required "promot(ing) experiences and types of development in the teachers that enable and motivate them to promote similar experiences and types of development in the children" (Schienfeld, 2008, p. 151). If teachers are fostering dispositions of "little scientists" in the children in their care, then mentors must also respectfully engage with teachers to construct questions to research.

As noted in the earlier vignette, a simple and effective beginning question for an early childhood teacher is, *How does [name of child] learn through play?* If the teacher does not have a question, invite the teacher into the process after first observing a child in his or her program. Then, share the stages of *observe—reflect—apply*, as identified with examples in Table 5.4.

Table 5.4 Beginning a Mini-Cycle of Inquiry

Mini-cycle of inquiry:
What am I wondering or what questions do I have?

Cycle One:
Mentor demonstrates inquiry process for teacher. Mentor observes a child and frames a simple inquiry question such as "How does Sam learn through play?"

OBSERVE *What is this child doing and saying?*	REFLECT *What does it mean?*	APPLY *What do I do to keep the learning going?*
Sam (20 months) is wearing a firefighter hat as he goes outside to play. He picks up a stick he finds on the playground. He points the stick at a plant and says "Brrrrrrr. Out, fire!"	Sam substitutes one object for another in pretend play. He is beginning to express himself in two-word phrases. (Reference: Teaching Strategies GOLD, 2010)	Mary Ann, the teacher, expands on what Sam says and to encourage him to express his ideas. She says,."I see that you have a hose to squirt the fire. Do you need a lot of water?" Sam replies, "Fire all wet. Gone!"
Mentor uses descriptive narrative or anecdotal notes as evidence. After taking anecdotal or narrative notes, highlight with the teacher the areas he or she is interested in understanding.	**Mentor uses program's resources to interpret observation.** Help the teacher choose one area of an observation to interpret. Remember, effective mentors do not overwhelm teachers.	**Mentor describes effective teacher–child interactions.** Ask questions and listen for new or different insights from the teacher. Model openness to multiple perspectives, and build on the teacher's ideas.

REFLECTION

After reading the stages of the inquiry process in Table 5.4, reflect on the mentor communication skills needed in each phase of inquiry. In which of the areas (e.g., observe, reflect, apply) do you feel most confident? What areas to you want to practice with another adult?

Observe–Reflect–Apply

In the *observation phase*, mentors should use their skills of listening, responding with empathy, noticing and supporting, and seeking more information or making plans for additional observation or evidence gathering. Moving to the *reflection phase* involves use of the communication skills for positive feedback, making connections, and establishing meaning. Finally, the *application phase* includes giving instructive feedback, ongoing affirmation, and encouragement to continue to reflect on the next steps. See Section I for review of these communication skills.

Questioning and Inquiry

Revisiting the same documentation evidence allows for the teacher and mentor to become more skilled in working together, as more detailed questions and more collaborative dialogue facilitate greater investigation and learning. Mentors working with teachers experienced in methods of assessment and teacher research, as detailed in Table 5.5 and Cycle Two, may choose to begin facilitating with more detailed questioning.

Table 5.5   Mentor and Teacher Revisit Observation

Cycle Two: Mentor and Teacher revisit and reexamine

OBSERVE ⇨	REFLECT ⇨	APPLY
Observation revisited: *What do you want to know?* *What are you curious about?*	*Reflective conversation:* *Making more meaning*	*Planning to engage more deeply with content or curriculum changes*
What do you find most interesting in this observation? *What other evidence should you collect (observation notes, work samples, photos, audio or video recordings, input from families, etc.)?*	*What does it tell you about the child's strengths, interests, development, temperament, or learning strategies (or other areas for interpretation)?* *To which child goals and objectives does it relate?* *What additional resources do you need to help you interpret what you document and the evidence you collect?*	*What might you do next?* *What do you want to plan for this child to support his development?* *What changes might you make to the environment, materials, schedule, routines, or to my interactions?* *What content or curriculum areas do you want to know more about before planning for this child?*
Mentor supports teacher to develop a research question and a purpose for continued observation and evidence gathering. Plans for more evidence gathering are made.	**Mentor uses questions that prompt the teacher to examine the observation and evidence gathered to answer the new teacher research question.**	**Mentor poses questions that help the teacher evaluate ways in which the plans that he or she made and the outcomes of those plans supported goals for the child. Mentor asks teacher what he or she would do the same or differently next time.**
Example of a new, more specific teacher-generated research question: *How do teacher–child conversations support Sam's language development?*	Example of teacher comment: *After reviewing my latest observations, I see that Sam's engagement in conversation is greatest when he is involved in back-and-forth conversations during dramatic play. He seems to have a strong interest in learning about water's properties.*	Example of teacher comment: *Looking at the videotape of Sam and me talking made me aware that I often ask him a lot of fact-based questions. I see from the language-development information you gave me that I might want to try more open-ended questions to encourage his language.*

REFLECTION

1. Reflect on the *process emphasis* (see definition in this box) of facilitating the *observe—reflect—apply* cycle of inquiry with a teacher. How does the role of the mentor change as the teacher and mentor move through a cycle of inquiry together?

> *Process emphasis:* Engagement in a process that promotes teachers to construct, examine, analyze, and communicate their ideas. The mentor is a facilitator of a teacher's research of children's understandings and interests. Just as teachers should support the representation of children's learning, mentors should support a parallel process for teachers engaged in professional development. Content is still very important, but it is arrived at through a protocol or process orientation (i.e., cycle of inquiry involving the use of many communication strategies).

2. Discuss the differences between a process emphasis and a content emphasis after reviewing the box that follows. Notice in the cycle the location of each emphasis, and consider the timing for using each approach.

> *Content emphasis:* Specific subject matter (math, science, setting up an environment for learning, etc.) is the focus. This is best done after a process is established. Consider the short- and long-term benefits of each emphasis. In a mentoring approach, content is often meaningless if the teacher does not know how to use it or apply it or if a learning relationship is not established with the mentor. Timing is key here. The skilled mentor knows when to link the teacher to specific information or technical assistance.

Using Documentation of an Inquiry Process to Communicate Learning to Families

Read the vignette labeled "Toddler Friendship." Do you think that you could facilitate an early childhood teacher's documentation and creation of a simple vignette like this? How would you help a teacher select notes from longer document that seems significant to, for example, a child's development? What resources would a teacher need for you to provide to interpret the meaning of his or her narrative notes? What questions do you still have about supporting the beginning of the development of documentation skills or fostering new curiosity in very accomplished teachers? Consider more elements that would add to this vignette (accompanying photos, video, learning goals, etc.).

> **Vignette: Toddler Friendship**
> Forming Toddler Friendships: Lori and Jamie's Cooking Experience
>
> **Selected observational notes:**
> *Lori:* I would like to have a picnic. You, too?
> *Jamie:* Yeah, I wanna come. I need to make tea for my baby!
> *Lori:* Okay. I will help, okay?
> *Jamie:* Yes, please! Thanks!
> *Lori:* Okay, I will get my bear and the puppy to sit with your baby.
>
> **Interpretation:**
> Lori is working together with Jamie to accomplish her goal for having a picnic for her stuffed friends and doll babies. They are cooperating and communicating with each other through multiple tasks such as cooking, cleaning, and setting the table. From their laughs, smiles, and conversation, I believe that they really enjoy each other's company and are learning what it means to be a friend.

Expanding the Cycle of Inquiry and Identifying Areas for Teacher and Mentor Development

After engaging a program or teacher with the three-part cycle of inquiry (observe, reflect, and apply), mentors may benefit from a self-assessment of knowledge, skills, and program conditions needed to facilitate teacher research. To sustain a teacher's learning after formal mentoring ends, ask yourself : *Who in the program models being a self-directed learner with a sense of confidence about his or her ability to solve problems and act with others to promote a child's development, a program's development, and the collaboration of parents?* (Schienfeld, Haigh and Schienfeld, 2008). Also, review specific gaps in teacher skills or knowledge by referring to Table 5.6. These gaps may prevent a teacher from making necessary changes to his or her practices.

Document Progress From the Teacher and Mentor's Perspective

The cycle of inquiry process requires a mentor to shift from an orientation of teaching children to facilitation of an adult learning process. Study Table 5.7, Teacher–Mentor Professional Development Plan, and reflect on progress from both the teacher and mentor perspectives to complete the Documenting Progress section.

Table 5.6   Assessment of Program Conditions to Support Teacher Inquiry

Inquiry Phase	Mentor Comments
Observe • Are teachers able to record what they see, hear, and observe? • What supports and barriers exist? • Describe how documentation or assessment skills need strengthening.	
Reflect • Are teachers able to infer meaning from the information that they gather? • Do teachers need more knowledge regarding child development, cultural competency, language acquisition, etc., to interpret their observations? • Is the disposition of the teacher as researcher understood and supported by the program? • What skills, disposition, or knowledge need strengthening?	
Apply • Does the teacher have practice and skills in making choices, sharing perspectives, and collaborating? • Is the program a safe place to share multiple points of view? • Who in the program has the skills to connect the perspectives of the teachers and parents to the development of the child and the program plans? • Does the teacher have experience in building upon children's interests and ideas? • Does the teacher know how to guess or anticipate possible responses of the children or parents to program plans? • Are parents and everyone involved in the program a part of the learning community?	

Based on professional development strategies detailed in Schienfeld, Haigh, and Schienfeld (2008).

Planning-Process Check-In

It is important to check the pulse of the learning relationship and goals after a few meetings or after an initial cycle of inquiry. On the basis of the first mentor–teacher observation, reflection, and application experiences together, do you or the teacher have any new insights to the suggestions and questions that follow?

• Review your goals. After your initial work together has gotten underway, do you still want to accomplish those goals, or do they need to be adjusted or changed?

Table 5.7   Teacher–Mentor Professional Development Plan

Documenting Progress	Teachers and Mentors Comments	
1. Implementing: Documenting Action Steps After They Occur (Example: Observed, documented, reviewed information, discussed choices, put into practice, offered feedback . . .)	Observations: Review of documentation, information collected: Put into practice:	
2. Status: What happened? Check-in date(s):	Progress toward goals:	Facilitation of learning:
3. Reflection	Mentee reflects on observations, documentation, and actions chosen.	Summary of mentor feedback:
4. Changes needed and next steps:	What was accomplished? What has changed? What still needs to occur? What needs to change? Next steps:	Evidence of making progress or meeting goals: What should change about the mentoring process? Next steps:

- Do you have any new insights into what short-term goals and program conditions are necessary to produce longer term outcomes?
- What resources are needed to begin the activities that you identified and to maintain the program supports necessary for the activities to be effective?

Mentor Development Parallels Teacher Development

Mentors also benefit from reflection by themselves or with others who are in similar professional-development roles. Disequilibrium may occur for the mentor just as it does for teachers who are learning and growing. When mentors take the time to journal, discuss, and reflect on how they are developing in the areas outlined in Table 5.8, they will model for teachers ways to seek growth in their professional practices. Results from periodic completion of a mentor self-assessment—for example, by the use of Table 5.8—may inform ongoing education for mentors (Casey & Claunch, 2005).

Table 5.8 Mentor Development Self-Reflection

Review the topics shown here. Note how you feel in your mentoring role, and add comments about what you are still wondering or areas in which you feel you need support. Circle the letter next to the statement that describes your feelings about your mentoring relationship(s) or skills.

I feel unsure (U), I am developing (D), I sometimes agree (SA), or I am confident (C)

U-D-SA-C	Comfort and trust exists in the PD relationship.
U-D-SA-C	Organization of time: Schedule of observations and/or meetings meets needs.
U-D-SA-C	Listening skills are growing.
U-D-SA-C	Questioning skills are growing.
U-D-SA-C	Communication during and between meetings is effective.
U-D-SA-C	Collaboration and collegiality exist.
U-D-SA-C	Ability exists to individualize and use multiple strategies to fit teacher's needs.
U-D-SA-C	Intentional mentoring practices are used. Reasons are given for facilitation choices.
U-D-SA-C	Timing of support fits teacher's needs.
U-D-SA-C	The mentoring process supports the strengths and resiliencies in the teacher.
U-D-SA-C	Teacher is an active participant and decision maker in his or her own learning.
U-D-SA-C	The mentor is able to separate the mentoring process from his or her personal agenda.
U-D-SA-C	The mentor facilitates and advocates more than directs and dictates.
U-D-SA-C	Personal mentoring style is emerging.
U-D-SA-C	Teacher's expectation of mentoring process is realistic.
U-D-SA-C	Adult-learning theory is understood, and effective teaching facilitation is used.
U-D-SA-C	The mentor is able to identify strengths and needed areas of development in the mentoring role.
U-D-SA-C	The mentor helps the teacher to connect observations, reflections, and actions.

Summary

Mentors need to be as aware of adult behaviors and comments just as teachers need to be aware of what young children do and say. The mentor's understanding of the stage of change that an adult may be in or the contextual factors that are preventing or supporting the adult's PD participation is essential in order for the mentor to facilitate individualized PD. Although it is always hard for an enthusiastic mentor to accept that a teacher may not be interested or ready to participate in PD, it is essential for the mentor to notice the signs of readiness for change on the part of the teacher and understand what they mean so that the mentor may respond effectively.

The process of mentors' joining with teachers to identify and research teacher questions requires support for planning a cycle of inquiry. An inquiry approach may lead to sustaining adult learning because it involves the qualities of the best of education. Inquiry is active, not passive, and is connected to reflection and analysis based on the collection of information and documentation of change over time. Knowledge and understanding are applied to a problem or dilemma while a mentor facilitates a teacher's thinking and analysis of his or her documentation. The mentor's role is to notice a teacher in the act of figuring out and constructing understanding. Just as teachers broadcast a child's learning processes, so too the adult mentor should try to understand the teacher's interests, skills, and view of personal accomplishments. When a mentor observes a teacher, the mentor is also looking for more than how the teacher interacts with children; the mentor is also looking for ways to join with a teacher in the learning journey. The inquiry approach has the potential to promote and sustain long-term change and develop effective thinking and teacher problem solving.

What do you still want to know about supporting teachers to research their questions? First, review the key ideas from Figure 5.2.

Figure 5.2   Summary of Readiness for Change and Learning Through Inquiry

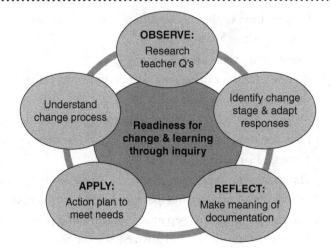

As a mentor, you need to support teachers so that they see themselves as capable of identifying a problem, collecting and analyzing observational notes and information, and making action plans based on what they learn. Keep the learning going by examining teacher research that is available from peer-reviewed professional publications and other teacher websites. Encouraging teachers to publish their learning stories about problems or investigations is especially affirming. Examples of how other teachers have reflected on their own questions about their everyday practices can be inspirational to teachers who are being mentored. Publications for teacher research include the following:

**The Center for Practitioner Research (CFPR) of the National College of Education at National-Louis University, http://www.nl.edu/cfpr
Links to a long list of teacher research websites

***Voices of Practitioners,* NAEYC,** http://www.naeyc.org/publications/vop
Contains helpful support for teachers (and other educators) to support teachers or college students to begin a process of teacher research

References

Casey, J., & Claunch, A. (2005). The stages of mentor development. In H. Portner (Ed.), *Teacher mentoring and induction: The state of the art and beyond* (pp. 95–108). Thousand Oaks, CA: Corwin.

Deci, E. L., & Ryan, R. M. (1985). *Intrinsic motivation and self-determination in human behavior.* New York: Plenum.

Dodge, D. T., Rudick, S., & Berke, K. (2008). *The creative curriculum for infants, toddlers & twos.* Washington, DC: Teaching Strategies, Inc. Retrieved from http://www.TeachingStrategies.com

Fenichel, E. (2001). From neurons to neighborhoods: What's in it for you? *Zero to Three, 21*(5), 8–15.

Fixsen, D. L., Naoom, S. F., Blase, K. A., Friedman, R. M., & Wallace, F. (2005). *Implementation research: A synthesis of the literature.* Tampa, FL: University of South Florida, Louis de la Parte Florida Mental Health Institute, the National Implementation Research Network (FMHI Publication No. 231). Retrieved from http://nirn.fpg.unc.edu/sites/nirn.fpg.unc.edu/files/resources/NIRN-MonographFull-01-2005.pdf

Fixsen, D. L., Blase, K. A., Horner, R., & Sugai, G. (February, 2009). *Scaling-up brief. State implementation & scaling-up of evidence-based practices.* FPG Child Development Institute, University of North Carolina at Chapel Hill. Retrieved from http://sisep.fpg.unc.edu/sites/sisep.fpg.unc.edu/files/resources/SISEP-Brief3ReadinessForChange-02-2009.pdf

Forman, G., & Hall, E. (2005). Wondering with children: The importance of observation in early education. *Early Childhood Research & Practice, 7*(2), 1–15. Retrieved from http://ecrp.uiuc.edu/v7n2/forman.html

Galinsky, E. (2010). *Mind in the making.* New York: HarperCollins.

Heroman, C., Burts, D., Berke, K., & Bickart, T. (2010). Teaching Strategies GOLD objectives for development & learning: Birth through kindergarten. Washington, DC: Teaching Strategies, Inc.

Jablon, J. R., Dombro, A. L., & Dichtelmiller, M. L. (2007). *The power of observation.* Washington, DC: National Association for the Education of Young Children.

Joyce, B., & Showers, B. (2002). Student achievement through professional development. In B. Joyce & B. Showers (Eds.), *Designing training and peer coaching: Our need for learning.* Alexandria, VA: Association for Curriculum and Supervision Development.

Metz, A., & Bartley, L. (2012, March). Active implementation frameworks for program success: How to use implementation science to improve outcomes for children. *Zero To Three* (pp. 11–18). Retrieved from: http://www.zerotothree.org/about-us/areas-of-expertise/reflective-practice-program-development/metz-revised.pdf

Perry, G., Henderson, B., & Meier, D. R. (2012). *Our inquiry, our practice: Undertaking, supporting and learning from early childhood teacher research(ers).* Washington, DC: National Association for the Education of Young Children.

Peterson, S. M. (2008). *Applying the Ttranstheoretical Mmodel of behavior change to child care providers enrolled in a professional development programs.* Rochester, NY: Children's Institute, Inc.

Peterson, S. M., & Baker, A. (2011). Readiness to change in communities, organizations, and individuals. In John A. Sutterby (Ed.), *The Early Childhood Educator Professional Development Grant: Research and Practice (Advances in Early Education and Day Care): Vol. 15,* pp. 33–59. Emerald Group.

Peterson, S. M., & Valk, C. (2010). Beyond babysitting: Challenges and opportunities in early childhood education. In S. B. Neuman & M. L. Kamil (Eds.), *Preparing teachers for the early childhood classroom: Proven models and key principles* (pp. 49–64). Baltimore, MD: Paul H. Brookes Publishing Co.

Peterson, S. M., Valk, C., Baker, A. C., Brugger, L., & Hightower, A. D. (2010). "We're not just interested in the work": Social and emotional aspects of early educator mentoring relationships. *Mentoring & Tutoring: Partnership in Learning, 18*(2), 155–175.

Prochaska, J. O., DiClemente, C. C., & Norcross, J. C. (1992). In search of how people change. Applications to addictive behaviors. *American Psychologist, 47* 1102–1114.

Prochaska, J. O., & DiClemente, C. C. (1982). Transtheoretical therapy: Toward a more integrative model of change. *Psychotherapy: Theory, Research and Practice, 19,* 276–287.

Prochaska, J. O., & Velicer, W. F. (1997). The Transtheoretical Model of health behavior change. *American Journal of Health Promotion, 12,* 38–48.

Reason, P., & Bradbury, H. (2001). *Handbook of action research: Participative inquiry and practice.* Thousand Oaks, CA: Sage.

Schienfeld, D. R., Haigh, K. M., & Schienfeld, K. (2008). *We are all explorers: Learning and teaching with Reggio principles in urban settings.* New York: Teachers College Press.

Shonkoff, J. P., & Phillips, D. A. (2000). *From neurons to neighborhoods: The science of early childhood development.* Washington, DC: National Academy Press.

Teaching Strategies. (2010). *Teaching Strategies GOLD.* Washington, DC: Teaching Strategies, Inc.

Weiss, I. R., & Pasley J. D. (2006). *Scaling up instructional improvement through teacher professional development: Insights from the local systemic change initiative.* Philadelphia: Consortium for Policy Research in Education (CPRE) Policy Briefs.

Zachary, L. J. (2000). *The mentor's guide: Facilitating effective learning relationships.* San Francisco: Jossey Bass.

CHAPTER 6

• •

Coaching to Connect Curriculum, Assessment, and Teaching

The chapter supports your growing capacity to

- understand choices to observe, gather information, and document learning;
- explore ways to reflect on observations and make meaning through dialogue, discussion, and use of professional resources;
- create curriculum and apply what you learn; and
- share a project, evaluate, and celebrate both teacher and mentor achievements.

It is wonderful to see children solve problems, talk about their emotions, show empathy for each other, and take power in their own learning. They learn so much every day and investigating that process is amazing to me.

(Preschool teacher in a Head Start professional
learning community, April, 2012)

No longer are teachers able to satisfy most program standards or even the questions of parents by simply saying, "I taught that skill" or "I set up this environment to support the children's play." Showing the planning sheet on the wall that identifies a theme or a content area to be taught on Wednesday morning isn't enough to explain a program's educational choices. Meeting the expectations of current early childhood state, national, and professional standards (NAEYC and NAECS/SDE, 2003) demands that teachers of our youngest children identify what a child knows and is able to do and translate that knowledge into plans and teaching strategies to continue the child's learning. A teacher needing support to make curriculum, assessment, and teaching connections requires an adult instructor who also models and understands these connections.

Just as children learn best from teachers who use responsive and intentional strategies, adult students learn from instructors who create a caring community of learners, teach to enhance development and learning, plan curriculum aligned with important learning outcomes, assess student growth and development related to those outcomes, and build positive relationships with students and stakeholders in the program.

(Lutton, 2012, p.13)

Specific professional knowledge and skills are needed to help teachers to grow in the area of linking curriculum, assessment, and teaching. The National Association for the Education of Young Children (NAEYC) and the National Association for Child Care Resource and Referral Agencies (NACCRRA) place this role under the responsibility

121

of a person with specific expertise, referred to as a *coach*. This definition adds some additional dimensions that are required beyond the foundational skills of a mentoring relationship. The role of the coach is ". . . to build capacity for specific professional dispositions, skills, and behaviors and is focused on goal-setting and achievement for an individual or group" (Lutton, 2012, p. 85).

The current era of educational accountability is sometimes interpreted in a cynical way by teachers who feel that they are forced to meet standards imposed by outsiders. Coaches have the opportunity to turn cynicism into empowerment by assisting teachers and programs to follow the culturally and developmentally appropriate program approach of their choice (e.g., High Scope, Reggio inspired, etc.), working with them to learn to demonstrate how and what the children are learning. Having the knowledge and skills to communicate ways in which higher quality teaching can improve child outcomes can be liberating for teachers. Coaches can demystify the many methods designed to both meet standards and stay true to preferred program approaches by embedding into the mentoring process the examination of ways in which curriculum, assessment, and teaching are integrally connected. Neuman (2010, p. 222) suggests that the underlying purpose of all early childhood education professional development (PD), regardless of the form it takes (e.g., workshops, courses, or one-on-one mentoring), must be to link child outcomes to any teaching and planning strategy used. In addition, the American Educational Research Association states that assessment should be aligned with the curriculum and the goals of instruction (AERA, 2004, p. 2).

Head Start, as the largest U.S. early childhood education program, has a child outcomes framework (USDHHS, ACF, & OHS, 2010) that influences Head Start preschool teacher curriculum and assessment decisions. Teachers who can explain their decisions by connecting these broad areas will have the tools to uphold the traditional early childhood values of facilitating play and emergent learning while also meeting national Head Start standards. When teachers are able to explain and present evidence about what children are learning in their play, they are able to explain the purpose and power in their teaching choices. Teachers who can defend their choices as the right ones for the children whom they actually teach may also be less susceptible to inappropriate curriculum fads. It is even more important that general early childhood teachers who work with early-intervention specialists to use assessment to inform and monitor their instruction be able to engage in classroom interventions designed to prevent learning disabilities later on (Coleman, Buysse, and Neitzel, 2006; Hemmeter, Joseph, Smith, and Sandall, 2001).

Producing confident teachers means coaching for planning, adapting curriculum, and choosing teaching strategies with the expertise of a teacher-researcher. Current studies have shown that ongoing coaching involving modeling and constructive feedback is associated with positive changes (Boyle, Lamprianou, and Boyle, 2005) in the understanding of broad areas of teaching practices.

Understanding Choices to Observe, Gather Information, and Document Learning

"Help me with planning curriculum that I can use tomorrow!" is a request that this author has heard consistently from working teachers who want immediate support. This is understandable because, like a restaurant chef with a dining room full of hungry people, the teacher is met each morning with children who always need to be engaged in something interesting. The challenge for the professional early childhood coach is to resist the quick-fix focus of the "make and take" curriculum requests of the working teacher. Instead, using a teacher's intense interest in the process of curriculum planning, the coach might begin by engaging teachers in wondering about who their children are. That is, what do they know? What can they do? What are they interested in? What are their preferred learning processes? What are their families' wishes and hopes?. Coaches might begin with a dialogue with a teacher interested in curriculum help and ask the following questions:

- What do you already know about this group of children?
- What children get your attention, and which ones do you feel you understand?
- What children do you not understand?
- What ways do you learn about the children in your group?
- What is puzzling you, and what do you want to gather information about?

Before explaining to the teacher that observation is the first step to curriculum planning, ask a teacher to remember a time that he or she has been particularly effective in teaching a child. By beginning with a teacher's personal memory of successful teaching, you are allowing the teacher to discuss what he or she already knows about the connection between teaching a child and understanding a child's prior knowledge. For example, ask the teacher these questions:

Do you remember a child you were not connecting with until you observed him or her or got more information? How did learning about what that child was doing and saying change your behavior toward him or her?

Thinking over recollections of successful uses of naturalistic or authentic assessment data is the best place to begin for most teachers because it is the most commonly used documentation method. However, other educators with broader experience in managing systems of multiple types of assessment could be asked the following:

Do you recall changing your mind about a child after carefully reviewing multiple sources of information and assessment data over time? How did this change your behavior toward the child?

After listening and taking notes on what a teacher shares about a successful memory of connecting to a child, draw three boxes on a piece of paper. Label the boxes *observation, curriculum,* and *teaching.* Listen carefully to a successful teaching story. Insert the facts of the story into the boxes that fit the details. The following is an example of a teacher recollection:

Oh yes, I remember when I thought the toddler Maureen was just a very bossy child— until I stopped and observed her at the sensory tub. She started dumping and pouring water into a water wheel, when two toddler boys came to the table. As soon as she saw them, she screamed, grabbed the water wheel, and began shaking her head and saying, "no . . . no . . . mine." Then, a teacher came over and told Maureen to share. This seemed to enrage her even more. After class, I shared my observation with the teacher. We decided that next time, we needed to intervene, before Maureen became upset, by doing a few things differently. We decided to have multiples of the same cups and other items in the tub. We also decided to talk to the children before they were upset. A third teacher gave us another idea; she said that Maureen might be given words to say to the boys, such as, "I am playing with this now. You can have it next." We tried this, and it worked! I knew that observing the scene was important because I was starting to get a negative view of Maureen's social skills. When I reflected on what I had seen, looked over the notes I had taken, and talked with other teachers, I then realized that Maureen was reacting to a situation that was beyond her coping ability. Even though she couldn't say the words I gave her, she seemed relieved that now I knew what she was feeling. We all made changes in our plans and behaviors, and Maureen's social skills grew.

A coach listening to this experience might summarize and diagram the teacher's comments as follows:

Observation:
Narrative notes on the interactions at the toddler water table for 10 minutes during the morning free play time.

Curriculum:
Goal: Support parallel play at the water table. Materials: Put out triple the number of cups, and limit the number of children at the sensory tub to three.

Teaching strategies:
Discuss dumping and filling with the children, and map each of their actions. Use vocabulary about how "we" are all playing. Move the group to new activities before they are frustrated and in conflict.

This exercise lets the teacher know that he or she already has successful experiences and skills for connecting these three areas. Now, the coach's role, like that of the teacher in the example, is to add to a repertoire of strategies in each area and encourage the teacher to use these skills and insights more consistently. Teachers who at first can't recall any successful experiences often do remember after listening to other teachers share their stories.

In the mentoring process, beginning with a focus on observation helps teachers to learn about some of their choices for gathering information about what children are doing and saying. This includes exploring the areas of documenting, investigating, and increasing awareness of biases that may prevent adults from seeing and understanding a child. In summary, work with teachers to understand how to

- find ways to observe what adults and children are doing and saying;
- recognize biases that prevent "seeing," or getting to know, a child;
- put together a cycle of documentation (or assessment), curriculum, and teaching

Finding Ways to Observe What Adults and Children Are Doing and Saying

The coach's role is to ask, "Do documentation skills by the teacher and other staff need strengthening or expanding?" This requires understanding the needs and strengths of a teacher to discern whether he or she knows ways of objectively gathering information about children in order to better understand and support a child's learning and development. Review Table 6.1 for definitions and examples of the many purposes, types, methods, and instruments of assessment of children. Individualized coaching requires an answer to specific questions about a teacher's understanding of assessment if the PD is to foster foundational knowledge and skills related to teaching young children. A coach should create a needs assessment from observing and dialoging with a teacher about the teacher's background knowledge in the areas outlined in the table.

In summary, there is great consensus in the early childhood education field that the link between observing what is taught and teaching what is assessed should be understood by early childhood teachers (Copple and Bredekamp, 2009; NAEYC & NAECS/SDE, 2003; Neuman, 2010). Infant teachers who shake an object near of a 2-month-old's face and observe as the baby turns his or her head to watch the object move across the air now know that the child is able to track objects. The infant teacher can offer the baby interesting objects to view and explore in order to keep development going. The toddler teacher who plays peek-a-boo with an excited 1-year-old can tell a parent that his or her child is enjoying exploring how people and objects appear and disappear. If these expected milestones are not occurring,

Table 6.1 Understanding Assessment Basics
....

What does the teacher understand about the following assessment basics?

Multiple Purposes of Assessment	• A continuous process of documenting a child's behaviors, skills, learning preferences, interactions, milestones, and competencies • Developmental screening and, if indicated, referral for diagnostic testing • Feedback on the planning of instruction and teaching choices • Program evaluation and other accountability requirements to meet standards • Communicating with parents and other teachers about a child's development and learning (See: WA OSPI, 2008)
Multiple Types or Methods of Assessment	**Naturalistic, authentic, or curriculum-based assessment** is the most commonly used teacher-administered observation method for observing children during play, in typical routines, and in familiar places with well-known persons, and involves • narrative information (e.g., running records, anecdotal records, jottings, diagrams, sketches, photos, audio, visual recordings); • procedures that count (e.g., checklists, participation charts); or • procedures that rate or rank (e.g., frequency charts, rating scales, rubrics). **Other types of assessment** include screening, diagnostic, readiness, and criterion-referenced instruments. Does the teacher know what reliability and validity are and how to choose research- or evidence-based tools? (See: NCCIC, 2005)
Multiple Contexts	• Indoors, outdoors, at home, at school, etc.
Multiple Sources	• Teachers, parents, peers, professional specialists, etc.
Some Common Pitfalls	• Lacks culturally and linguistically appropriate methods or understandings of the context or sources of information • Special needs not understood; instrument not appropriate • Documentation has unfounded biases or assumptions about an individual, which have clouded the judgments of the teacher (See: NAEYC & NAECS/SDE, 2003)

documenting that delay indicates to the teacher that it is time to inform parents to consider consultation with a doctor or other professional. Preschoolers taking on dramatic-play roles are ready to have a teacher plan experiences that allow them to think abstractly about things not concretely present. Early-primary students who are sounding out words benefit from teachers who routinely record the specific phonemes that their students are able to decode. Successful teachers of children of all ages know what their children know and are able to do. They then consistently record that information in order to plan to extend learning through effective teaching strategies or seek referral for possible developmental delays.

It is important for a coach with specific expertise in assessment, curriculum, and instruction planning, who is engaged in encouraging a teacher to observe and document children's learning and development, to participate in the parallel process of documenting what the teacher knows and is able to do in these areas. Use Figure 6.1 to support improvement of coaching practices designed for the mentor to learn the needs of teachers in order to align their teaching strategies with what they know about a child.

Figure 6.1 Coaching to Understand the Needs and Strengths of Teachers
. . . .

Complete responses to these questions during a coaching session with a teacher.

- *What is the content about which the teacher is interested in learning?*
- *How will the coaching process link a teacher's specific interest to the importance of aligning observation, curriculum planning, and teaching strategies?*
- *What authentic (naturalistic) assessment or curriculum-based assessment tools does the teacher and program understand and use?* Do the teacher's skills need strengthening in order for the use of this tool to be more effective?*
- *What program and child observation tools do the teacher or other program staff use and understand?*
- *What is the overall quality of the classroom? of the program? Does the coaching process involve observing the program to give the mentor a baseline of information about the quality of the program?*
- *Which program evaluation tool will be used (e.g., CLASS, ELLCO, ECERS**, etc.)?*
- *After observing a teacher, does the coach consider and share with the teacher what the mentor believes is especially effective? What professional-development needs have been identified by the coach and by the teacher? Do the two align?*
- *Is the coach modeling informed-consent practices by obtaining permission from the program for use of any evaluation tools?*

*A Short List of Frequently Used Early Childhood Instructional (authentic curriculum-based) **Instruments**

- *Assessment, Evaluation, and Programming System (AEPS),* Paul H. Brookes Publishing Co.
- *Carolina Curriculum for Infants and Toddlers,* Paul H. Brookes Publishing Co.
- *Carolina Curriculum for Preschoolers,* Paul H. Brookes Publishing Co.
- *Teaching Strategies GOLD,* Teaching Strategies, Inc.
- *Dynamic Indicators of Basic Early Literacy Skills (DIBELS),* University of Oregon Center on Teaching and Learning.
- *Hawaii Early Learning Profile (HELP),* VORT.
- *High Scope Infant Toddler COR,* High/Scope Press.
- *High Scope Preschool COR,* High/Scope Press, The Work Sampling System, Pearson Early Learning.

**A Short List of Frequently Used Early Childhood Program Evaluation Tools and Resources

- *Classroom Assessment Scoring System (CLASS),* University of Virginia Press.
- *Early Childhood Environmental Rating Scale Revised Edition (ECERS-R),* Teachers College Press.
- *Early Childhood Classroom Observation Measure (ECCOM),* D. Stipek & P. Byler, Stanford University School of Education.
- *Early Language and Literacy Classroom Observation Tool (ELLCO),* Paul H. Brookes Publishing Co.
- *Family Child Care Environmental Rating Scale—Revised Edition (FCCERS-R),* Teachers College Press.
- *Infant Toddler Environment Rating Scale Revised Edition (ITERS-R),* Teachers College Press.
- *School Age Care Environment Rating Scale (SACERS),* Teachers College Press.
- *Supports for Early Literacy Assessment (SELA).*

REFLECTION

1. One promise that observation holds for teachers is a better relationship with the children whom they educate and care for. When teachers really know children, they are better able to individualize their curriculum plans. Would this outcome (or others, such as information to communicate to

parents or to identify children needing referrals for diagnostic evaluation or for program evaluation) motivate a teacher you know to observe and document children's interactions or other aspects of a program? Think of a particular teacher to interview, or recall what has motivated the teacher to document what children do and say.

2. Look back at your own learning experiences. Remember a person whom you misunderstood until you got to know him or her well. How and why did your views change?

3. Observation and assessment can intimidate early childhood teachers who have never had formal education about its purposes, methods, and uses. Considering the coaching principle of always starting from the strengths of the teacher, how might you begin to engage a teacher in authentic assessment as an ongoing process to inform his or her instruction and other program plans?

Recognizing Biases That Prevent a Teacher's "Seeing" or Getting to Know a Child

If a group of teachers need support understanding the basics of narrative documentation (e.g., running records and anecdotal notes), the teachers may progress more quickly if they learn as a group by taking notes independently and then sharing their narratives of observed children in a staff meeting or in another type of professional-learning group. Learning to record only what is seen and heard, without interpretation or judgment, takes practice, repetition, and feedback from others with more experience. Mentors working with multiple staff members of one program should emphasize the basics of narrative recording by sharing the need to

- write exactly what is seen and heard without interpretation, avoiding categories and labels (e.g., *smart, shy, irritating, always doing this, loves to push my buttons*);
- describe—rather than guess at motives and emotions, or hint at past or future behaviors—and stay in the moment, noting only what is observed;
- find other methods such as videotaping a specific episode or period of interest when a teacher finds it challenging to find time for taking notes while teaching; or

- have a *focus* and a *guiding question* for the observation, designed to answer the question, *Why am I gathering information?* For example, consider the following:
  - *Focus:* Block area during free-play time.
  - *Question:* How do the children learn about math concepts when they play with blocks?

After a teacher observes for a time, the mentor should critique the teacher's work to strengthen his or her authentic assessment skills. Jablon, Dombro and Dichtelmiller's *The Power of Observation* (2007) is an example of an easy-to-use resource to encourage teachers to open their minds to the potential of every child by taking the time to observe. This simple message is important to be reiterated even for very experienced teachers who understand multiple types of assessment. All teachers are at risk for being too busy or stressed to take the time to focus on what a child is able to do. Jablon et al. suggest having an attitude of openness, which includes strategies such as

- letting go of opinions and interpretations when first observing;
- describing actions and behaviors in detail;
- listening to children and recording what they say and do;
- tuning in to individual children or whatever is the focus of the observation; and
- documenting over a long enough period to gather needed information.

Examine with teachers what they bring to observing, and acknowledge that, although we strive to be free of bias or judgment, complete objectivity is impossible because we all come with specific backgrounds that inform what we notice. Ask teachers to consider a child who puzzles them.

Weave into your discussions, or suggest a journal reflection about, their perspectives to encourage more teacher self-awareness. Rephrase the following question in the way that best fits an individual teacher:

What are your lenses of culture, experience, beliefs about child rearing, ways to communicate, your temperament, interests, or feelings that may be causing you not to "see" what a child is doing or is capable of doing?

If expressing this matter in question form does not seem right for a specific teacher, make some observations that encourage reflection, such as, "I am noticing that you are very direct in your approach to people. Have you observed other styles of interacting in the children and families whom you work with?" Discuss factors that may increase the chance that a teacher will be able to document to get to know his or her children. These factors include

- observing regularly and making authentic documentation a continuous process; and
- ensuring that enough information is gathered (from multiple sources, methods, contexts, and including the family's views) for the teacher to avoid making snap judgments about specific children.

  This may require knowledge in the use of a specific instrument or tool for assessment;
- understanding how beliefs are informed by culture and other aspects of identity, which may help a teacher separate observation from interpretation;
- separating what is believed about a child from the "factual" information being recorded. This is essential. Being present in the moment and clearing the mind of other distractions is a skill to be cultivated when observing;

- combining mentoring with training or a course in observation methods—an ideal way to support teacher skills and knowledge.

Additional review of basic ideas foundational to assessment is helpful for most teachers (Kagan, Scott-Little, and Clifford, 2003). Experienced and new teachers benefit from a mentor's asking them questions about their choices. Ask them whether they are familiar with the concepts outlined next (Council of Chief State School Officers, 2004; Macy, Bricker, and Squires, 2005).

- *Reliability:* Is it dependable, trustworthy, and consistent information? If another person observed what I observed, would he or she come up with the same information? Are my biases so great toward this child that I cannot reliably observe him or her?
- *Validity:* Am I observing what I think I am observing? If we are focusing on indicators of physical development, for example, are we observing at the right time of day or during the right type of activity that we may learn about a child's abilities? Or, for example, did the observation of a teacher's asking a child to jump three times really confuse the child's ability to jump with his or her language ability to understand the directions?
- *Permission and Confidentiality:* What does this mean for our professional responsibility to receive informed consent from parents for us to assess a child and to then safeguard and communicate with others about information learned? What are the program policies in this area? Do they need strengthening?

Putting Together a Cycle of Documentation (or Assessment), Curriculum, and Teaching

Coaches should begin with the area of authentic assessment and make the observation process simple at first by breaking it down in a way that encourages even the busiest of teachers to gather information (Howell and Nolet, 2000). In the beginning, the goal for the coach should be to build a comfortable relationship with the teacher that reduces feelings of intimidation and the often-heard anxious comment, "I don't have the time to do this!" There are a variety of ways to engage a teacher in a process that involves

- *asking questions about what the teacher wants to learn about a child, a program, or some other entity;*
- *observing, listening, and taking notes;*
- *reflecting on the meaning of these notes by using professional resources; and*
- *responding with a change, a plan, or a new approach.*

  Jablon et al. (2007).

The coaching process should include an overview of the cycle, but the power of mentoring lies in tailoring support for the area in which an individual teacher needs help. After going through a cycle of observation, interpretation, and application, consider which areas need strengthening for a teacher. Does the teacher have the knowledge, skills, and resources for

- interpretation of notes or evidence (i.e., identification of developmental milestones, understanding children's learning processes, etc.);
- reflection, asking questions to interpret evidence (i.e., dialogue with peers and/or mentors, and use professional criteria and curriculum-based assessment resources);

- planning a response to the information (i.e., determining changes to class-room materials and environment, planning next experiences, and adjusting teaching strategies and professional resources to support these choices)?

Of course, coaches need to have foundational understanding of these areas themselves (see Jablon et al., 2007) and should also have received training in a specific curriculum-based tool to use in order to educate others to reliably document children's interactions, as well as help in their own instruction. Knowing which instrument to select can be confusing and requires specific education and expert consultation for both mentors and teachers. See *A Short List of Frequently Used Early Childhood Instructional Instruments* in this chapter.

Observing is a natural process that starts with an infant's intense gaze on the faces and attention to the sensory input all around him or her. Coaches have the opportunity to bring the passion back to teachers and encourage curiosity and wonder about what children are feeling, thinking, and learning.

The payoff for teachers is in having more information to build positive relationships with children and positive child outcomes as a result of the teachers' documenting, reflecting, and responding to what they learn. Although observation gives teachers more knowledge to inform instruction and monitor children's progress, teachers also need to be very aware of common pitfalls to their process, even when authentic assessment is the best choice in most situations (Neisworth and Bagnato, 2004). Coaches should remind teachers of such variables in children as fatigue, hunger, illness, and temperament, as well as the complexities of home language(s), culture, and family contextual factors that may be understood only through a combination of methods and multiple sources of information over time. Understanding documented behavior and progress made toward established goals is best accomplished through the use of a variety of developmental checklists, rating scales, caregiver interviews, and portfolios of children's work. Using multiple ways to learn about a child is essential for prevention of potentially inappropriate decisions resulting from misinterpretation of assessment data (NAEYC, 2005).

Observation requires making choices about what information to collect, as well as how many sources, methods, and contexts to use. The mentor needs to help teachers understand that, usually, the more information they have, the more complex and accurate picture they will get of a child or a program.

Beginning considerations include the following:

- *Source:* Focus on the child, the parent, other children, specialists, records about the child, other adults, and any other useful sources.
- *Method of observation:* Share a tool with teachers that fits their documentation needs and their ability to use the method in their context. Set them up for success.

Narrative	Counting	Rating or ranking
Running records Anecdotal notes Jottings, diagrams Sketches, photos Audio or digital recordings	Checklists Participation charts	Frequency charts Rating scales Rubrics

- *Context:* What context is best for the collection of information (e.g., indoors or outdoors, home or school)?

REFLECTION

1. Understanding the difference between observation and interpretation is a place to begin with teachers who confuse documenting their opinions with just what they can see and hear when observing a child. Compare and contrast the short narrative observations that follow. Consider why it is important to mentor teachers to record only what children are doing and saying and to remove judgments that may be biased. Why should observation and interpretation be clearly identified and separated in a child's file? When interpreting observational notes, how can professional resources support applying appropriate meaning to notes?

    Example of documenting without bias or interpretation: The teacher says, "What happened to you, Mary?" Mary replies, "Jimmy pushed me down, and I hurt myself."

    Example of adding interpretation that may be biased: The teacher takes Mary's hand and walks over to Jimmy, who is angry and feeling sorry for himself. Jimmy is a very forceful child who often responds with aggression.

2. If we accept the notion that, as human beings, we are unable to be truly objective, how can we work with a teacher to increase his or her attitude of openness?

Exploring Ways to Reflect on Observations and Make Meaning Through Dialogue, Discussion, and Use of Professional Resources

Once a teacher has practiced taking observational notes of only what a child is doing or saying, it is time for a mentor to support a teacher in interpreting the notes. Beginning with a curriculum-based assessment tool, such as *Teaching Strategies GOLD* (2010), can scaffold a teacher to understand how research-based criteria should inform the linking of observational notes to developmental milestones. Going deeper in analysis of documented child evidence requires a mentor to consider the following questions: *Is the teacher*

- able to infer or recognize themes, interests, and ideas in his or her documentation?
- in the habit of consulting with other staff, parents, and specialists to make meaning from the that information he or she gathers?

- needing more knowledge or professional resources regarding child development, cultural competency, language acquisition, or some other content area essential to understanding a child's development and learning?

One way to foster making meaning from examination of documentation and collection of a child's work products is through a professional group process explained in Figure 6.2 and referred to by Abramson (2008) as *co-inquiry*. Abramson suggests, in this Reggio-inspired process for sharing teacher documentation (Gandini and Goldhaber, 2001), that everyone listen carefully to the presentation and then have an equal chance to respond. The three-stage structure is detailed in Figure 6.2.

Figure 6.2   Co-Inquiry Meetings
....

1. **Sharing Focused Documentation:** A teacher begins by presenting documentation on which he or she wants group comments. The presentation involves sharing the question, dilemma, and focus, which inspired and guided the observation—for example, "Why are the preschoolers not choosing to play in the block area?" The power of this process is in the sharing of a specific focus that involved collecting relevant documentation, rather than in the discussion of a topic area, such as early mathematics, without evidence from the teachers program.
2. **Communication:** Each of the teachers in the group gives feedback to the issue and helps interpret the meaning of the documentation presented, or notes an interesting aspect of the evidence about which he or she wants to learn more.
3. **Action:** As teachers continue to talk, the group is asked to shift to suggest possible actions to take (i.e., instructional strategies, changes to the environment, etc.). On the basis of the comments, questions, and ideas from the co-inquiry session, the presenting teacher works to refine his or her interpretation of the documentation. The presenting teacher then creates a plan to put into action during the next week. Documentation of the new plan for classroom experiences is discussed in the next inquiry meeting.

Expanding on Abramson's group protocol, a coach who is facilitating a *co-inquiry* session might add to its power and the effectiveness of its outcomes if the group had a common understanding of research-based criteria to interpret documented evidence. Yet, a group dialogue session can do even more than that. Creativity and innovation in teaching responses may also be encouraged when many ideas are generated to address the interpreted evidence and teacher goal. As with any group process, a facilitator would be needed to remind the group of basic ground rules such as the following:

- No criticism or judgment of people is allowed. Focus on ideas and solutions.
- Listen to and extend other's people's ideas.
- Ask questions to clarify what is shared.

Coaches can guide group discussions to consider times at which specific technical assistance may be needed (e.g., regarding health and safety issues) to improve a situation or to obtain a professional referral for a child who exhibits developmental red flags. For the more common classroom scenarios requiring creative ideas for engaging children in experiences to meet developmental milestones (e.g., expansion of oral language), a group brainstorm may be very motivating to a teacher who is sharing child evidence. Teacher discussion groups, such as the one described, can sustain the individual work started by a mentor. Inspiring creative teaching solutions is another outcome. Usually, a teacher is invigorated and inspired to experience the sharing of other teachers, with high levels of interest, in the details of a situation that was previously only his or her concern. Creative problem solving in many professional work settings is sustained when peers listen and brainstorm together over time. Sustaining and motivating creative problem solving requires a work environment that has such supportive characteristics (Csikszentmihalyi, 1996).

REFLECTION

How do you as a mentor motivate a teacher to make meaning of evidence and brainstorm solutions?

1. Imagine that you are a mentor who has supported a teacher to document the words and actions of children in her program. You have helped this teacher to identify a question of interest. You have noticed that the teacher is now frustrated because she does not know how to interpret this interesting information or otherwise what to do with it. She also says that she does not have time to do anything with the notes. How can you motivate this teacher to use relevant resources to make meaning of her gathered documentation?

2. Most of us are weary of hearing the tired phrase, "Think outside of the box." However, we all get into daily routines of doing things the same way, even when they do not work. Trauma or feeling as if we have nothing to lose can shake us up to change. In less dramatic circumstances, it may be more difficult for us to get motivated. How have you changed a pattern and come up with a new idea? How have you inspired another person to take the risk to come up with a new way of doing things?

Coaching Reflections: Evaluating Progress Through Ongoing Documentation of Practices

The notion of *parallel process* is emphasized in this book in order for coaches to remember to also model strategies that are suggested for teachers. Documentation is another important activity encouraged for teachers and also being identified by researchers as a means to increase the effectiveness of early childhood mentors. Wright (2010, pp. 208–217) describes the use of *online coaching logs* as a means of isolating the specific coaching strategies associated with improving teacher practices. For coaches working in a project with strategies defined for a specific area, such as promoting early literacy, answering the question, "Were the strategies modeled with fidelity or as planned?" requires a coach to note what was done. Even in more general mentoring and coaching programs with individualized or differentiated content to fit a variety of teacher goals, documentation of strategies is important. Documenting strategies, as suggested in Figure 6.3, is also a way for mentors to gather evidence for their own reflection on what seems to work and what does not.

Figure 6.3 Coaching Process Documentation

Every coaching project will have specific goals, but common questions about the process include the following:

- How did coaches and teachers negotiate specific goals or desired outcomes?
- What focused observations occurred? Did they relate to the goals?
- What content was shared with the teacher (focus area)?
- What ethical standards did the mentor and teacher review (confidentiality, etc.)?
- Is a coaching agreement in place to clarify roles and responsibilities?
- How did observed or gathered information help to guide the teacher's reflection?
- How often were meetings scheduled (frequency)?
- How long was each meeting with the teacher (duration)?
- What research-based strategies were used (observing teacher–child interactions, feedback on teaching, modeling, demonstrating, promoting reflective conversation, co-planning, etc.)?
- Is the professional learning relationship based on teacher goals designed to improve child outcomes?
- How will progress over time be documented and reviewed?
- How did goals turn into an action plan?
- How will the teacher know when his or her goal has been achieved?
- What assessment or other tools will support the teacher?

Buyssee & Wesley (2005) also suggest that coaches ponder broader reflective questions, and this activity may be facilitated by a coaching supervisor in a group setting, or the mentor may keep a reflective journal.

Self-reflection questions to consider periodically and over time should include taking the pulse of the relationship by asking the following questions:

- Is the coach forming a true learning partnership based on trust with the teacher?
- Did the teacher and coach negotiate and clarify their roles and responsibilities?
- Are goals for teacher learning at the center of the partnership?
- Have documentation or assessment tools been chosen?
- Is the coach able to remain flexible during implementation?
- Are conversations focused on problem solving, and is reflective feedback occurring?
- Does the coach encourage reflection and learning through open-ended and probing questions?
- Are the teacher and coach able to state how they will know that they have accomplished planned goals?
- Does every coaching session end with brief notes on ideas for next steps?

Coaches, like teachers, may feel that they do not have the time to keep such detailed notes. If detailed notes of each visit do not seem feasible (e.g., due to lack of paid time for this task), then consider using a set of more abbreviated prompts to gather the basic data that will allow mentors to stay on track and meet the needs of the teachers with whom they are working.

Figure 6.4   Coaching Notes After Each Visit Brief coaching notes after each visit

- Needs and interests of teacher
- Purpose of visit
- Focus of inquiry or discussion
- Strategies discussed
- Strengths and resources of teacher
- Next steps and timeline

Applying What You Learn

A focus on coaches engaging teachers to plan for changes in teaching strategies and program approaches includes an examination of how to facilitate feedback from peers and share teacher learning and research. A final reflection on the effects of mentoring on both the mentor and the teacher is explored in these topics:

- Taking action and making decisions about what to implement
- Steps to facilitating peer group discussions with two different models— *Critical Friends* and *Professional Learning Communities*
- Reflection on the effect mentoring that has had on the mentor and the teacher

Taking Action and Making Decisions

The work of identifying a question to investigate, observing what children do and say, and interpreting and analyzing the gathered information informs what teachers have been awaiting: implementing learning experiences! Taking action and making decisions about what to implement should be connected to what was observed and the goals that were set. A form to connect all three areas is found at Chapter 6, Appendix A. This tool is adapted from the work of McTigue & Wiggins backwards planning logic (2004). The form is not a typical planning form because it helps teachers think about both what they need to learn as well as what the child needs to learn, according to prior observed evidence. It has three stages to the plan, requiring the mentor to guide the teacher through a thought process that has the following logic:

1. If the *desired result* for the child is to . . . (learn classroom rules);
2. Then, *observational evidence* of the child should show . . . (confusion about routines);
3. And the *learning experiences* will need to . . . (engage in experiences that allow the child many ways to hear stories and repeat, describe, and act out a sequence of daily events used in the classroom community)

The form can be used in parts only, for short-term or for long-term goals, observation, and learning experiences. The purpose of the form is as a tool to help the teacher see how alignment or connection of these three big areas is the key to positive child outcomes. A strong caution against using this form with teachers who do not have any experience or formal education in curriculum planning is needed here. Coaches working with early childhood teachers in this situation should use the form only as a guide in their mentoring process. For many teachers, it will be far more effective to discuss the three areas sequentially, or separately, connecting them only at the end. Another way to support teachers to learn about aligning these areas is through a group presentation of their observation to fellow teachers who dialogue about its meaning and possible uses in planning experiences for children. See the next section for those strategies.

Action Steps: Coaching to Support a Teacher to Make Decisions

NAEYC (2010) teacher-preparation standards call for teachers to collaborate with colleagues on their own classroom research and to engage in continuous professional development and collaboration for increasing teaching skills. In some programs, this commitment to continuous learning is easier to encourage than to accomplish. Mentors need to recognize the conditions in an early childhood program that either support professional growth or make it very challenging. Coaches will not see the insights that they have facilitated in individual teachers implemented in their classroom practices unless supportive structures are in place. Coaching programs that include involving in the learning as many as possible of a program staff, and especially the administrative personnel, increase positive program outcomes (Dickinson and Caswell, 2007). When supporting implementation of a teacher's choices, consider these question: Is the program a safe place to brainstorm possible next steps? Are teacher thoughts and ideas valued in this program? Ask yourself the following to check your perceptions:

- Is there an atmosphere of openness, sharing perspectives, or being a collaborator?
- Do staff members promote a sense of well-being by respecting each other's views?
- Are parents and everyone involved in the program a part of the learning community?
- Does the staff have practice and skills in collaborative dialogue?
- What skills are needed, and who should facilitate dialogue?
- Who on the professional team has the skills to link the evidence collected, including the perspectives of the teachers and parents, to the development of the child and the program plans?
- Who seems able to understand and support the growing competencies of the children and build on the children's interests? Who is skilled at altering the environment to fit children's learning needs?
- Does this teacher still need more tools for planning involving the details of implementation?
- Does this teacher still need more tools for hypothesizing or imagining likely responses of the children, teachers, and parents to the activities or program plans?

Regardless of the growth fostered by the work of a mentor, sometimes, more professional development offered in a different way (i.e., courses, discussion groups) is still needed to continue the learning required for a teacher to gain the confidence to actually implement what he or she knows is needed, as suggested by the documentation and interpretation of the evidence. Here is where yet another form or discussion group may be helpful.

Steps to Facilitate Peer Group Discussions With Two Different Models

Critical Friends and Professional Learning Communities

How does an early childhood program keep the professional development and learning going when the relationship with the outside mentor ends? The process of co-inquiry was explored in this chapter. A similar process for the mentor to teach the group and model for them is an inquiry process called *Critical Friends*.

The Annenberg Institute for School Reform at Brown University first developed this model as a protocol to support critical dialogue among teachers (National School Reform Faculty, 2011; Bambino, 2002). *Critical Friends* may be used with teachers in one setting or with colleagues who come together, for example, as part of a professional organization. Potential benefits are similar to those of co-inquiry groups, but this protocol especially emphasizes offering different points of view through questioning to encourage a teacher to think more deeply about ideas presented. The *Critical Friends* process focuses on developing collegial relationships and encouraging reflection, which may involve creating a more democratic leadership structure. It is ironic that the positive value put on harmony in the early childhood work setting may serve to encourage early childhood teachers to talk around and avoid difficult issues or even to entirely avoid exploring common dilemmas. The *Critical Friends* process is a way to both receive and give feedback to promote reflection. The feedback given in discussions is described (Burak, 2010, p. 38) as follows:

Warm—supportive statements
Cool—offers other ways to think about the issue or raises questions
Hard—expands ideas and/or raises concerns

The questions and issues that a presenter may offer come from issues that they have not been able to find a solution to by themselves. Roles in the *Critical Friends* process, in suggested small groups of 6–12 people, are as follows:

- Facilitator—sets time limits, goes over protocol, keeps group on track;
- Presenter—listens after presenting an issue, and does not speak during feedback;
- Participants or discussants—give feedback to presenters and about references.

The protocol for *Critical Friends* involves (Burack, 2010, pp. 37–41) the following:

1. Facilitator Overview (approximately 3–5 minutes)
   - Facilitator explains roles and time limits.
2. Presenter Overview (approximately 5 minutes)
   - Presenter shares an issue, provides context, and describes an issue for discussion.
3. Probing or Clarifying Questions (approximately 5 minutes)
   - Group members ask questions to learn about the issue.
   - Facilitator reminds group that no advice should be given at this point.
4. Participants or Discussant's Group Discussion (approximately 10 minutes)
   - Group discusses issue (both warm and cool) while the presenter is silent, taking notes.
   - Group may now give suggestions related to the issue.
5. Presenter Response (approximately 5 minutes)
   - Presenter responds to feedback.
6. Debriefing (approximately 5 minutes)
   - Facilitator leads the summarizing discussion and the critique of the process.

Professional Learning Communities (PLC) as described by Servage (2008) are another way to structure collaborative, collegial dialogue that involves inquiry and problem-solving about daily teaching practices. Using dialogue to promote professional development may also promote caring and collegiality (DuFour, 2004) not unlike those felt in a nurturing family. The PLC model may benefit collective work and shared responsibility while also meeting relationship needs. The literature on PLC's is vast, as K–12 school districts have adopted this model in large numbers. The key concept for beginning early childhood mentors to consider seems to be the notion that their impact may be very limited if the teachers they mentor are not connected to some sort of ongoing professional-learning community. This need for connection may be met by the teachers' enrolling in a degree program at a local college, joining an early learning professional organization, and by establishing a program protocol for ongoing reflection on their work with children and families.

In any professional-development learning community, there is a tension between solving immediate problems and considering big issues or long-term implications involving work with children and families. Servage (2008) suggests that we should support teachers to do both but not to be limited to only technical discussions of the immediate problems. The goal of conversations about issues should be not to just apply solutions in a technical manner but to find questions that, over time, may push the professional-learning community closer to its potential role as a site of transformative learning for participants.

Sharing a Project, Evaluating, and Celebrating Both Teacher and Mentor Achievements: Reflection on the Effect That Mentoring Has Had on the Mentor and the Teacher

After reviewing the *Critical Friends* protocol, spend a few minutes exploring the format with a director, administrator, or teacher whom you know in a program. Ask whether he or she can imagine staff or colleagues using the protocol. If it seems too formal for this or other early childhood program settings, would another tried-and-true method, such as the "talking stick," support collegial dialogue? The "talking stick" is a simpler process of appointing a facilitator to support one teacher in describing an issue. An object is used to designate the person holding it as the only person to speak until the object is passed to another person. This helps others to remember to listen to the person holding the object. The key idea is to leave a group with some protocols for continued dialogue and feedback. When have you done that? How did it work?

Becoming comfortable with reflection on the effects that mentoring has had on the mentor and the teacher is crucial to the process. If you are going to be a mentor, you must increase your comfort with receiving feedback from teachers. No one enjoys receiving criticism. However, if you open yourself to hearing what teachers have to say to you, over time, you will notice patterns of strengths and areas to explore. Especially in a mentoring relationship, you must practice what you are preaching. Getting feedback is essential to your effectiveness.

Evaluation and Reflection

Have I benefited from my coaching experience? In your work with children and families, reflect on whether you (a) strongly agree; (b) agree; (c) disagree; (d) are unsure with the following statements:

1. I understand my strengths and areas for growth better.
2. I can look at problems from different perspectives.
3. I am able to use feedback from my mentor.
4. I am better able to set goals for making changes.

5. I am more confident in solving problems.
6. I am better able to work with other adults to make changes.
7. I have developed new approaches or skills.
8. I was comfortable working with a mentor.

Overall, I liked best:
Overall, I liked the least:

Based in part on concepts in: Buyssee & Wesley (2005). Consultation in early childhood settings. Baltimore: Paul H. Brookes Publishing Co.

REFLECTION

Discuss the following questions with participants in large or small groups:

How comfortable are you with having your coaching process evaluated?
What makes feedback easier for you to hear?
What support do you need to use feedback in a productive way?

Coaches need to be self-aware of their emotional and social competencies and in what ways these competencies are required for the their role as mentor. Navigating interactions with teachers in a mentoring relationship requires what Goleman (1995) described in terms of personal and social competences. The following should be considered as essential abilities in the mentoring toolkit:

* **Emotional Self-Awareness**—Mentors know their strengths and areas for growth.
* **Emotional Self-Management**—Mentors use their emotions in a positive and productive way, are open to others, admit mistakes, are adaptable, and remain positive while handling stressful situations; are humble and interested in learning.
* **Social Awareness**—Mentors are empathetic and aware of the feelings of others; they understand social forces in groups and institutions.
* **Management of Social Situations and Relationships**—Mentors notice others' strengths and the need for change, advocate for others, respect multiple perspectives, and solve problems while remaining a group member

A coach with these abilities will more likely be able to foster resiliency skills in a teacher including; ". . . listening, reflecting, counteracting self-doubt, making meaning, prioritizing, developing a learning mindset, creating alliances, forming positive social connections, reaching out for help, staying on task, generating new ideas, and accepting and adjusting to change." (Jackson and Gregory, 2011, p. 180).

REFLECTION

1. Coaches are comfortable in taking time to work with someone and feel rewarded by helping teachers link their passions and beliefs with their actions in their work with children and families. After reviewing the competency areas of emotional and social intelligence, what areas do you think are your strengths and your areas for growth?

   Who do you know and trust who could give you feedback on areas for your growth in the role of mentor? How might a mentoring–coaching support group help raise your awareness about emotional-climate issues present in the role and activities of a mentor?

2. Explain the role of the coach in facilitating a teacher to connect observation, interpretation, and teaching. What questions do you still have?

3. Describe ways to join with an early childhood teacher to explore questions and interests.

4. Explain the differences between observation, critical reflection, and interpretation of information gathered in the early childhood program setting.

5. Identify ways to evaluate gathering and using program information.

6. Review methods to plan for changes in teaching strategies and program approaches.

Summary

Review Figure 6.5, which summarizes the big ideas explored in the preceding pages. Then jot down your first thoughts that complete these phrases:

I learned . . .

I am surprised by . . .

I want to say . . .

I am interested in learning more about . . .

Figure 6.5 Summary of Coaching to Connect Curriculum, Assessment, and Teaching

Just as teachers today need to be able to share with parents and programs what an individual child knows and is able to do, so mentors need to be able to support teachers to translate their knowledge about children into plans and teaching strategies to continue the child's learning. Today, teachers need to make curriculum, assessment, and teaching connections. Refer to Appendix 6A at the end of this chapter as a tool to explore aligning curriculum (i.e., learning experiences) and teaching plans (see Section III) with assessment (see Section II) and overall goals (see Section I). This means that they need to be supported by adult instructors who also model and understand these connections.

References

Abramson, S. (2008). Co-Inquiry: Documentation, Communication, Action. In *Voices of Practitioners—Co-Inquiry Meetings for Facilitated Professional Interchange*. Retrieved from http://journal.naeyc.org/btj/vp/pdf/Voices_Abramson_Co-Inquiry.pdf

Abramson, S., & Atwal, K. (2003). Teachers as co-inquirers. In *Next steps in teaching the Reggio way*, J. Hendrick (Ed.), pp. 86–95. Englewood Cliffs, NJ: Merrill.

American Educational Research Association (AERA). (2004). Position statement concerning high-stakes testing in pre-K–12 education. Washington, DC: Author.

Bambino, D. (March, 2002). Redesigning professional development: Critical Friends. *Educational Leadership, 59*(6), pp. 25–27.

Bowman, B., Donovan, S., & Burns, S. (Eds.). (2001). Eager to learn: Educating our preschoolers. Washington, DC: National Academy Press.

Boyle, B., Lamprianou, I., & Boyle, T. (2005). A longitudinal study of teacher change: What makes professional development effective? Report of the second year of the study. *School Effectiveness and School Improvement, 16*(1), 1–27.

Burack, C. (2010). *New paradigms for faculty rewards: Resources and an action planning workshop to support engaged scholarship.* Northern New England National Campus Compacts. Retrieved from http://www.compact.org

Buyssee V., & Wesley, P. (2005). Consultation in early childhood settings. Baltimore: Paul H. Brookes Publishing Co.

Coleman, M. R., Buysse, V., & Neitzel, J. (2006). Recognition and response: An early intervening system for young children at risk for learning disabilities. Executive summary. Chapel Hill: The University of North Carolina at Chapel Hill, FPG Child Development Institute. Retrieved from http://www.recognitionandresponse.org

Copple, C., & Bredekamp, S. (Eds.). (2009). *Developmentally appropriate practice in early childhood programs serving children from birth to age eight.* Washington, DC: National Association of Young Children

Council of Chief State School Officers. (2004). The words we use: A glossary of terms for early childhood education standards and assessments. www.ccsso.org/eceaglossary

Csikszentmihalyi, M. (1996). Creativity: Flow and the psychology of discovery and invention. New York: Harper Collins.

Dickinson, D., & Caswell, L. (2007). Building support for language and literacy in preschool classrooms through in-service professional development: Effects of the Literacy Environment Enrichment Program (LEEP). *Early Childhood Research Quarterly, 22,* 243–260.

DuFour, R. (2004). What is a professional learning community? *Educational Leadership, 61*(8), 611.

Espinosa, L. (2005). Curriculum and assessment considerations for young children from culturally, linguistically, and economically diverse backgrounds. *Psychology in the Schools, 42*(8), 837–853.

Gandini, L., & Goldhaber, J. (2001). Two reflections about documentation. In L. Gandini & C. Edwards (Eds.), *Bambini: The Italian approach to infant/toddler care,* pp. 124–45. New York: Teachers College Press.

Goleman, D. (1995). *Emotional competence: Why it can matter more than IQ.* New York: Bantam.

Hemmeter, M., Joseph, G., Smith, B., & Sandall, S. (Eds.). (2001). DEC recommended practices program assessment: Improving practices for young children with special needs and their families. Longmont, CO: Sopris West and Division of Early Childhood/Council for Exceptional Children.

Howell, K. W., & Nolet, V. (2000). Curriculum-based evaluation: Teaching and decision making. Belmont, CA: Wadsworth Thomson Learning.

Jablon, J. R., Dombro, A. L., & Dichtelmiller, M. L. (2007). *The power of observation.* Washington, DC: National Association for the Education of Young Children.

Jackson, V., & Gregory, W. H. (2011). Resilience for leaders in times of change. In G. Blau & P. R. Magrab, (Eds.), *The Leadership Equation: Strategies for individuals who are champions for children, youth and families* (pp.167–197). Baltimore: Paul H. Brookes Publishing Co.

Kagan, S., Scott-Little, C., & Clifford, R. (2003). Assessing young children: What policymakers need to know and do. (pp. 5–11) In C. Scott-Little, S. Kagan, & R. Clifford (Eds.). *Assessing the state of state assessments: Perspectives on assessing young children,* Greensboro, NC: SERVE. Retrieved from http://www.tats.ucf.edu/docs/ASSA.pdf

Lambert, L. (2005). What does leadership capacity really mean? *Journal of Staff Development, 26*(2), 38–40.

Lutton, A. (Ed.). (2012). *Advancing the profession: NAEYC standards and guidelines for professional development.* Washington, DC: NAEYC.

Macy, M. G., Bricker, D. D., & Squires, J. K. (2005). Validity and reliability of a curriculum-based assessment approach to determine eligibility for Part C services. *Journal of Early Intervention, 28,* 1–16.

McLean, M. (2005). Using curriculum-based assessment to determine eligibility: Time for a paradigm shift? *Journal of Early Intervention, 28*, 23–27.

McTighe, J., & Wiggins, G. (2004). *Understanding by design: professional development workbook.* Alexandria, VA: Association for Supervision and Curriculum Development.

National Association for the Education of Young Children (NAEYC). (2010). *NAEYC standards for initial & advanced early childhood professional preparation programs.* Retrieved from http://www.naeyc.org/files/ncate/file/NAEYC%20Initial%20and%20 Advanced%20Standards%206_2011-final.pdf

National Association for the Education of Young Children (NAEYC), & National Association of Early Childhood Specialists in State Departments of Education (NAECS/SDE). (2002). Early learning standards: Creating the conditions for success. Joint position statement. Washington, DC: National Association for the Education of Young Children.

National Association for the Education of Young Children (NAEYC), & National Association of Child Care Resource and Referral Agencies (NACCRRA). (2011). *Early childhood education professional development: Training and technical assistance glossary.* Washington, DC: National Association for the Education of Young Children. Retrieved from http://www.naeyc.org/GlossaryTraining_TA.pdf

National Association for the Education of Young Children, & National Association of Early Childhood Specialists in State Departments of Education. (2003). Early childhood curriculum, assessment, and program evaluation: Building an effective, accountable system in programs for children birth through age 8. Joint position statement. Washington, DC: National Association for the Education of Young Children.

National Association for the Education of Young Children, & National Association of Early Childhood Specialists in State Departments of Education. (January 2005). Screening and Assessment of Young English-Language Learners: Draft Recommendations. Joint position statement in supplement to early childhood curriculum, assessment, and program evaluation: Building an effective, accountable system in programs for children birth through age 8. Washington, DC: National Association for the Education of Young Children.

National Child Care Information Center. (June, 2005). Assessment and evaluation: Becoming an educated consumer. Part III: Accountability systems. Retrieved January 26, 2008, from http://nccic.acf.hhs.gov/pubs/goodstart/assess-eval3.pdf

National Research Council & Institute of Medicine. (2002). From neurons to neighborhoods: The science of early childhood development. Committee on integrating the science of early childhood development. J. Shonkoff & D. Phillips, (Eds.), Board of children, youth, and families, commission on behavioral and social sciences and education. Washington, DC: National Academy Press.

National School Reform Faculty (NSRF). (2011). *Critical Friends Groups at the National School Reform Faculty, a Professional Development Initiative.* Harmony Education Center, Bloomington, IN. Retrieved from http://www.harmony.pvt.k12.in.us/www/cfg1.html

Neisworth, J. T., & Bagnato, S. J. (2004). The mismeasure of young children: The authentic assessment alternative. *Infants and Young Children, 17*, 198–212.

Neuman, S. B. (2010). The research we have. In S. B. Neuman & M. L. Kamil, (Eds.), *Preparing Teachers for the Early Childhood Classroom: Proven Models and Key Principles* (pp. 221–236). Baltimore: Paul H. Brookes Publishing Co.

Servage, L. (2008). Critical and transformative practices in professional learning communities. *Teacher Education Quarterly, 35*(1), 63–77.

Teaching Strategies. (2010). *Teaching Strategies GOLD.* Washington, DC: Teaching Strategies, Inc.

Washington State Office of Superintendent of Public Instruction. (2008). *A guide to assessment in early childhood:Infancy to age eight.* Olympia, WA: Washington State Office of Superintendent of Public Instruction.

U.S. Department of Health and Human Services (USDHHS), Administration of Children and Families (ACF) Office of Head Start (OHS). (2010). The Head Start child development and early learning framework promoting positive outcomes in early childhood programs serving children 3–5 years old. Retrieved from http://eclkc.ohs.

acf.hhs.gov/hslc/ttasystem/teaching/eecd/Assessment/Child%20Outcomes/HS_Re-
vised_Child_Outcomes_Framework(rev-Sept2011).pdf

Wright, T. S. (2010). A tool to monitor fidelity of implementation in large-scale interventions. In S. B. Neuman & M. L. Kamil, (Eds.), *Preparing Teachers for the Early Childhood Classroom: Proven Models and Key Principles* (pp. 207–220). Baltimore: Paul
Brookes Publishing Co.

Chapter 6 — Appendix

Planning Form to Guide the Process of Connecting Curriculum, Assessment and Teaching

Curriculum Goals and Plans, Assessment, and Teaching Strategies

Coaches may want to use this form to document and guide their support of teachers
in connecting curriculum goals, assessment, and teaching strategies. The form is too
complex to give to a teacher to use alone. It may be used either with collaborative
support to work through each section or as a tool for only the Coach to use, which
will serve to guide the Coaching process.

A teacher's focus or goal may be related to a standard, competency, or other
desired and appropriate child outcome. The form can be used with any curriculum
approach and professional resource to guide goals, assessment, and teaching strategies. In the beginning, using a commonly available curriculum-based tool, such as
Teaching Strategies GOLD (2010), will scaffold teacher learning by suggesting ways
to link documented milestones to planning for learning experiences.

I. Section One - Begin with the end in mind, and plan for preferred results. Write one phrase.

My broad goal is to explore the developmental domain, subject area, or "big idea" of:

Example: *Promote social–emotional development* or *have warm, supportive relationships in a caring community of learners.*

My goal relates to a professional value, standard, or competency, or is influenced by this professional source or reference:

Example of source: *"Create a caring community of learners," Developmentally Appropriate Practice in ECE Programs Serving Children Birth to 8* (Copple & Bredekamp, 2009, pp. 16–17).

A. Specific Teacher Objective	B. Specific Child(ren)'s Objective
1. What will I (the teacher) eventually be able to do consistently?	**1. What will the child(ren) eventually be able to do?**
Examples: *Promote a positive climate in my preschool classroom community, establish a classroom routine, facilitate problem solving between preschoolers, have guidance talks with individual children, etc.*	Examples: *Problem-solve social conflicts with support from the teacher, follow a daily routine, ask for help, understand classroom rules, show empathy for others, etc.*
Source: _____	**Source:** _____
Use a child guidance reference or classroom evaluation tool with specific teacher interaction suggestions, (e.g., Gartrell, 2011; Pianta et al, 2008)	Use social–emotional development milestones or other child standards or curriculum objectives, such as Head Start Child Outcomes or Teaching Strategies GOLD (2010).
2. What do I (the teacher) need to understand and be able to do to be more effective? Examples: Ways to . . . a) *build supportive relationships by encouraging children with specific feedback;* b) *model respectful interactions by using culturally relevant greetings and social interactions;* c) *use proactive child guidance by clearly communicating expectations.*	**2. What specific issues or content do the children need to learn?** Examples: a) *What rules are there in my classroom community, and why do we have them?* b) *How can I work with my classmates?* c) *What is a friend?*
3. What am I especially wondering about, or what misunderstandings do have? a) *Developmentally appropriate limits vs. punishment* b) *Preventing conflict by establishing classroom agreements vs. reacting to challenging behavior* c) *Importance of modeling positive behavior vs. talking to children about class rules*	**3. What skills do the children need to practice in their everyday interactions? Use verbs to describe what you hope to see or to discuss with the children.** Examples: Children will be able to . . . *Give examples of . . . how to share materials with their friends.* *Describe . . . how to play on the playground so that everyone is safe.* *Observe . . . the feelings that another person is Expressing, and react in a caring way.* *Compare and contrast . . .* *Draw . . .*

d) *Differences between expectations in school*
   and in a child's home

<u>*Play the roles*</u> . . .

<u>*Examine the similarities and differences*</u> . . . .

II. Section Two—Assessment Evidence: *How will I document what I (the teacher) and the children already know?*

What do I already know about . . . ?

What will I document, take anecdotal notes about, videotape, collect, etc.?

What resources do I need in order to interpret the interactions that I describe or the information that I collect?

How will I compare and contrast what happened before and after my planned changes?

A. Teacher Evidence	B. Child(ren)'s Evidence
BEFORE	**BEFORE**
Examples:	Examples:
• *In previous interactions . . .* • *I tried before . . .* • *Another teacher suggested based on . . .* • *I noticed . . .* • *I videotaped myself . . .* • *Another teacher observed me . . .* • *My supervisor used a checklist of "best practices" and noted my strengths and areas for growth are . . .*	• *My summary of anecdotal notes on children's behaviors, comments is . . .* • *I have noticed . . .* • *Checklists of participation indicated . . .* • *Video and audio recordings show . . .* • *The parents of this child have noticed . . .* • *Another teacher gave me her notes about . . .* • *Work samples of drawings show . . .*

AFTER

Reflect on the teacher–child interactions in the areas of planned activities or planned changes to achieve both the teacher and child goals and objectives. What other evidence (e.g., work samples, observations, journals, pictures) will be used to demonstrate achievement of desired goals for both the teacher and child(ren)?

Cite Sources used to interpret the meaning of the results after examining evidence. For example:

Gartrell, D. (2011). A Guidance Approach for the Encouraging Classroom. Belmont, CA: Wadsworth, Cengage Learning.

Teaching Strategies (2010). *Teaching Strategies GOLD.* Washington DC: Teaching Strategies, Inc.

Pianta, R., La Paro, K., & Hamre, B. (2008). Classroom assessment scoring system (CLASS) manual K–3. Baltimore: Paul H. Brookes Publishing Co.

III. Learning Experience:

What strategies did I use in the past?

How will I teach, facilitate, or alter the environment to support planned learning?

What strategies and child experiences do I anticipate will happen? What are my alternative plans?

A. Teacher Strategies	**B. Child(ren)'s Experiences**
BEFORE: Describe one or more strategies that you plan to use?	**BEFORE:** Describe what you anticipate the children doing.
AFTER: What strategies were used? How did you demonstrate the desired understandings? How will reflection and self-assessment occur?	**AFTER:** Describe what happened. What other evidence (e.g., work samples, observations, journals, pictures) demonstrated achievements and other outcomes related to the desired goals?

Learning Activities/Instructional Strategies:

- What learning experiences and instruction will enable the teacher and children to achieve the desired results?

- How will the design support the the teacher and children to . . .? (Use action words such as *observe, attempt, practice, refine, listen, watch, question, take notes, answer, give a response, construct, examine, compare, classify, collaborate, connect, brainstorm, explain, argue, revise, and reflect.*)

Resources:

- What materials do you need?

Final Reflection:

- How did you (the teacher) use what you knew about the children (assessment) to support and monitor their learning goal?

- Compare and contrast your teaching strategies used before this learning experience and after. Have you changed anything?

- What was especially effective that you want to continue? If you were to do this over, what would you do more of, or less of, or differently?

Concepts based on: McTighe, J., & Wiggins, G. (2004). *Understanding by design: Professional development workbook.* Alexandria, VA: Association for Supervision and Curriculum Development (p. 30).

Alternate - Short Planning Form to Connect Goals, Evidence and Learning Experience Use this simplified form with a teacher just beginning to learn about planning.

One: Teacher and Child Goals: What will we be able to do if we are successful?

Teacher Goal: What will teacher eventually be able to do consistently?	**Child(ren's) Goal:** What will the child(ren) eventually be able to do?

Two: Evidence: What will I observe, videotape, collect, etc.? What does it mean?

Teacher Evidence	**Child(ren's) Evidence**
BEFORE: In previous interactions or I tried before....	**BEFORE:** Brief summary of anecdotal notes, or what you noticed previously.
AFTER: Reflect on the teacher-child interactions. I noticed that......	

Three: Learning Experience: What will happen? What did happen? Next steps are...

Teacher Strategies	**Child(ren's) Experiences**
BEFORE: Describe one or more strategies the teacher plans to use.	**BEFORE:** Describe what you anticipate the child(ren) will do.
AFTER: What strategies did you use? Next time I will.....	**AFTER:** Describe what happened.

CHAPTER 7

Supervisors and Teacher-Leaders as Mentors or Coaches

The chapter supports your growing capacity to

- compare reflective supervision to the mentoring and coaching process;
- transfer skills and abilities from supervision or teaching to mentoring and coaching;
- meet the needs of a specific professional development (PD) context by choosing technical or innovative strategies; and
- contribute to the growth of authentic mentors, coaches, and leaders.

This chapter will focus on supervisors and teacher-leaders as mentors or coaches of early childhood teachers. The process of *reflective supervision* is explored for its power to promote increased competence in early childhood professionals while providing a process for respectful partnership and open communication among staff in the same program.

> *A teacher was leaving her position; and on her last day, our director sang our goodbye song to her. I started to cry and so did the teacher who was leaving. Our director finished the song and looked at the children and said, "They are crying because they love working and being together. It can be hard to say goodbye." The children seemed to accept the emotions of their teachers because they knew why we were sad and could empathize with us. I have learned a lot from that director. She modeled the way to build relationships and mentored others through her actions.*
>
> (Teacher interview about being mentored by a supervisor, May 2012)

Matching mentoring or coaching responses to program conditions requiring compliance with technical requirements and adapting work to support a focus on producing innovative change are examined. The chapter uses the NAEYC and NACCRRA (2011) definitions for *mentoring* and *coaching*. Throughout this book, for ease of reading, the term *mentor* has been used when either term (*coach* or *mentor*) could correctly be applied to the strategies described. In this chapter, both terms, *mentor* and *coach,* will be used to emphasize the combination of the specific skill set needed by a curriculum coach and the general adult learning facilitation skills of the mentor.

Mentoring

A relationship-based process between colleagues in similar professional roles, with a more experienced individual with adult learning knowledge and skills, the mentor, providing guidance and example to the less-experienced protégé, or mentee. Mentoring is intended to increase an individual's personal or professional capacity, resulting in greater professional effectiveness (Lutton, 2012, p.84).

Coaching

A relationship-based process led by an expert with specialized adult-learning knowledge and skills who often serves in a different professional role than the recipient(s). Coaching is designed to build capacity for specific professional dispositions, skills, and behaviors and is focused on goal-setting and achievement for an individual or group (Lutton, 2012, p. 85).

Reflective Supervision and Mentoring or Coaching

The literature on early childhood mentoring and coaching cautions against supervisors' taking on the additional role of educational mentor or coach to the teachers and professionals in their schools, programs, and organizations (American Institutes for Research, 2001, pp. 24–26). The supervisor's taking on the role of mentor or coach may be problematic because supervisors usually participate in hiring, firing, and conducting official evaluations. Teachers may worry that when directors, principals, or other direct supervisors act as mentors or coaches, shared concerns could be misused as evidence of teachers not meeting existing program or teaching standards. Supervisors also tend to focus on the program's big picture and are results oriented. A mentor or coach needs to put the teacher's learning first while individualizing support to meet specific learning needs over time. The roles would seem to be frequently in conflict.

However, access to support for a teacher in a job-embedded one-on-one mentoring or coaching experience may impose barriers of cost, access, and the time needed for participation. Additionally, many teachers prefer to learn alongside, and be mentored by, a trusted professional from their own organization or school, whom they already know well. Issues of cultural and linguistic relevancy or other important aspects of finding the best "fit" between a teacher and a mentor sometimes point to a supervisor or teacher-leader as a mentor of choice by a teacher in a program.

Strong supervisor–teacher relationships have the potential to meet a teacher's needs in emergent contexts that formal mentoring programs cannot address. Daily check-in meetings, staff meetings, and individual conferences offer both parties frequent opportunities for reflective analysis of, for example, especially intense interactions with children and families. In some situations, the frequent mentoring needs of a teacher—along with the willingness and availability that a trusted supervisor or a teacher-leader has to mentor that teacher—may make this the optimal learning relationship. In many childcare, preschool, or Head Start settings, an appropriate teacher-mentor may be the program manager or another experienced teacher who has an official role of overseeing curriculum, instruction, or other specific program responsibilities, such as home visiting or family support services.

Supervisors who have a reputation for collaboration and who are seen as having a strong commitment to ongoing learning facilitation, are often viewed as leaders from whom other teachers want to learn (Lieberman and Friedrich, 2010, pp. 95–102). In the birth-to-age-3 program area, as well as in related human services and mental health roles, a tradition of providing *reflective supervision* is well established and has responsibilities and characteristics similar to mentoring (Eggbeer, Mann, and Seibel, 2007). The traditions of both early childhood mentoring and reflective supervision differ from the broader duties of general supervision because they focus on offering empathy and support to staff, and facilitated reflection on staff reactions to their work (Parlakian, 2002; Weatherston, Weigand, & Weigand, 2010). These qualities are intended to promote professional growth over time and are described in this recollection:

> The best supervisors I've had listened intently, found something to value, and then recast what I told then, embellishing it with something of their own. The experience of good supervision is like finding a fellow traveler on a challenging journey, a companion worthy of trust who has visited similar destinations. This fellow traveler knows many routes to our goal but is open to discovering a different path, a path we walk together, often with me in the lead, except when I miss the flowers to smell or when I stumble or can't find my way. Then, the supervisor is there to guide, even to prod a little, to bolster my courage and to help me regain my footing and focus, to help me find my strength.
>
> (Shahmoon-Shanok, 1992, p 37).

REFLECTION

1. Jeree Pawl, an infant mental health expert, says, "Do unto others as you would have others do onto others" (Pawl and St. John, 1998, p. 7). She cites professionals who work with parents, treating the parent the way that they hope the parent will interact with his or her child. Recall a time when you were supervised in a way that modeled for you how to teach children and work with their parents. If you have not had that experience, consider whether you have provided this experience for other adults. How has supervision that promotes reflection on your work also acted as professional mentoring for you? Were there also pitfalls to viewing a supervisor as a professional mentor?

What Is Reflective Supervision?

Supervisors who take the responsibility to guide teachers' decision-making through reflection are engaged in a form of apprenticeship or on-the-job mentoring known as *reflective supervision* (Scott Heller and Gilkerson, 2009). This means that supervisors who are teacher-leaders (i.e., professional peers who are more experienced than the teacher-mentee and who are responsible for overseeing curriculum or another program area) use some of the same mentoring techniques in staff meetings and emergent discussions with teachers that mentors use with teachers in a formal professional-development or mentoring relationship. Consider the following question:

1. *What conditions are required for teachers to experience effective mentoring by a supervisor or teacher-leader?*
   - Relationships between supervisors and teachers are built on nurturance, empathy, and shared experiences. All involved have a shared desire to

learn and support each other. Both mentors and teachers are comfortable being explicit about their role at any given time, as well comfortable with the question, "*What hat are you wearing now, supervisor or mentor?*"

- The person acting as mentor is able to apply skills for promoting reflection and professional growth in a teacher, without judgment or criticism.
- The process of *reflective supervision* is facilitated by someone who has demonstrated professional competencies (and has an interest in continuing to grow and learn), as identified by the *Best Practice Guidelines for Reflective Supervision/Consultation* in the following areas: ". . . wondering, responding with empathy yet sharing knowledge if a crisis arises, inviting contemplation rather than imposing solutions, recognizing parallel process, supporting curiosity, remaining open, and recognizing the power of relationship as it affects health and growth" (Michigan Association for Infant Mental Health, 2004 as cited in Weatherston, Weigand, and Weigand, 2010, p. 25).
- The teacher is willing to accept, and voluntarily accepts, the supervisor or leader in the role of helping them reflect on immediate daily experiences. The teachers feel that sharing their thoughts, feelings, and responses to what they are observing and doing with children and families will be helpful to promoting both the children's and their own growth and development.
- The supervisors, or teacher-leaders, clearly identify when they have power and control (i.e, requiring the use of an assessment tool or specific curriculum approach). Supervisors or leaders are trustworthy and do not have any "secret agendas." They also identify what hat they are wearing (i.e., mentor or supervisor) and are able to shift to the mentoring or reflective supervision stance by listening to and facilitating, for example, ways in which a curriculum approach is being adapted to the specific context of a teacher's classroom.
- The teachers and supervisors, or program leaders, have a history of successful problem-solving experiences and have mutually decided that they want more time together (e.g., official release time from usual work duties) to examine these or similar questions:
  - *What tensions, issues, or problems exist?*
  - *What is already working?*
  - *What are the teaching and program strengths and existing competencies?*
  - *What teaching and program areas need strengthening?*

2. *How should the supervisor or teacher-leader acting as mentor begin to promote reflection on daily work?*
  - Don't assume anything. Begin to mentor by listening and asking plenty of questions. Remember, your role is to support a shift in a teacher's understanding by helping a teacher to solve his or her own problems.
  - Practice giving undivided attention to the person being mentored. Parlakian (2002, p.3) notes that *being present* as a mentor is the place to begin.
  - Promoting a teacher's reflection on his or her practices means that a supervisor acting as a mentor should take the following actions:
    - *Stop and listen to the teacher:* Avoid multi-tasking, and focus on listening and paying attention to the teacher seeking mentoring. This is hard to do at first but is essential. Turn off the phone, close the door, and listen.
    - *Look and learn from the teacher:* Consider this question: *What is the teacher telling you with his or her nonverbal cues?* Do not rely on what you think you already know about this teacher's background, temperament, or experience. Your goal is to learn what is important to this teacher, how he or she thinks and feels, and what he or she is doing about it.

- *Listen and wonder together:* Ask yourself, *What are the perspectives and emotions surrounding the teacher's issue?* Visualize this teacher as competent and capable, and listen to his or her perspective. Ask questions and make comments for the purpose of clarifying and understanding the teacher's point of view, not yet for solving a problem or directing a solution.
- *Respond that you have heard and understood:* Check with the teacher to ascertain whether or not your understanding is correct. The most important goal is for the reflective supervisor to let the teacher know that he or she is heard and understood.
- *Check: What is this teacher's timeline?* Learn from the teacher the answer to this question: *Is this an emergency requiring immediate discussion about the teacher's hypothesis for a specific situation? Does the teacher need immediate support analyzing and planning for a response? Or can the mentor and teacher make an appointment for future action planning?* Remember, this timeline is based on the teacher's perceptions of need.
- *Plan for future action steps:* Make a plan, or simply make an appointment to make a plan. The action phase requires time to brainstorm together questions to investigate (i.e., collecting more information or observing). Plan goals together. As you learn more, modify your questions, and keep researching and talking. Collaborate to engage in a cycle of observing, reflecting, and responding described in earlier chapters.

Transferring Skills and Abilities From Supervising or Teaching to Mentoring and Coaching

Supervisors and teachers who have learned how each relationship affects another (e.g., a supervisor's interactions with the teacher affect that teacher's interactions with a child) have the raw ingredients needed for reflective supervision. The disposition and the critical ability to analyze the importance of all relationships in an early childhood program are essential to the reflective supervision process.

Is Reflective Supervision a Way to Mentor Teachers?

Not all supervisors or teacher-leaders should mentor teachers in their own programs. First, consider the list of reflective supervision competencies based on those developed by the Michigan Association for Infant Mental Health (2004) as shown in Table 7.1. Next, recall an occasion when a supervisor or teacher-leader in your experience has demonstrated these competencies, and jot down examples with children and/or adults. Finally, reflect on how consistently these competencies were modeled. Interview the person whom you are thinking about for this role—or reflect on yourself—and ask, *Does the supervisor or teacher-leader consistently, sometimes, or rarely exhibit these competencies?* Put a "c," "s," or "r" next to each competency example.

Taking the time to consider the characteristics of a leader who is able to support reflection in a teacher is the first step to understanding how a supervisor supports teachers to accomplish their goals through mentoring. Part of the function of leadership in an early childhood program setting is the simple act of positively influencing the people in the program environment. Facilitating the development of teachers and empowering them are also roles of a mentor.

Table 7.1   Competency Checklist for Supervisors and Teacher-Leaders

Does the supervisor or teacher-leader have the following competencies? Recall evidence of behaviors with children and adults.

Competency	Describe an example of a teacher-leader with <u>children</u> (when acting as a teacher)	Describe an example of a teacher-leader with <u>adults</u> (when acting as a supervisor)
Listens well, does not interrupt, and respects the pace of the other person		
Is able to wait for others to discover solutions, form own ideas, and reflect		
Asks questions that encourage details		
Is aware of and comfortable with his or her feelings and the emotions of others		
Is responsive to others		
Guides/nurtures and supports/ empathizes		
Integrates emotion and intellect		
Fosters reflection or wondering by others		
Is aware of how others' reactions affect a process of dialogue and reflection, including sensitivity to bias and cultural context		
Is willing to have consistent and predictable meeting times and places		
Is flexible and available		
Is able to form trusting relationships		

Based on the work of Michigan Association for Infant Mental Health (2004). *Best practice guidelines for reflective supervision/ consultation.* Retrieved from http://www.mi-aimh.org/reflective-supervision

Leader, Manager, or a Teacher: How Do These Roles Relate to the Role of Mentor?

Ideas about the differences between leaders and managers were once framed as opposites. The well-known quote by Warren Bennis (1989) that "managers do things right while leaders do the right thing" situated *managers* as concerned mostly with completing tasks, whereas the work of setting visions and goals was inspired by *leaders*. In programs for children that operate with processes of *distributed leadership*, supervisors or teacher-leaders usually have qualities of both leaders and managers. In a distributed leadership style (Spillane and Diamond, 2007), hierarchical relationships of power over others are replaced by a more democratic process. Leaders and managers are both focused not only on *why* to do something (leadership function) but also on *when* to do it (management task). Both maintaining and developing teachers through *inspiring trust* (leadership) and *communicating bottom lines* of budget, regulatory, or other constraints on decision-making (management) are required supervisory abilities in most early childhood education (ECE) programs. Long- and short-term considerations are integrated by supervisors when they help teachers to see how the immediate needs of children can be connected to the hopes and dreams of their parents and to a teacher's vision for the children's long-term healthy development and learning. Excellent supervisors both model tried-and-true strategies for teachers and encourage new and novel ideas to be developed by them.

If the role of the supervisor or other key leaders in a program is to be focused on day-to-day issues as well as on inspiring the attainment of goals, then where do mentoring teachers fit into these responsibilities? Is it also appropriate for the supervisor to be a leader in learning or a mentor to teachers? Antonacopoulou and Bento (2004) describe the role of learning as being at the heart of leadership: "Leadership is not taught and leadership is not learned. Leadership is learning." (p. 82). This view would indicate that, at a minimum, the supervisor should model a learning disposition for the teachers in a program or school. Fullan (2008), an expert in school and other organizational change, states that "you can achieve consistency and innovation only through deep and consistent learning *in context*" (p. 86). If deep learning does not occur in a vacuum and cannot be simply transmitted to someone in an adult-education classroom, then improving teaching practices must occur in a social context (Lave and Wenger, 1991), and methods to that end should be constructed by the learner (Bruner, 1996; (Vygotsky & Cole, 1978). Consideration of these ideas about learning, as well as reflection on the suggested competencies needed for mentoring, will help a supervisor to evaluate whether serving as both leader and mentor is appropriate in a given context.

REFLECTION

1. Consider a time when you or someone you have closely observed has taken on the duties of managing or leading in an educational organization. Discuss several of the duties and skills of a manager who effectively keeps a school running. Then, discuss a few strengths that you have observed in a leader who is able to help teachers identify and discuss the vision and direction in which a children's program should go. Have you seen all of these skills present in one person? Finally, do you think it is possible for persons acting as managers or leaders in a school to also act as mentors to teachers? Have you witnessed such dual roles in action? What questions do you have about juggling multiple roles and responsibilities? What cultural or community considerations are important as the functions of leading, managing and mentoring are considered? Keep these questions in mind as you read the next section.

Leaders Acting as Mentors: *What Do They Want to Have Happen?*

Any tensions existing between the two functions of leading and mentoring teachers may be brought to the surface by the supervisor's answering a few initial questions:

- What do I want to have happen?
- How do I hope to influence or inspire this teacher in areas in which he or she wants to learn?
- How will I also monitor and direct the teacher in areas that are not negotiable?

If the supervisor's answers point to using a *facilitative style* of leadership, which involves using a leader's *power for* the benefit of the teacher's learning (and not as only *power over* the teacher), the responses might include something similar to any of the following:

- I will first focus on noticing the emerging interests, abilities, and questions of the teacher.
- After listening, observing, and dialoguing with the teacher, I will support him or her with resources and opportunities to explore the area of interest.
- If what the teacher wants to learn is outside of my area of expertise, I will find another teacher in the program to work alongside him or her as a peer mentor.
- Understanding what a teacher wants and needs to learn might evolve into big changes or simply new skills for the teacher, but we will negotiate the areas for continued learning.
- I will be clear as to times when I am acting as a supervisor who needs to direct all staff to comply with a policy and times when I am acting as a mentor.
- If I find it too challenging to keep these different roles clear in my mind, I will remove myself from the mentoring role.
- If the teacher prefers to increase his or her professional development through another method (e.g., a course, community mentor program, teacher learning group, then) I am willing to support the teacher's preferred way of learning and growing as a professional.

If the supervisor is less accustomed to the role of mentor, then his or her responses might be centered around an initial and continuing desire on his or her part for a focus on *evaluation*, *monitoring*, and *directing* the teacher in a step-by-step way. Although a new teacher may need and want technical direction, the key disposition for a supervisor acting as a mentor is to focus first on supporting the teacher in a way that allows the teacher to feel comfortable in taking the risk to grow and learn. This is sometimes called a *servant leadership* style (Greenleaf and Spears, 2002) and is characterized by a leader who meets organizational needs by serving others before focusing on his or her own needs and goals. However, a mentor is much more than a servant to a teacher. The supervisor acting as mentor should also focus heavily on facilitating teamwork and collaboration for the purpose of supporting learning.

The teacher interested in having a supervisor act as the professional-development mentor should ask the questions that follow. The teacher should, of course, feel free to keep his or her answers confidential and for use only as a personal self-reflection tool.

- Am I concerned that I could be punished for noncompliance if I don't follow the professional-development advice of my supervisor?
- Do I admire and respect this supervisor and think that I can learn something from him or her?
- Do I understand the specific areas and situations in which the supervisor has the right to direct my behavior and prescribe my choices?

If teachers are nervous about compliance, do not feel that they will learn what they hope to learn, and do not have high regard for the supervisor, the learning relationship may not be effective (Zeece, 2003). Also, when teachers are worried that they will be confused about compliance if they are working with a supervisor as mentor or if they are not in a situation allowing for an open conversation about their learning, then a mentor who is not the supervisor will be a better choice for them. The feelings of the teacher are important to consider. Attitudes often change over time, even toward the same supervisor. Respecting a teacher's feelings by allowing him or her to end a formal mentoring relationship with a supervisor is a delicate situation for both persons. However, supervisors who respect teachers' needs to be mentored by someone else should remember to offer the teacher the opportunity to be part of a mentoring relationship with them later, when the time is right. A leader who is flexible and is able to change when the teacher's situation or needs change is modeling *situational leadership*. This sort of leader is using his or her emotional intelligence, or awareness of how a teacher feels, and is translating that knowledge into respect and understanding (Bruno, 2009).

Supervisors who sincerely want to inspire and influence teachers to be more effective and are emotionally aware of the feelings and aspirations of their staff have the potential for transforming the way the staff approaches complex problems. Sullivan (2010) notes that the early childhood education profession is a field of mostly women, many of whom value putting the needs of others above their own. Considering the prevalence of low-pay and high-turnover conditions in the early childhood field, it seems important to weigh the benefits and challenges of helping supervisors and teacher-leaders to see themselves also as mentors. Reflect on whether imposing multiple roles might be another way to overburden professionals who are already overextended in their support of teachers in classrooms, programs, and family and community organizations. There are no simple answers to this question.

REFLECTION

Consider the scenarios that follow. Imagine that one participant is the mentor and that the other is the ECE teacher, director, or other staff person in these scenarios. Choose one scenario to role-play or write about, and describe the possible reactions of both the supervisor and the teacher who is being mentored in the scenario. Reflect on the feelings, skills, and knowledge needed for the learning relationship to be productive and successful for all involved (teacher, supervisor, and others noted).

1. Servant leadership *that facilitates the growth of others*. Consider a teacher-leader who mentors another teacher in how to use problem-solving techniques with preschoolers.

2. Situational leadership *in which a teacher takes on a new style to fit the demands of the situation*. A health or safety crisis requires directive behavior by a program manager or family childcare owner who usually has a facilitative style.

3. *Long-term relationships in an ECE program that offer an opportunity for transformational change*. A teacher takes a college course on creating a

program for dual-language learners. He or she then works with a supervisor and several teachers with bilingual education expertise who mentor him or her in applying the new learning to fit the needs of the enrolled children.

Meeting the Needs of the Situation by Choosing Technical or Innovative Strategies

Business models of leadership and supervision often do not reflect the values or the vision promoted by the early childhood education field. Rather than a tradition of competitive individualism, most early learning settings maintain the vision of creating and maintaining a caring and interdependent community. Although these ideals are not always achieved, behaviors of collegiality and advocating for children and families are traditional values and strengths of most early childhood program supervisors. The toolbox of a leader who has thrived while navigating the many challenges of leading an early learning program contains the strategies needed to cope with a very complex set of professional variables. The experiences of a supervisor or teacher-leader who has met challenges requiring technical responses (e.g., implementing new health department food safety protocols) or innovative responses (e.g., fostering greater partnerships with families of enrolled children) to needed change are also very relevant to a mentoring process.

When supervisors act in the role of mentor, they are able to help teachers reframe their questions so that problems can be solved through inquiry (Schon, 1983; Cochran-Smith and Lytle, 2009). This style of mentoring requires the ability to motivate, to encourage participation, and to innovate for or adapt to a changing situation (Kagan, Sockalingham, Walker, and Zachik, 2010). A supervisor may also have a wealth of technical knowledge that is just right for a teacher who needs to increase specific skills. A key decision point for supervisors acting as mentors is to recognize the difference between *technical* and *innovative/adaptive* support needs. If a teacher is concerned about a lack of participation of Spanish-speaking families in a school's open house events and requests mentoring on family involvement strategies, both technical and adaptive responses are appropriate. Does the teacher want to learn the process for translating information flyers into Spanish (technical response), or does he or she want the supervisor to facilitate his or her work with other teachers as part of a family partnership team (innovative or adaptive response)? The second response will require skills in the mentor for supporting a cycle of observation, interpretation of information gathered, and planning for action. Most teacher learning challenges require both technical and adaptive work to be solved. However, not all supervisors are skilled in the complexities of adaptive work.

REFLECTION

1. Review Table 7.2. Notice the different characteristics of the challenges offered to supervisors and teachers who are working on issues needing technical or innovative responses. After reading the chart, consider a time when you were acting as either a teacher or a supervisor (or other leader)

and you were dealing with a work-based dilemma. Remember—or interview a supervisor or teacher who can recall—when

- technical work was needed;
- innovative or adaptive work was needed; or
- some of both responses were needed to address an issue or problem.

2. Review the chart one more time as you consider the following: What are your areas of strength, and in what areas do you have little experience? In what area would you like to increase your abilities to be able to respond to workplace challenges and/or to mentor others to do so?

Table 7.2 Leader Acting as Mentor

What response should be used for the learning issue or problem of the teachers being mentored?

Characteristics of challenges for leaders and teachers	Technical Response Needed	Innovative or Adaptive Response Needed
	A clear and defined response is needed to a specific problem.	The problem is not clear or defined, and many points of view, challenges, and solutions need to be examined.
Values, beliefs, and perspectives in a work-based problem	Goal is to move teachers to share the same point of view and reproduce results with fidelity to a research-based protocol.	Goal is to bring out all the voices present on a topic and move staff to generate solutions that best fit a program issue.
	Specific sources of information must be examined.	A safe discussion climate encourages participation.
	Topic example: Health and safety practices.	*Topic example:* Family involvement programs tailored to the local community.
Issues and action needed	The issue is understood by all, or technical assistance is given to provide understanding. Need exists for organization, delegation, and clear direction.	Collaborative learning processes should be facilitated to support new learning. Need exists for establishing a climate that motivates and encourages new ideas.
	Issue example: A program fundraising dilemma with a short timeline.	*Issue example:* Compliance with new education standards that honor the philosophy of the teachers in the program.
Assets of participants Involved	Participants have answers and authority or responsibility to comply with regulations. Control or power issues are involved.	Questions and facilitation of inquiry should be implemented. Collaboration is sought after group agrees on a solution.

	Situation example: A federal review of a Head Start program uncovers dangerous playground conditions.	*Situation example:* Teacher-leaders support staff to document children's actions and interpret their possible meanings.
Leader: Solutions and decisions	Leader has solutions and makes decisions.	Leader seeks solutions with others through a process for decision-making.
	Response example: Owners of family childcare programs involved in an administration study group later inform enrolled families that tuition must be raised to maintain the quality of care.	*Response example:* A weekly discussion with teachers working on new home-visiting strategies.
Process and vision	Day-to–day routines and challenges are explained.	The big picture is explained and patterns described.
	Response example: Established routines are described to a new teacher.	*Response example:* The program vision is contrasted with actual observed practices. This dilemma is presented without solutions, for staff discussion.

Based on Heifertz, 1994; Heifertz & Linsky, 2002; Heifertz, Linsky & Grashow, 2009.

Assessing a situation for the appropriate response is what both leaders and teachers do on a daily basis. Having a respected supervisor make visible their process for making decisions is invaluable to a teacher being mentored. The courage and integrity that a supervisor displays in identifing gaps in performance and in taking responsibility to join with teachers on their learning journeys can be dangerous if the supervisor does not have corresponding skills or does not recognize that there are many ways to respond to teacher dilemmas. Before supervisors agree to mentor a teacher, they need to take inventory of their own technical and adaptive facilitation skills. Teachers and supervisors are capable of holding multiple professional identities (including supervisor and mentor) in mind for both for themselves and for others by clearly identifying roles and supporting each other's daily interactions in "communities of practice" (Wenger, 1998). Conversely, a self-aware supervisor knows when to delegate mentoring or other adult education functions, to another person to better fit what a situation needs.

Growing Authentic Leaders and Mentors

In *The Power of Mentoring. Taking the Lead: Investing in Early Childhood Leadership for the 21st Century,* Elliott et al. (2000) suggest the importance of recruiting emerging or grassroots early childhood leaders as mentors from candidates who represent and understand a community. Some of these mentor candidates will be acting within the supervisory and teacher-leader roles. Early childhood education and experience qualifications must also include understanding the community context and having cultural competency skills. In some settings, that will mean that no one person will have all of the qualities, education, and relevant experience needed. Mentoring teams or partnerships of mentors are another way to collectively ,meet the qualifications for effectively working with teachers.

Another model is for one mentor to work with small groups of teachers in order to facilitate the power of peer-to-peer sharing, which may have a greater impact than several one-on-one mentoring relationships. Questions that relate to meeting the challenge of providing culturally responsive mentoring include the following:

1. Is the planning group for a mentoring program made up of members of the local community and cultural groups?
2. Does the mentoring program take into account cultural values or standards that should influence the nature or design of the program?
3. What languages should mentors be able to speak?
4. Should teachers choose their own mentors?
5. What qualities do local early childhood teachers seek in a mentor?
6. Do potential mentors understand the socio-economic issues in the community?
7. If the mentor is qualified to support learning in a specific early childhood content area, does he or she understand the program context of the teacher (e.g., family childcare, center care, for-profit or nonprofit organization, federally or state-funded preschools)?

Based on Elliot, K., Farris, M., Alvarado, C., Peters, C., Surr, W., Genser, A., & Chin, E. (2000). *The power of mentoring. Taking the lead: Investing in early childhood leadership for the 21st century*. Boston: The Center for Career Development in Early Care and Education at Wheelock College.

REFLECTION

1. How could mentoring teams facilitate growth together when one mentor alone might not have the background needed to be effective?

2. Image that you and several early childhood teachers whom you know are going to become a mentoring team. First, consider and list the knowledge and experience that you bring, both from your life's journey to date and from your formal education, that might be used to support another early childhood educator's professional growth and development.
Examples of relevant strengths might be that some people in your group have family and center childcare experience, some speak languages other than English, and others have worked extensively with school-age children or infants. Other valuable knowledge may have been acquired from relevant college courses and degrees or through extensive work with specific curriculums. After compiling these skills, knowledge, and relevant experiences, consider the gaps. What other set of skills, knowledge, or experiences might be needed to create a mentoring team that reflects and meets the needs of your local early-learning community? What professional development might your group need? What additional recruitment is needed of mentors with different strengths?

Summary

Early childhood program supervisors or teacher-leaders are often asked to wear many hats. After reviewing key ideas identified in Figure 7.1, list the implications to the mentoring process of the mentor's serving multiple roles as a supervisor or teacher-leader and as a mentor or coach.

Figure 7.1   Summary of Issues Surrounding Supervisors and Teacher-Leaders Serving as Mentors or Coaches

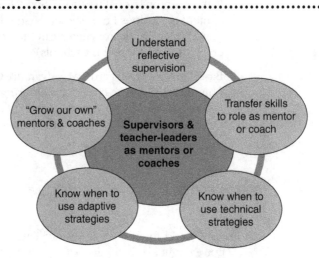

For a person to simultaneously serve in management, leadership, and mentoring roles is not uncommon. The overarching question that this chapter has considered is, *Is it a good idea to try to fill so many roles at once?* A chorus of professionals will say *No!* due to the predictable pitfalls of mixing up evaluation with mentoring, or directive supervision with fostering learning about questions or topics of interest. However, another large and growing body of evidence from the birth-to-3 profession of the home visiting, human services, and mental health fields have identified *reflective supervision* as an appropriate set of dispositions, behaviors, and processes that do support the efforts of a supervisor to also successfully mentor teachers. Supervisors who understand their skills sets, who know the difference between the need for technical or innovative responses to problems, and who have strong, trusting relationships with teachers may be successful as mentors. These leaders, acting in the tradition of the best teachers, have learned that "reflection (on) personal experience is empowering for learners because they confront the contradictions of everyday life" (Austin, 2009, p. 160). Finally, the need for a program or community to grow its own leaders and mentors is facilitated by supervisors who model and explicitly mentor others in the process of critically reflecting on daily dilemmas. The support of "sustained professional development that encourages a deep dive into content rather than surface level exploration" is what early childhood teachers are looking for today (Galinsky, 2012, p. 27). Being part of a learning community facilitated by a trusted and skilled supervisor or teacher-leader is one option to explore when the conditions are right for refocusing a supervisory relationship to put the spotlight on a teacher's learning.

References

American Institutes for Research. (2001). *Putting the PRO in protégé: A guide to mentoring in Head Start and Early Head Start.* Washington, DC: U.S. Department of Health and Human Services, Head Start Bureau, Administration for Children and Families.

Antonacopoulou, E. P., & Bento, R. F. (2004). Methods of "learning leadership": Taught and experiential. In J. Storey (Ed.), *Leadership in organizations: Current issues and key trends* (pp. 80–102). London: Routledge.

Austin, L. (2009). Reflective teaching strategies for a reflective educator. In A. Gibbons & C. Gibbs (Eds.), *Conversations on Early Childhood Teacher Education: Voices from the Working Forum for Teacher Educators* (pp. 160–166).Redmond, WA: World Forum Foundation and New Zealand Tertiary College.

Bennis, W. (1989). *On becoming a leader.* Reading, MA: Perseus Books

Bruner, J. (1996). *The culture of education.* Cambridge, MA: Harvard University Press.

Bruno, H. E. (2009). *Leading on purpose: Emotionally intelligent early childhood administration.* Boston: McGraw-Hill Higher Education.

Cochran-Smith, M., & Lytle, S. L. (2009). *Inquiry as stance: Practitioner research in the next generation.* New York: Teachers College Press.

Dewey, J. (1933). *How we think: A restatement of the relation of reflective thinking to the educative process.* Boston: D. C. Heath.

Eggbeer, Mann, & Seibel. (2007). Reflective supervision: Past, present and future. *Zero to Three, 28*(2), 5–9.

Elliot, K., Farris, M., Alvarado, C., Peters, C., Surr, W., Genser, A., & Chin, E. (2000). *The power of mentoring. Taking the lead: Investing in early childhood leadership for the 21st century.* Boston: The Center for Career Development in Early Care and Education at Wheelock College.

Fullan, M. (2008). *The six secrets of change.* San Francisco: Jossey-Bass.

Galinsky, E. (2012). Learning communities: An emerging phenomenon. *Young Children, 67*(1), 20–27.

Goffin, S. G., & Washington, V. (2007). *Ready or not: Leadership choices in early care and education.* New York: Teachers College Press.

Greenleaf, R. K., & Spears, L. C. (2002). *Servant leadership: A journey into the nature of legitimate power and greatness.* New York: Paulist Press.

Heffron, M., Grunstein, S., & Tiemon, S. (2007). *Exploring diversity in supervision and practice. Zero to Three, 28*(2) 34–38.

Heifertz, R. A. (1994). *Leadership without easy answers.* Cambridge: MA. The Belknap Press of the Harvard University Press.

Heifertz, R. A., & Linsky, M. (2002). *Leadership on the line: Staying alive through the dangers of leading.* Boston: Harvard Business School Press.

Heifertz, R. A., Linsky, M., & Grashow, A. (2009). *Practices of adaptive leadership; tools and tactics for changing your organization and the world.* Boston: Harvard Business Publishing.

Kagan, E., Sockalingham, S., Walker, J. A., & Zachik, A. (2010). The work of leadership in systems change for human services and education. In G. M. Blau & P. R. Macgrab (Eds.), *The Leadership Equation: Strategies for individuals who are champions for children, youth and families.* Baltimore: Paul H. Brookes Publishing Co.

Lave, J. & Wenger, E. (1991). *Situated learning: Legitimate peripheral participation.* New York: Cambridge University Press.

Lieberman, A., & Friedrich, L. (2010). *How teachers become leaders: Learning from practice and research.* New York: Teachers College Press.

Linksy, M., & Heifetz, R. A. (2007). Foreword. In S. G. Goffin and V. Washington, *Ready or not: Leadership choices in early care and education* (pp. ix–xi). New York: Teachers College Press.

Lutton, A. (Ed.). (2012). *Advancing the profession: NAEYC standards and guidelines for professional development.* Washington, DC: NAEYC.

Mazutis, D., & Slawinski, N. (2008). Leading organizational learning through authentic dialogue. *Management Learning, 39*(4), pp. 437–456.

Michigan Association for Infant Mental Health. (2004). *Best practice guidelines for reflective supervision/consultation.* Retrieved from http://www.mi-aimh.org/reflective-supervision

National Association for the Education of Young Children (NAEYC) and National Association of Child Care Resource and Referral Agencies (NACCRRA). (2011). *Early childhood education professional development: Training and technical assistance glossary.* Washington, DC: National Association for the Education of Young Children. Retrieved from http://www.naeyc.org/GlossaryTraining_TA.pdf

Neugebauer, B., & Neugebauer, R. (Eds.). (2008). *The art of leadership: Managing early childhood organizations.* (Rev. ed.) Redmond, WA: Exchange.

Parlakian, R. (2002). *Look, listen, and learn: Reflective supervision and relationship-based work.* Washington, DC: ZERO TO THREE.

Parlakian, R. (2002). *Reflective Supervision in Practice: Stories from the field.* Washington DC: ZERO TO THREE.

Pawl, J., & St. John, M. (1998). How you are is as important as what you do. In *Making a positive difference for infants, toddlers and their families.* Washington, D. C.: Zero to Three National Center for Infants, Toddlers, and Families.

Schon, D. (1983). *The reflective practitioner: How professionals think in action.* New York: Basic Books.

Scott Heller, S., & Gilkerson, L. (Eds.). (2009). *A practical guide to reflective supervision.* Washington, DC: ZERO TO THREE.

Senge, P. M. (1990). *The fifth discipline: The art and practice of the learning organization.* New York: Doubleday.

Shahmoon-Shanok, R. (2006). Reflective supervision for an integrated model: What, why and how? In G. Foley and J. Hochman, (Eds.), *Mental health in early intervention: A unity of principles and practice.* San Francisco: Jossey-Bass.

Shahmoon-Shanok, R. (1992). The supervisory relationship: Integrator, resource and guide. In E. Fenichel (Ed.), *Learning through supervision and mentorship to support the development of infants, toddlers, and their families: A sourcebook* (pp. 37–41). Arlington, VA: ZERO TO THREE.

Shahmoon-Shanok, R., Gilkerson, L., Eggbeer, L., & Fenichel, E. (1995). *Reflective supervision: A relationship for learning.* Washington, DC: ZERO TO THREE.

Spillane, J. P., & Diamond, J. B. (Eds.). (2007). *Distributed leadership in practice.* New York: Teachers College Press.

Sullivan, D. (2010). *Learning to lead: Effective leadership skills for teachers of young children.* (2nd ed.) St. Paul, MN: Redleaf Press.

Vygotsky, L. S., & Cole, M. (1978). *Mind in society: The development of higher psychological processes.* Cambridge, MA: Harvard University Press.

Weatherston, D., Weigand, R., & Weigand, B. (November, 2010). Reflective supervision: Supporting reflection as a cornerstone for competency. *Zero to Three, 31*(2), 22–30.

Wenger,E. (1998). *Communities of practice: Learning, meaning and identity.* New York: Cambridge University Press.

Yukl, G. (2002). Leading change in organizations. In *Leadership in organizations.* Upper Saddle River, NJ: Prentice-Hall.

Zeece, P. D. (2003). The use and abuse of power in child care programming. In Bonnie Neugebauer and Roger Neugebauer (Eds.) (Rev. ed.), *The art of leadership: Managing early childhood organizations* (pp. 25–29). Redmond, WA: Exchange Press,.

● ●

CHAPTER 8

Mentoring and Leadership for Professional Development

The chapter supports your growing capacity to

- grow your own effective early childhood professional development (PD) leaders;
- understand adaptive leadership and learning communities;
- strive for inclusive and multicultural groups and organizations;
- plan for systems of selecting, planning, and modifying a mentoring design; and
- evaluate and advocate for effective PD.

"Leadership is open to anyone who has the courage and the skill to try to mobilize people to address their most difficult issues, what we call their Adaptive Challenges."

Linsky & Heifetz (2007), In Forward to Goffin & Washington,
Ready or Not: Leadership Choices in Early Care and Education, p. ix.

"I gained so much knowledge for myself—I never saw myself as a leader."

Early childhood teacher after 8 months in a leadership
learning community (Brown-Kendall, Aubel & Koetje, 2011, p. 72).

Growing Our Own Effective Professional Development Leaders
● ●

The field of early childhood education values collaborative professional leaders who want to support others to achieve their goals though an "ethic of care" (Noddings, 1984). "Care" here refers to reciprocal PD relationships for growing new leaders.

Teachers who value engaging—with both children and adults—with sensitivity and responsiveness also expect professionals taking on the work of leadership to have high regard for the perspectives of others (Hard, 2004). This means that effective leaders model a willingness to seek out others in their professional communities in order to form partnerships that support a connection between what early childhood teachers want to learn and what children need in order to grow and develop. Additionally, early-learning practitioners who are current in their understanding of educational policy and how it intersects with requirements and standards serve important leadership functions. Teachers are increasingly asking to join with other practitioners to make informed decisions about how to meet rigorous professional standards without compromising their values and their understanding about what they know is good for children. Connecting policy to research-based practices and understanding the leadership and administrative support required to make change happen (e.g., adequate resources, implementation teams, ongoing mentoring or coaching, assessment-based decision-making) are key to setting the wider program conditions necessary to sustain improvements in teacher practices over time (Fixsen & Blase, 2008).

Issues and ideas related to leadership are often confused by the fact that people have very different assumptions of leadership's functions, styles, and definitions. The multiple and overlapping, as well as contrasting, definitions of *leadership* comprise a large body of scholarly work. This chapter will specifically examine *leadership*, not as a trait or as situated in an official role, but as a process demonstrated by individuals and groups engaged in guiding the direction of improving teaching and learning. Additional assumptions about PD leadership involving strategies to create needed change, known as *adaptive work*, include the understanding that the values, attitudes, skills, and behaviors of individuals and groups matter when decisions are made (Heifertz, Linsky, and Grashow, 2009). A *distributed leadership* style is proposed as a way to use and value the expertise in all members of inclusive early childhood programs and organizations to achieve shared visions and goals (Spillane, Halverson, and Diamond, 2001).

Current early childhood practitioners whose positions involve engaging in educational leadership functions (e.g., directors, principals, program managers, teacher-leaders, teacher-educators, and community trainers) are in the position to know many teachers in their community who demonstrate the best of professional ethics, values, skills, and dispositions. Teachers who act with humility, show a willingness to be uncomfortable, take risks in order to learn, and recognize their own gaps in knowledge and experiences are often the people who have the potential to inspire others to gain these desirable teaching dispositions for ongoing professional learning (Chu and Carroll, 2010, pp. 19–20). This chapter will focus on the activities of early childhood PD leaders in selecting, planning, modifying, and evaluating mentoring projects.

Adaptive Leadership and Learning Communities

Mentoring is used here, for ease of reading, as an inclusive term to refer to broad mentoring processes or specific coaching strategies (Lutton, 2012, p.84–85). Mentoring, in this sense, and planning for mentoring systems are the first steps to encouraging teachers with the time, interest, and effective teaching skills and dispositions to contribute to their professional communities. A professional learning community may be an ideal place to grow future mentors and professional-development systems leaders. One way to refocus those in our field on both nurturing professionalism and improving teacher and child learning is to bring teachers together into *professional learning communities*. A supportive context to grow early childhood PD leaders is defined here:

> A learning community is a group of people who come together to learn with and from each other and then seek to act on what they learn. Their reason for being is ongoing inquiry for the sake of improvement (Galinsky, 2012, p. 21).

A promising model of PD leadership is seen in the active involvement of teachers in designing mentoring systems or in assisting in professional-learning communities with colleagues. Yet, barriers exist in supporting early childhood teachers to become PD teacher-leaders. One of the biggest barriers is a teacher's own view of his or her roles and potential. Research for over 20 years on K–12 teachers suggests that if teachers are recognized by their colleagues and supervisors for their informal mentoring and dispersed styles of leading, they may shift their views of their own capabilities for leadership (York-Barr and Duke, 2004). Could the same concept hold true for growing PD teacher-leaders in the many different program contexts in early childhood education? Some emerging cases suggest that it may.

When a National Association for the Education of Young Children (NAEYC) affiliate group in the western United States recently identified the need to "grow their own" early childhood teacher-leaders, the group decided to use a nonhierarchical, developmental approach. The group engaged in the same process that many teachers use with children; that is, the group members became colearners and empowered others in the process (Brown-Kendall, Aubel, and Koetje, 2011). A leadership academy was formed that served as a monthly learning community of experienced and new teacher-leaders for 8 months. Some of the many outcomes of this academy were as follows: Teachers organized and gave PD presentations at local conferences, and led book discussions with colleagues as part of team development meetings. Some teachers became NAEYC affiliate board members. At the conclusion of the 8 months of the academy, the members felt that they had become a community of learners who had increased their professional knowledge and use of effective practices though reflection on current professional literature. Their story seems to illustrate what Linsky and Heifertz (2007, p. ix) identify as the three steps of adaptive and innovative leadership: *observation, interpretation,* and *intervention.* The process should sound very familiar to an early childhood teacher. It is the same three steps that many teachers use when they are confronted with a classroom dilemma calling for more than a quick technical solution. When the answer is unknown and creativity is needed, adaptive or innovative leadership may be required (Goffin and Washington, 2007).

The cycle of adaptive leadership in the NAEYC PD group is illustrated in Figure 8.1. The cycle unfolded first when the group brainstormed to discover what seemed to be the problem. The group decided that the NAEYC affiliate members were overworked due to lack of sufficient participation by the overall membership in leadership activities. A goal to build new PD leadership capacity and effectiveness from teachers in the community was set.

Figure 8.1 Anatomy of an Organizational Problem

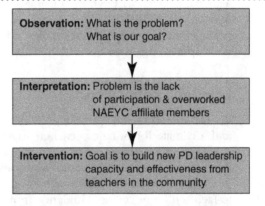

The group then moved to the next phase of the cycle and began to look for ways to *answer or interpret* the question, *What skills and knowledge (technical solutions) and new (adaptive) solutions are needed to meet the identified challenge?* The group analyzed its collected facts regarding the lack of interest in leadership activities and identified the following conclusion:

- Learning is required to grow new teacher-leaders. The group needed to use critical inquiry into professional-leadership topics of intense interest to allow teachers' voices, opinions, and expertise to be shared in a collegial atmosphere.

Members moved to take action in the final phase of *intervention*. They asked themselves, *What actions will we take based on what we now know?* They decided to have a PD response to a PD dilemma. They acted to

- recruit future teacher-leaders through a leadership academy;
- study leadership, communication styles, and other related topics; and
- meet once a month for 8 months, with mentor-facilitators, for discussion and learning about topics such as power and its uses and leading with compassion.

The process employed by the group was in itself a PD experience in how to engage in responding to future professional dilemmas in the group members' own early-learning programs. They moved from *observation (What is our problem and goal to resolve it?)* to *intervention (What skills and knowledge are needed?)* to *interpretation (What actions will we take on the basis of what we learned?)* (Linsky and Heifetz, 2007).

Dalli (2008, p. 183) found in her examination of early childhood teachers' views of professionalism in New Zealand that teachers had a need to express strong views on their daily realities related to pedagogy, professional knowledge, teaching practices, and collaborative relationships. Respectfully engaging teachers in daily realities, as did the NAEYC affiliate group discussed previously, may be a way to bridge classroom leadership to a broader early childhood PD leadership. The NAEYC Affiliate early childhood leadership academy experiences were summarized by participants and mentors in the group as follows:

> It has brought us closer together as an organization and as a community of learners. We more readily accept new voices and conflicting opinions. The Affiliate grows stronger as we learn to compromise, collaborate, and reflect on our work. We mentor each other and our new leaders. We talk about "the whole teacher" or "the whole leader" in the same way we talk about nurturing the whole child (Brown-Kendall, Aubel, & Koetje, 2011, p. 73).

These team-based learning, community styles of mentoring for professional leadership must go beyond "niceness" or meeting only the needs of social connection. Hall (2006) found that conformity and compliance, rather than a stronger professional learning identity, result if critical inquiry is not a part of the professional development processes.

Learning Communities

Common functions of learning communities are that they strive to create conditions and a climate for bringing teachers together, with enough time set aside for them to reflect on how to test out and implement new ideas. Guidance and support from peer teachers or mentors with relevant expertise and experience (Hamre, Downer, Jamil, & Pianta, 2012). The new educational learning community may be in a face-to-face setting or online. Guidance from other teachers with more knowledge and experience in a targeted area of need and interest has been identified by early childhood teachers themselves as an important way to receive support (Ryan and Whitebook, 2012). Experience alone is not enough to improve teaching practices, without the active examination of concrete ways to improve practice. Intentional reflection, along with being socialized into a community of practice (Lave and Wenger, 1991), allows teachers the opportunity to make sense of their work with fellow teachers. Learning communities usually function, in part, to remind teachers to pay attention to their actual behaviors and compare and contrast them with their vision for teaching.

The work environment is key to influencing any teacher's ability to reflect on practice. Because teachers are not paid, in many early childhood education settings, for time spent on collaboration with other teachers, an external learning community that reaches out to teachers most needing and interested in involvement is important. Teachers without job embeded mentoring may find professional learning communities will help them to apply their learning from from books, classes and workshops (Galinsky, 2012).

Learning communities may focus on peer-to-peer exchanges, or they may be the vehicle for inviting in experts to offer specific knowledge and skills for the burning issues that the group identifies. They are also a context for planning for how to intersect with required or mandated PD and for forming ideas for adapting approaches to best fit their communities. Learning communities of teachers also serve a collective leadership function when they forward their views to college, state, or other advisory groups who influence policy and practices in the early childhood field.

REFLECTION

1. Consider a time when you have been part of a professional learning community or when you encouraged another teacher to join one. This could have been, for example, a few teachers from the same program talking together once a month about emergent issues, or a formal PD group sponsored by a professional organization with specific goals and objectives to increase early literacy practices. What would you do differently now?

2. Do you think that a learning community intended to support early childhood teachers to gain the knowledge, confidence, and skills to form a mentoring system would work in your community?

3. If a mentoring system is designed by an outside organization or is mandated by a state or program directive, how might a teacher learning community contribute to its implementation?

Collaboration

Adaptive work that has the potential to motivate others toward positive change is also referred to as *transformational leadership* (Bass and Bass, 2008). In order to promote the goal of positive change, the hard work of collaboration needs to be understood and embraced. A literature review of over 40 studies (Mattessich, Monsey, and Murray-Close, 2001) found that the most important factors facilitating collaboration among human services, government, and other nonprofit organizations were

- mutual trust, respect, and understanding;
- a broad cross section of individuals and/or organizations; and
- frequent and open communication.

This research indicates that participation alone is not sufficient for collaboration to occur. Creating processes that build trust and respect, and that offer opportunities for meaningful contributions from participants who have different skill sets and a stake in the outcomes are essential ingredients to facilitating, directing, and inspiring others.

REFLECTION

1. Recall a time when you were part of a group for which the old adage *The sum is greater than its parts* seemed to hold true. In other words, when have you accomplished more as a team than you did separately? When have you experienced "two heads being better than one"? What conditions seemed to facilitated the collaboration?

2. In contrast, have you ever had to recruit new members to a PD or other type of professional planning team because the team did not represent the people that it was designed to serve or because you needed a new perspective?

3. Have you ever helped a small group of teachers increase its ability to communicate more openly?

Striving for Inclusive and Multicultural Groups and Organizations

When early-learning professionals join together to plan for their PD, the strategies of mentoring individual teachers needs to be raised to the organizational or group level. Building common ground and a shared and inclusive vision should be the first task for a group facilitator. One way to successfully engage in this task is by being mindful of the social environment. Begin with identifying common agreements for confidentiality, respect, and listening. The reason to take the time to document common agreements is to promote feelings of being valued, as well as modeling an equitable process for sharing ideas and resources. Practical considerations—meeting the group's expectations and using the participants' time well—can also be addressed in discussions about initial agreements. Maintaining an awareness of teachers' need for room and time to participate in ways that fit their individual and culturally influenced communication and participation styles is needed to support openness and learning from the start. This is more easily accomplished if the group itself represents the diversity of the wider community. For example, having a sufficient number of bilingual teachers participating in the group will increase the chance that the perspective of the needs of dual-language learners is represented. At the beginning is the time to ask the group, "Who is not here from our professional or wider community who should be here to support our understanding of an important perspective?" Finally, if group norms and decision-making processes are clear, dialogue can begin.

Next, defining a large goal of collaborating for a shared professional-development vision will set a purpose for the remaining work. Imagining what shared interests the group has by looking to the future to find common "dreams and goals" often motivates teachers. Making another list of PD areas that the group feels that it needs to address, yet is not excited to deal with, is important, too. For example, a group may come to consensus that its members are very interested in focusing on ways to promote oral language(s) in preschoolers. The members may also feel that it is important—yet may be less enthusiastic to understand—the national kindergarten *Common Core Standards for English Language Arts*. This is why having a diverse professional group that represents the range of professional positions and expertise in an early-learning professional community pays off. By breaking down the typical isolation of teachers, the members may open up to moving though challenging and initially less inviting areas of learning. Taking the time to establish some areas of common agreement may lead to a shared and inclusive PD vision and may also set the stage for the activities requiring collaboration for ongoing learning. The accompanying graphic shows the foundation for an inclusive PD plan. Notice that the arrow goes both ways because the process is dynamic, requiring groups to maintain all three areas to plan for PD.

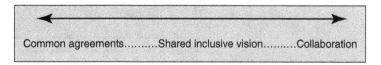

Common agreements..........Shared inclusive vision..........Collaboration

However, at all times, there are elements that work against learning and collaboration. Teaching systems are composed of elements that interact and reinforce the known and that sometimes make change difficult to achieve.

> In a system, all the features reinforce each other. If one feature is changed, the system will rush to "repair the damage," perhaps by modifying the new feature so it functions the way the old one did (Stigler & Hiebert, 1999, p. 97).

Models of multicultural organization development may help a group to keep in mind how individual members experience their participation. Jackson and Holvino (1988) and Jackson (2005) propose a progression of stages through which organizations or groups often move. The following is an organizational progression described to this author in a community early childhood conference planning group that worked together over the course of a decade.

1. *Exclusion and bias unjustly prevent certain people from belonging:* Conference flyers were never sent to Latina teachers who worked for a large bilingual childcare program.
2. *"The Club" that poses barriers to participation:* Planning meetings were held during the day, the very time when nearly all family childcare providers were unable to attend.
3. *Compliant organization:* A few individuals from the two previously excluded groups joined the "team." They were congratulated for being easy to work with, showing up on time, and being "team players." Unfortunately, most of the new members from the previously excluded groups did not return the next year.
4. *Affirming organization:* A large number of childcare providers from the previously excluded groups were recruited, and they joined the planning group at the same time. Meetings were changed to the evening, and a Spanish-language track was established at the conference to meet the PD needs of bilingual and monolingual Spanish-speaking teachers. Monolingual

English-speaking teachers serving Latino children and families also excitedly attended the new PD sessions. New ground rules were established, and an outside facilitator supported the planning process.

5. *Redefining organization:* Most of the diverse planning group members, who by this time fairly represented the linguistic and cultural diversity of the community at large, decided to take a course together on diversity from the new bilingual early childhood education department chair at the local community college. Many members also engaged in leadership training from a nonprofit group in the local town. The conference planning team was now made up of a range of professionals, including students preparing to be early childhood teachers, as well as a director of a multi-site Head Start program system. The group wrote its history, recalling its progression from an exclusionary to a redefining group. Group members also noted that they heard that some teachers were still uncomfortable with the idea of joining the group because they thought it was a college "club." The group members knew that their work would always be in progress. However, they felt that their community now had a superior conference with trusting relationships on the planning team and excellent program collaborations throughout the year.

Exclusionary organization	The "club"	Compliant organization	Affirming organization	Redefining organization
←				→

The journey of this group over a decade took its members from an inclusion/exclusion model of "Who should be here?" to an affirming organization asking, "Who needs to be part of designing what this group should become?" (Mor Barak and Travis, 2009). The practices became, over time, more in line with a culturally competent vision (Nybell and Gray, 2004) for early childhood practice.

REFLECTION

1. Consider the PD or other early childhood education groups and organizations to which you have belonged and you currently belong. Choose one that you feel is moving from exclusionary to redefining in nature. Would different people have different views of where this organization is along the multicultural organizational development continuum?

Planning for Systems of Selecting, Planning, and Modifying a Mentoring Design

Mentoring competencies in the areas of adult learning, building relationships, change, communication, assessment, professional development, and professional relationships are associated with effective mentoring (Minnesota Center for

Professional Development, 2009a; 2009b). However, the idea of developing these competencies can be intimidating for teachers who are just beginning to consider a mentoring role or who have been asked to join a team to plan for a mentoring. When recruiting potential teacher-leaders to join the ranks of mentors or PD planning groups, consider recruiting those who have basic mentoring assets already in place. This should include those without all of the specific knowledge and skills but who have demonstrated the dispositions for gaining them. Teacher-leaders who have demonstrated a *growing capacity* for engaging with others (children and adults) in ways detailed in Table 8.1 may be great candidates for a "grow our own" PD mentoring/leadership learning community. These teacher assets are adapted from Chu and Carroll's (2010) identification of teaching dispositions, and from others as cited.

REFLECTION

Who in your early childhood teacher community has assets (see Table 8.1) that could be more fully developed in a learning community designed to promote the growth of new mentors and/or teacher-leaders?

When recruiting early childhood professionals to consider for the PD mentoring or coaching ranks, share the questions and indicators of mentoring competencies detailed in Table 8.1.

REFLECTION

The well-known Green Bay Packer football coach, Vince Lombardi, is often quoted as having said, "Leaders aren't born, they are made." (Retrieve from: quotationsbook.com/quote/22874/) After reviewing *Self-Assessment for Becoming an Early Childhood PD Teacher-Leader*, do you believe that we can say of early childhood education mentors, "Leaders aren't born, they are mentored"? Why or why not?

Planning for PD

Once a group is formed to design a PD plan for a small staff, a system of programs, or an entire early childhood community, consider the ingredients needed to spark the passion for the work of planning. Looking to well-established teacher roles around

Table 8.1 Self-Assessment for Becoming an Early Childhood PD Teacher-Leader

Facilitating Adult Learning	Building Relationships
Do you have interest and experience in forming partnerships?	***Do others see you as caring?***
Examples of indicators:	**Examples of indicators:**
Collaboration with others to foster learning	Having an "ethic of care" involving sensitivity and responsiveness (Noddings, 1984)
Demonstrating the ability to listen, learn, observe, and form partnerships	Valuing human diversity as a resource (Vavrus, 2002)
Persisting until mutual goals are realized	Developing relationships characterized by receptivity, relatedness, and responsiveness (Noddings, 1984)
Having a commitment toward pursuing connections, implications, and relationships among ideas and practices	

Understanding Change	Communicating to Understand, Learn, and Teach
Do you have a willingness to question your own views?	***Are you interested in understanding and sharing different perspectives?***
Examples of indicators:	**Examples of indicators:**
Being willing and able to question one's own perspective	Demonstrating the ability to share with others one's experiences and personal ways of making sense of the world (Gay, 2010; Cochran-Smith, 2004; Ladson-Billings, 1994)
Taking on challenges	
Recognizing and being willing to explore how power differences affect contexts of learning and development (Freire, 1985)	Listening more than speaking when trying to understand another's views
Acting with humility, showing a willingness to be uncomfortable, being willing to take risks in order to learn and acknowledging gaps in one's own knowledge	Speaking a language other than English
	Varying ways of communicating to fit the needs, cultural context, and purposes of specific adult and child interactions

Valuing the Role of Assessment

Do you document what you do and then reflect on how this information should inform your decisions and actions?

Example of an indicator:

Showing interest in learning new research-based tools to evaluate personal/program progress towards goals

Commitment to Professional Development for Oneself and Others	Using Relationship-Building Skills to Build Professional Relationships
Does your battery get recharged by learning from others and facilitating others' learning?	***Do you avoid a deficit approach with others?***
Examples of indicators:	**Examples of indicators:**
Showing regard for others' points of view and a willingness to learn from them	Taking a positive strength-based view of persons
Having a growing vision of great teaching–learning	Recognizing that the world view that one grows up with is not universal but is influenced by life experiences and aspects of gender, race, ethnicity, and social–class and cultural background (Darling-Hammond & Bransford, 2005; Villegas & Lucas, 2002; Darder & Torres, 2002)
Developing or recognizing competence in a specific content area of early childhood education	
Having a commitment to exemplary teaching–learning contexts that embrace diversity and promote social justice	
Fostering program and community relationships that promote a culture of learning	Behaving in ways consistent with professionalism; is confidential, ethical, and knowledgeable about professional guidelines and practices (Feeney, 2012)

children's play may act as an inspirational metaphor or may suggest an initial place to engage teachers. Children first learn how to take on difficult challenges through their play. They try on different roles and persist in solving problems in scenarios negotiated with their play partners. Jones and Reynolds (2011; 1992) classic work *The play's the thing* identifies the different roles that teachers take on to support children's play, including acting as stage managers, players, assessors, planners, scribes, mediators, and communicators. The experienced adult scaffolds the child's gaps in knowledge and is available to support the child to reach another level of understanding by supporting, collaborating, and participating in their play (Bodrova and Leong, 2007; Vygotsky, 1962).

Inspiring the development of a plan for adult learning may also be a joyful and creative process for an implementation team with similar "player" support roles. The supporters of adult learning need to "play" and join together to explore and integrate their best thinking. Creating a joyful, productive, and cooperative learning environment supports teachers to open their minds to new ideas (Fredrickson, 2004). When teacher's needs for *relatedness* (a sense of being valued and connected), *competence* (a sense of mastery, skill, and ability) and *autonomy* (a sense of freedom, control, and choice) are met, the teachers tend to engage and learn more (Clement and Vandenberghe, 2000; Deci and Ryan, 1985, 2000).

The National Implementation Research Network released a report (Fixsen, Naoom, Blase, Friedman, & Wallace, 2005) that summarized research findings on implementation *drivers* of changes in practices in education and human services. The Network found that integration of cycles of improvement in increasing the competence of staff must be connected to accountability for building capacity of the organization as well as the individual. One way to sustain a PD planning team is to make it fun, engaging, and inspiring.

Becoming a PD Player

As you read about the players in any well-designed PD project or system, consider these questions: If you were on a planning team for setting up a system of mentoring for teachers in a school or a community, what role would you play? Who do you know among your professional peers who could play other roles (which will be described in the next section)? Where are the gaps in knowledge among members of your imaginary planning team? What education do you think is needed to support planning for teacher mentoring? Could a learning community on leadership support the skills needed to form a mentoring or PD planning team? Use Table 8.2 to help prospective mentors consider this new role.

Selecting, Planning, and Modifying a Mentoring Design

This text is designed to help mentors and those planning for mentoring programs to become aware of and to practice the foundational skills and competencies needed to be effective. It can serve as an overarching resource for a mentor to gain these foundational adult-learning, communication, and other skills. However, it may also be used along with a specific research or evidence-based mentoring or coaching protocol and curriculum. The Center on the Social and Emotional Foundations for Early Learning, for example, has specific content and coaching protocol that might be chosen for use in a mentoring project designed for teachers of infants and toddlers focusing on improving their social and emotional development. Isner, Tout, Zaslow, Soli, Quinn, Rothenberg, and Burkhauser (2011) suggest that early childhood mentoring and coaching projects "begin with the end in mind" and take the

Table 8.2   Play as a Metaphor for Planning for Professional Development: Inspiring a Playful Professional-Development Process

. . . .

PD planning team PLAY roles: *What roles or perspectives are needed on a mentoring planning team?*	**Contributions:** *What "role" contributions does the team need from this team member, such as interest, knowledge, skills?*
Stage manager Position might be administrator, program manager, teacher-leader, supervisor, principal, or anyone with the contributions noted in the right-hand column in this row.	**Facilitates professional development choices to fit individuals/groups:** Choices include mentoring, coaching, consultation, technical assistance, college courses, learning communities, and so on. Able to facilitate a connection or link the • **desired results** (goals/objectives) to the • **plan for instruction** (mentoring, coaching) with a • plan for **collection of evidence** for understanding
Player Includes teachers and all participants	**Builds professional relationships through** • understanding and responsiveness to diversity and culture; • seeing the adult as a whole person with social, emotional, cultural, and intellectual experiences that inform their learning; • ways to share, reflect, and demonstrate understanding through real-world application; • respecting that the learner needs to feel safe and valued, and have choices to make sense of the content; • supporting others to achieve a sense of mastery or growth; and • recognizing the need to feel like a collaborator and not a person being judged
Scribe, communicator, mediator	**Models and facilitates giving attention to many ways to communicate:** • technology • relevant resources used • individual differences accommodated (skill levels, interests, ways of learning) through a variety of ways of communicating • strategies to negotiate tensions between mandates and teacher-centered interests • policies as well as teachers' views • ways to support, challenge, and articulate a vision
Assessor	**Understands the importance of documenting the process of change over time:** • assessment of child and adult learning objectives • adult self-assessment encouraged • prior knowledge, skill levels, and misconceptions shared and explored through active learning • ways to share, reflect, and demonstrate understanding through real-world application

| **Planner** | **Knows that the adult teaching–learning process should emphasize these factors:** (McTighe & Wiggins, 2004; Bransford et al., 2000):
• relevant problems, issues, or challenges to engage the learners
• learning linked to goals
• instructor/facilitator/mentor/coach guides learner inquiry
• uncovering important ideas and processes by exploring essential questions and application
• time for trial and error, reflection, and revision of ideas and/or skills explored
• considers how frequently a mentor should work with a teacher
• opportunity to rethink, revise earlier work or ideas
• cycles of "model—try—feedback" refine and anchor the learning
• collaborative activities
• plan to check for understanding
• modeling, giving examples of ideas and skills relevant to a diversity of learners
• variety in work and methods for learning
• choices and flexibility for ways to participate
• relevance to participant's culture, language, and other areas of learner diversity
• understanding and application of the content emphasized through active and experiential modalities |

(Jones & Reynolds, 2011)

time to do the following activities and answer the following questions in order to plan for gathering data to allow for evaluation of a project's effectiveness:

- Describe the context of any mentoring or coaching project.
- Describe the needs and the assets present.
- Indicate the problem to be solved or the indicators or evidence for the problem.
- Identify the interested stakeholders and ways in which they will they be involved.
- What are the mission, vision, values, mandates, and resources?
- What are assumptions underlying the project, or is your project influenced by a theory or framework?
- Is your mentoring or coaching support based on a particular model?
- Does your program aim to duplicate the mentoring or coaching approach used in a particular project or study?
- How was the coaching model designed, determined, or chosen?
- How closely do you follow this model?
- How much freedom do coaches have to make changes to the model or do things differently?
- Is there a manual or set of materials that explain the model?

Based on Isner, T., Tout, K., Zaslow, M., Soli, Quinn, K., Rothenberg L., & Burkhauser, M. (2011). *Coaching in early care and education programs and Quality Rating and Improvement Systems (QRIS): Identifying promising features.* Child Trends. Retrieved from http://www.headstartresourcecenter. org/assets/files/Collab%20meeting%20OCTOBER%20Resources%20Coaching_Promising_Features.pdf

When specific planning to respond to a workplace or professional dilemma begins, identifying a *theory of change, program theory,* or *theory of action* (Weiss, 1995) is one way to make transparent and align the goals, activities, and expected outcomes of a project involving mentoring. Nearly all funders, including school districts, Head Start programs, and other grant sources, expect measurement of outcomes related to a project's goals and activities. Individual schools or programs engaged in designing a way to use mentoring and coaching of teachers to improve child outcomes may also find that a visual summary of the overall project will make clear how the planned activities may be associated with expected results. The visual depiction of a project usually contains the following components:

1. **inputs**, or the resources (including time, money, partners, etc.) and research, including the mentoring model informing the project's choices;
2. **outputs**, or activities and processes; and
3. **expected outcomes**.

Using a theory of action planning process reminds a group to: identify their underlying assumptions or research basis and monitor how resources, activities and intended results align.

Make Your Project Visible

Begin first with a description of a problem and the situation surrounding that problem. Then, describe the inputs, outputs, and expected outcomes. Table 8.3 is one example of a way in which this author worked with a community college planning group to make visible the group's *theory of change.* While theoy of action charts can become very complicated, table 8.3 has been kept to the basic components to shows that any group can participate in this process and increase its possibility of meeting its goals.

> *Problem:* During a community college survey of local preschool-teacher educational needs, a majority of the teachers expressed frustration that they did not have the skills or knowledge to prevent the most common challenging behaviors of their enrolled children.

Table 8.3 is a response to this problem by a community college planning group made up of faculty, local preschool teachers, and an early childhood nonprofit grant agency. The group's goal was for preschool teachers to increase their skills and knowledge in child guidance strategies. Group members identified resources and activities and aligned them with the improved outcomes that they hoped to see in children. They also identified the mentoring-coaching competencies needed to educate the mentors, as well as features of the mentoring-coaching approach. Ways to assess and monitor the plan were added.

Putting Your Plan Into Action

1. How might making a mentoring project's available resources (e.g., the assets that include time, money, partners, research, and available mentoring expertise) visible allow for thoughtful review by a planning team before, during, and after the project?
2. How would identifying a mentoring project's activities and processes (e.g., observing documenting, reflecting, analysis, application, feedback, goal-setting, and modeling) allow for adjustment before, during, and after a project?

Table 8.3 Example of Using a Theory of Change Model to Plan for PD

Inputs	Outputs		Outcomes		
Resources (time, money, partners, etc.) & research or model	Mentor-coach education & support activities	Mentor-coaching activities & processes	Short-term outcomes or changes in teacher skills, practices, & interactions	Intermediate outcomes or changes in teacher practices & interactions	Long-term child outcomes/changes
Early-learning mentoring coaching grant funding	Education in mentor competency areas of goal-setting, communication, adult learning, etc.	Observe/Document Reflect/Analyze Apply feedback Goal-setting: individual, classroom, program	Teacher–child interactions will be more consistently positive, responsive, and sensitive.	Teachers will use more proactive child guidance strategies	Children will have improved social and emotional outcomes.
Community college early childhood education expertise in meeting mentoring competencies and collaboration with community childcare programs	Mentor supervisors trained in use of *reflective supervision* practices (monthly meeting with mentors)	Modeling Videotaped interactions			
Center on the Social & Emotional Foundations of Early Learning (CSEFEL) Pyramid	Training in observation protocol (Reliable in *CLASS* assessment) Training in *Teaching Strategies GOLD* CSEFEL Resources for Trainers/Coaches	Monthly 3-hour visits to each enrolled teacher's classroom, & monthly virtual coaching	Measured by the *CLASS* assessment	Documented by mentor-coach classroom observation	Measured by *Teaching Strategies GOLD* developmental continuum or other tools as indicated

Assessment sources cited in the plan are in the reference list at the end of this chapter: CSEFEL, CLASS, Teaching Strategies GOLD

Table 8.4 Planning for Mentoring and Coaching With a Theory of Change Model

The problem is:

If the intervention is effective, we hope to see changes in:

Inputs	Outputs		Outcomes		
Resources (time, money, partners, etc.) & research or model	Mentor coach education & support activities (Circle all that apply, and add missing information.)	Mentor coaching activities & processes (Circle all that apply, and add missing information)	Short-term outcomes or changes in teacher skills, practices, & interactions	Intermediate outcomes or changes in teacher practices & interactions	Long-term child outcomes/changes
Mentoring-coaching funding:	Review education in mentor competency areas of: adult learning, building relationships, change, communication, assessment and PD relationships.	Observe/Document Reflect/Analysis Apply Feedback Goals setting: individual, classroom, program Modeling Videotaped interactions	Teacher-child interactions will be more consistently effective in the area of . . .	Teachers use strategies that are effective in promoting . . .	Improved outcomes for children will be . . .
Existing expertise of mentors, coaches, teachers or others in community members:	Mentor supervisors trained in use of *reflective supervision* practices and or . . .	Other primary activities not mentioned prevously areFrequency (how often) and duration (how many months) of mentor activities will be:			
	Frequency (how often) and duration (how many months) of mentor training will be:				
Resources, research or underlying assumptions inspiring and informing this project:	Observation or assessment tool is . . .		Measured by . . .	Documented by . . .	Measured by . . .
	Curriculum for children is.				
	Other resources for mentors, trainers, or coaches are . . .				

3. How does identifying the expected outcomes for both children and adults involved in a mentoring project increase the chance that the outcomes will be met?
4. Identify a real or imagined problem in an early-learning setting. Put the problem in the form of a statement—for example, *Teachers are frustrated that they do not have the skills or knowledge to prevent common challenging behaviors of their enrolled children.*

Imagine that you will be given all of the funds that you need to implement an intervention for the problem if you simply complete the items presented in Table 8.4. Complete as much of the form as you are able to. It is acceptable if you cannot complete everything.

REFLECTION

What expertise or technical leadership do you need to complete a project chart such as the one in Table 8.4?

1. What sections did you find easy to complete? What sections did you not complete? What was easy to understand? What was confusing?

2. If, for example, you do not know of an assessment tool or observation method to measure the desired teacher and child outcomes, who in your early learning community could advise you on the matter?

3. What professional development do you and your planning group need in order to be effective? What consultation do you need to make a mentoring project's inputs, outputs, and outcomes visible and aligned?

Evaluation and Advocacy

Developing Leadership for Change

Early childhood teachers who have studied progressive theorists and program approaches (Bredekamp, 2011, pp. 106–128) usually point to learning in children as being developmental, with knowledge being constructed by interacting with the people, situations, and environments all around them. Uncovering your own views toward how you have constructed your assumptions about the way adult teachers learn and develop is also developmental in nature. You have a lifetime of experiences that contribute to your responses to situations. Even more important is to compare what you state you believe with what you actually do in different situations. Consider the list in Figure 8.2. Instead of positioning this list as a set of

Figure 8.2   Leading for Empowerment or Leading to Direct or Control
....

In what professional situations do you tend to	and when do you usually:
• Talk at people	Engage in dialogue
• Control others by making all of the decisions	Facilitate decisions
• Feel that you must know all of the answers	Work with others to find the answers
• Instill some fear to increase competence	Inspire commitment and creativity
• Point out errors	Solve problems
• Delegate responsibility	Support accountability by all
• Create structures and procedures	Create vision, promote flexibility within boundaries
• Do things right	Do the right thing
• Focus on the bottom line	Focus on the process that gets to the bottom line

Based on Nolan, M. (2007). *Mentor coaching and leadership in early care and education.* Clifton Park, NY: Thompson Delmar Learning.

Crane, T. (2001). *The heart of coaching: Using transformational coaching to create a high performance culture.* San Diego: PTA Press.

good-and-bad opposites and describing it by saying, "Old-style early care and education leaders believe this" or, "new-style transformative leaders believe that" (Nolan, 2007, p. 66; Crane, 2001), consider in what situations you (or a teacher whom you are mentoring) have made these opposite choices. When has the choice on either end of the continuum been appropriate for fostering another teacher's learning and professional growth? When has the choice silenced a teacher or not met the teacher's learning needs?

It is not simple to examine the power, stress, and contextual factors that make it hard for teachers to trust enough to collaborate, delegate, and wonder about new solutions to everyday situations. Mentoring for leadership requires that teachers experience what we hope they will also provide for others. The next section examines the organizational capacity and conditions needed to promote successful learning mentoring and leadership.

Evaluating Reflective Supervision, Peer Mentoring, and Program Conditions for PD

Mentoring for leadership requires supporting supervisors and teachers to reflect on the dynamics of a program or school. The questions in Table 8.5 could be used by a staff as a collaborative self-study. It is essential to first establish confidentiality protocols and to identify the exact intended uses of the collected responses. If teachers are uncomfortable sharing together, an outside facilitator could interview teachers separately, and if permission were acquired from participants, the facilitator could later share the aggregate responses.

Analysis of the responses to the questions in Table 8.5 could involve checking for patterns consistent with Parlakian's (2002) indicators of programs with conditions conducive to ongoing professional learning and growth.

Once a program's conditions for learning have been examined, designing interventions to meet the needs of a program can begin. The process of mentoring and coaching shares some of the same functions as that of the early childhood college instructor who is overseeing quality field experiences for 2- and 4-year degree programs. The National Association for the Education of Young Children (NAEYC, 2011)

Table 8.5   Reflecting on Conditions Conducive to Reflective Supervision and Professional Learning

Gathering and reflecting on information about the capacity of an organization to support professional learning, reflection, and mentoring

Questions *Please give an example from your experience in this program or school.*	Response examples of conditions conducive to reflective supervision and professional learning (Parlakian, 2002)
When have you developed shared goals and responsibilities with others?	• Collaborative mission statement • Evidence of shared responsibility and control of power
Do teachers have a commitment to spend time reflecting on their work? *Can you recall a time when you felt you grew professionally?*	• Supervisors support learning from experience • Goals, needs, and values aligned with mission and vision • Routine and regular exploration of work in discussion • Time invested to achieve long-term goals • Regular opportunities to wonder, explore, and brainstorm possible responses to dilemmas
Do regular individual or group meetings occur? *What happens at meetings?* *How does it feel to be in these meetings?* *What do you take away from the meetings?*	• Empathy, support, encouragement, collaboration • Administrative tasks and program issues discussed • Challenges discussed • Emergent issues, updates • New topics discussed • All discussions not dominated by daily responsibilities • Telling someone what to do not seen as best way to be effective • Learning to apply concepts • Listening to all • No one seen as the only expert • Discussion that is centered around what is happening rather than around questions about problems • Understanding that staff changes require time to build new relationships
How do you show respect and trust for each other?	• Acceptance of strengths and vulnerabilities • Recognition of strength in diversity; learning about each other's cultures, communication styles, and histories; allowing for many ways to communicate; noticing whether one style is dominating staff discussions, resulting in some staff doing most of the talking while others remain silent. • Parallel process; supervisor and staff reflection; supportive conversations among teachers and children; regular conversations among families and staff • Understanding that teachers must experience reflective support in order to give it • Open, supportive interactions with peers and supervisors the norm
Is there sensitivity and responsiveness between teachers and children and between teachers and supervisors?	• Staff cannot be sensitive to children if they are not treated with respect by their supervisors.
Do you understand the professional standards in your program? *How are they developed, or from where do they come?*	• Excellence and norms are defined and clearly communicated; the ways to achieve these are negotiated in the group.
Is it safe to have open communication? *Are the professional skills in place to facilitate discussion?*	• Thoughts, ideas, and feedback are valued. • Active listening and thoughtful, open-ended questions are usual. • Individual and group supervision, facilitation occur regularly.

Based on: Parlakian, R. (2002). *Reflective Supervision in Practice*. Washington, DC: ZERO TO THREE.

has broad guidance for field experiences in such teacher-preparation programs. Although job-embedded mentoring or coaching is almost always focused on objectives that are narrower than those of a college career preparation program, NAEYC guidelines for field experiences serve as an important reminder to mentors or coaches to consider the quality of their facilitated mentoring experiences.

Does the Mentoring Process Facilitate Experiences Allowing a Teacher to

- observe, implement and receive constructive feedback;
- integrate theory, research, and practice;
- make meaning of his or her experiences and to evaluate those experiences against standards of quality;
- provide positive models of early childhood practice consistent with NAEYC standards;
- be provided with other models and/or experiences (when settings used for field experiences do not reflect high-quality standards); and
- include field experiences with cultural, linguistic, racial, and ethnic diversity in families and communities NAEYC, 2011, P. 59)?

Providing Models That Don't Exist in a Program Setting

1. If a program has gaps in indicators of its capacity to support professional learning, reflection, and mentoring, how might a mentor support teachers to observe or experience features of a program that has greater capacity? Would a field trip, viewing of videos of effective and supportive teacher interactions, or modeling of new and different interactions be something that you might want to try? What other ways might support a staff and a program to increase their capacity to become more of a learning organization? Would first working with the supervisor, administrator, or program manager to increase his or her skills in reflective supervision (see Chapter 7) be the best place to start? Or, would working with an entire staff be more effective? Consider different program settings with which you are familiar and the best choices for mentoring for increasing the learning potential of these programs.

2. *Virtual mentoring or coaching* is another option for connecting teachers and entire early-learning programs with other settings that may offer models for high-quality program practices. When programs are too far away to visit or staff does not have time to leave sites, mentoring dispersed teachers as a *virtual pair* or *virtual group* is an option to consider. Have you ever connected adult learners across distances via the telephone or email or used programs designed to support videoconferencing over the Internet? Dialoging in real time—and continuing the learning on discussion boards in between live chats—is one option for providing needed models of practices and conditions and the ongoing reflection that may be missing from a teacher's environment. What is your experience in working over long distances with teachers? What do you want to learn? Who can support you to increase your skills in this area?

Document Your Mentoring Process

Teacher learning.   As a mentor engaged in encouraging a teacher to observe and document children's learning and development, you need to engage in the important parallel process of documenting what the teacher knows and is able to do in this area. As mentoring progresses, complete responses to the next set of questions.

Mentoring Plan at the Beginning

By creating a visual representation, or a *theory of action* plan, or by simply detailing ways in which the goals, resources, activities, and outcomes of a mentoring project are connected, you can more easily monitor and review the project for effectiveness. Some initial questions for those planning mentoring projects to consider and document are as follows:

- What is the purpose of our mentoring project?
- Who will participate?
- What information should be gathered from teachers interested in participating? Examples include education level, experiences with young children, beliefs about their work, type of early learning program, and involvement and support of supervisors.
- What incentives and/or benefits might the participants experience?
- How will accomplishments and challenges be documented?
- Who are partners in this project, and what will they contribute?

Documenting Mentor Experiences

A form for documenting the planned and actual experiences of mentors is given in Figure 8.3.

Figure 8.3   **Documenting the Mentoring Process**
....

Number of teachers per mentor:
- Mentors are working with _____ (#) teachers each.

Frequency of contact:
- Mentors are in contact with teachers every (e.g., week, month) _____ (how often).

Duration of contact:
- Mentors work with teachers during each contact time (e.g., # of minutes, hours) for _____ (how long).

Strategies used by mentors:
- Mentors are using the strategies planned for the project.

(Example: observation and feedback)
- Mentors are individualizing strategies used and varying from the model or protocol planned for the project. Provide details here:

Mentor competencies: Identify specific areas of strength or areas needing support and education. Identify whether the method used was observed or self-reported, or otherwise how knowledge was acquired.
- Early childhood content knowledge _____
- Mentoring process skills, knowledge and abilities in:

  - adult education
  - building relationships
  - communication
  - assessment
  - change process
  - professionalism areas
  - cultural responsiveness and knowledge of bias issues
  - other

Does reflective supervision for mentors occur? (Provide details here.)
Evidence of progress toward desired results is (provide details here):
Changes needed are _____because (provide details here):

Table 8.6 Documenting Mentoring Strategies

··

Mentoring Visit Record

Complete each section with brief anecdotal notes.

Mentor_____ Teacher _____ Date: _____

Purpose, Focus, or Goal Area

- Underline one:
  - Goal negotiated with mentor
  - Mentor suggests goal
  - Goal assigned
- Primary focus or goal: (I will be able to . . . when . . .)
- Emergent issues, needs, or interests of the teacher also explored:

Frequency: How often do we meet?

Duration: How long do we meet for each visit?

Mentoring and/or Coaching Tools	Mentoring Strategies and Teacher Response
Observe	
Observed interactions Documented with: • video • photos • narrative notes • anecdotal notes • assessment tool • checklist • collected data	Noted purpose of visit Watched, listened, sought information, noticed, empathized
Reflect	
Gave feedback about observed interactions or other focus	Used positive feedback, open-ended or clarification questions Made reflective comments Helped make meaning and connections with previous concepts Identified new concepts, challenges, and successes
Apply	
Modeled or demonstrated Co-planned Co-taught Engaged in problem solving Role-played Provided resources Collaborated by:	Had an instructive conversation and ended with an affirmation Reviewed progress toward goal

Progress Toward Goals: What is going well, and what is challenging?

Next Time: The action steps (including timeline and people responsible) are:

Taking the Pulse of the Mentoring Relationship

I am still wondering or I need support about (relationship building, communication, assessment, goal-setting, adult learning strategies, content resources, etc.):

Documenting Mentoring Strategies During Every Contact

Wright (2010) and Rowan et al. (2004) have published examples of mentoring, coaching, and teacher daily logs for the purpose of monitoring whether mentors are using effective and agreed-upon strategies for a specific project. Wright suggests that teacher daily logs can be kept online to allow for easier monitoring and data gathering. Keeping documentation brief will encourage mentors to quickly note their major strategies. Table 8.6 will help you to document your mentoring strategies and progress toward the teacher's goal. Briefly reflecting on what is going well during each visit models the reflective practice encouraged by relationship-based PD.

Document Teacher Experiences During Mentoring Over Time

Mentoring for promoting positive change in an early-learning teacher's interactions or for improvement of overall program practices includes a broad range of activities. It is important to document the details of the mentoring process with teachers to allow for planning, monitoring, and evaluation. Mentoring for technical competence, for example, in promoting high-quality or developmentally appropriate practices through increased knowledge of curriculum, assessment, and teaching is foundational to increasing positive outcomes for children. Professionals also need to engage in ongoing learning to support their understanding of how research findings may be translated into practices with children. Important areas to document are included in Figure 8.4.

REFLECTION

When have you systematically engaged in documenting your work with another adult or child, for the purpose of reflecting on it, monitoring it, and evaluating it for effectiveness? If you have not, who do you know who could support you or collaborate on using the documentation and evaluation tools in this chapter?

Advocacy

One of the most profound outcomes of mentoring for leadership is the increased confidence and ability of early-care and education professionals to see themselves as advocates for views. An advocate is a person who is passionate about an issue and has evidence to back up his or her enthusiastic perspective. It may be an effective classroom practice or an issue that has national implications (Sullivan, 2010, pp. 113–115) that the advocate shares broadly. When you advocate for more mentors who represent their community and have the skills and insights to support effective PD, you are an advocate for quality early childhood programs. Refer to Table 8.7 for ideas on supporting a mentor's PD.

Figure 8.4 Documenting Teacher Experiences

- *Content:*
  - What is the content that the teacher is interested in learning?
- *Aligning:*
  - How will the mentoring process link a teacher's interest to the importance of aligning observation, curriculum planning, and teaching strategies?
- *Observation tools:*
  - What program and child observation tools does the teacher or other staff in the program use and understand?
  - Does the mentoring process involve observing the program to give the mentor a baseline of information about the quality of the program? Will a program evaluation tool be used (e.g., CLASS, ELLCO, ECERS)?
- *Quality:*
  - What is the overall quality of the classroom? of the program? What tool will the mentor use to gather information on program quality?
- *Strengths:*
  - After observing a teacher, does the mentor consider these questions: What is the teacher doing that is especially effective? What are the PD needs identified by the mentor and by the teacher? Are they the same or different?
- *Feedback:*
  - What tool or criteria will the mentor use to evaluate and inform the feedback given to the teacher?
  - Is detailed, individual feedback for teachers given?
- *Modeling:*
  - Are suggested practices modeled? How?
  - After modeling, discussing, and working with a teacher on a specific goal area, what teacher gaps in knowledge, skills, and attitudes remain unchanged?
- *Change:*
  - What practices changed quickly?
  - What practices did not change?
  - What differences or patterns were there among teachers who began using more effective practices?
  - To keep the learning going, was reference to developing a long-term PD plan completed?

Summary

Becoming involved in mentoring others to uphold early childhood professional values and guidelines by supporting teachers to be more knowledgeable, reflective, and aware of their own perspectives is both rewarding and challenging. Shulman (2004) summarizes the complexities of teaching and hints at how overwhelming the work of trying to increase classroom quality can feel at times:

> I have concluded that classroom teaching . . . is perhaps the most complex, most challenging, and most demanding, subtle, nuanced, and frightening activity that our species has ever invented. In fact, when I compared the complexity of teaching with that much more highly rewarded profession, "doing medicine," I concluded that the only time medicine even approaches the complexity of an average day of classroom teaching is in an emergency room during a natural disaster (p. 504).

Table 8.7 Plan for promoting professional development of the mentor

Mentoring and leadership activities, skills, knowledge, and dispositions	Plan for promoting professional development of the mentor
	An example of something I will try is:
Describe one teaching skill or consideration that is also important in mentoring and leadership. How will you encourage yourself or others to try to implement this skill or practice when mentoring another teacher?	
What are some benefits and challenges of encouraging others or engaging yourself in an early childhood learning community?	
How can exemplary teachers be encouraged to view themselves as capable of engaging in mentoring and leadership activities?	
Identify strategies for creating a mentoring PD team that meets the needs of the community and cultural context.	
Explain ways to document and evaluate the mentoring process.	
What new evidence will you share with others about the potential power of mentoring?	

The mentoring and coaching process seems especially suited to engaging in understanding these early-education complexities. As a learning relationship that focuses both on *what* to know and *how* to teach, mentoring shows great promise when certain features are present. Zaslow, Tout, Halle, and Starr (2010) remind us that a growing research-based consensus is building that effective PD involves an ongoing focus on early-educator practices and knowledge with specific objectives involving other teachers from the same program and aligned with standards and assessment of practices. These PD criteria may seem daunting for a teaching force that is underpaid, under-resourced, and often lacking the opportunity for professional education. Mentors with specific early childhood expertise seem uniquely situated to successfully support teachers to meet these lofty professional goals if the mentors also have specific, demonstrated competencies for engaging teachers in empowering learning relationships.

Traditional early childhood values of building trust and respect in relationships are central to the power of mentoring. Teachers need to be able to feel comfortable communicating their concerns to the mentor when suggested strategies conflict with their values or expressing to the mentor what they feel is needed for the families and communities they know well. Mentors have the opportunity to engage in the parallel processes of teaching and learning when they are supported to also grow professionally through ongoing, reflective supervision. Positive outcomes for the children and families who are touched by a more effective teacher are really at the heart of the purpose of the professional mentoring relationship. Finally, *growing our own* more diverse and representative professional-development leaders through mentoring within supportive learning communities has the power to engage early childhood teachers in informed advocacy for *all* young children and the early childhood profession itself.

REFLECTION

1. What are several themes from your reading and reflection on the mentoring process that have affected your *head* (ideas), your *heart* (feelings), and your *hands* (ways to apply what you feel and know)?

2. What do these themes mean to you as person who is passionate about supporting the learning and development of the adults and children involved in early childhood education? Choose one of the areas in Figure 8.5, and make an action plan.

Figure 8.5   Summary of Mentoring and Leadership for Professional Development

References

National Association for the Education of Young Children (NAEYC). (June, 2011). *NAEYC Standards for Initial & Advanced Early Childhood Professional Preparation Programs*. Washington, DC: NAEYC. Retrieved from http://www.naeyc.org/files/ncate/file/NAEYC%20Initial%20and%20Advanced%20Standards%206_2011-final.pdf

Bass, B. M., & Bass, R. (2008). *The Bass handbook of leadership: Theory, research, and managerial application* (4th ed.). New York: Simon and Schuster.

Bloom, P. (1997). Commentary. In S. Kagan & B. Bowman (Eds.), *Leadership in early care and education* (pp. 34–37). Washington, DC: NAEYC.

Bodrova, E., & Leong, D. J. (2007). *Tools of the mind: The Vygotskian approach to early childhood education* (2nd ed.). Upper Saddle River, NJ: Pearson Education/Merrill.

Bransford, J., Brown, A., Cocking, R. (Eds.). (2000). *How people learn: Brain, mind, experience, and school* (Expanded ed.). Washington, DC: National Academy Press.

Bredekamp, S. (2011). *Effective practices in early childhood education: Building a foundation*. Boston: Pearson.

Brown-Kendall, R., Aubel, C., & Koetje, M. L. (2011). The growth of an affiliate: The birth of the leadership academy. *Young Children, 66*(3), pp. 72–73.

Center on the Social and Emotional Foundations for Early Learning (CSEFEL). (2012). *Resources for trainers/coaches*. Retrieved from http://csefel.vanderbilt.edu

Chu, M., & Carroll, D. (2010). *Fostering a culture of learning that advances knowledge, embraces diversity, and promotes social justice*. A report of the Teacher Education Recruitment and Retention Task Force, Woodring College of Education, Western Washington University. Retrieved from http://www.wce.wwu.edu/FacStaff/Publications.shtml

Cochran-Smith, M. (2004). Stayers, leavers, lovers, and dreamers: Insights about teacher retention. *Journal of Teacher Education, 55*, 387–392

Clement, M., & Vandenberghe, R. (2000). Teachers' professional development: A solitary or collegial adventure?. *Teaching and Teacher Education, 16*, 81–101.

Crane, T. (2001). The heart of coaching: Using transformational coaching to create a high performance culture. San Diego: PTA Press.

Dalli, C. (2008). Pedagogy, knowledge and collaboration: Toward a ground-up perspective on professionalism. *European Early Childhood Education Research Journal, 16*(2), 171–185.

Darder, A., & Torres, R. D. (2002). Shattering the race lens: Toward a critical theory of racism. In A. Darder, M. Baltodano, & R. D. Torres (Eds.), *The critical pedagogy reader* (pp. 245–261). New York: Routledge.

Darling-Hammond, L., & Bransford, J. (Eds.). (2005). *Preparing teachers for a changing world: What teachers should learn and be able to do*. San Francisco: Jossey-Bass.

Deci, E. L., & Ryan, R. M. (1985). *Intrinsic motivation and self determination in human behavior*. New York: Plenum Press.

Deci, E. L., & Ryan, R. M. (2000). The "what" and "why" of goal pursuits: Human needs and the self determination of behavior. *Psychological Inquiry, 11*, 227–268.

Feeney, S. (2012). *Professionalism in early childhood education: Doing our best for young children*. Boston: Pearson Education.

Fixsen, D. L., & Blase, K. A. (2008). Drivers framework. Chapel Hill, NC: The National Implementation Research Network, Frank Porter Graham Child Development Institute, University of North Carolina.

Fixsen, D. L., Naoom, S. F., Blase, K. A., Friedman, R. M., & Wallace, F. (2005). *Implementation research: A synthesis of the literature*. Tampa, FL: University of South Florida, Louis de la Parte Florida Mental Health Institute, National Implementation Research Network. (FMHI Publication No. 231).

Fredrickson, B. L. (2004). The broaden-and-build theory of positive emotions. *Philosophical Transactions of the Royal Society, B*(359), 1367–1377.

Freire, P. (1985). *The politics of education: Culture, power and liberation*. New York: Bergin & Garvey.

Galinsky, E. (2012). Learning communities: An emerging phenomenon. *Young Children, 67*(1), 20–27.

Galinsky, E. (2010). *Mind in the making: The seven essential life skills every child needs*. New York: Harper Collins.

Gay, G. (2010). *Culturally responsive teaching: Theory, research, and practice*. New York: Teachers College Press.

Gofffin, S., & Washington, V. (2007). *Ready or not: Leadership choices in early care and education*. New York: Teachers College Press.

Hall, L. (2006). *How is leadership understood and enacted within the field of early childhood education and care.* (Doctoral dissertation, Queensland University of Technology, Australia). Retrieved from http://eprints.qut.edu.au/16213/1/Louise_Hard_Thesis.pdf

Hamre, B., Downer, J., Jamil, F., & Pianta, R. (2012). Enhancing teachers' intentional use of effective interactions with children: Designing and testing professional development interventions. In R. Pianta (Ed.), *Handbook of early childhood education.* New York: Guilford Press.

Hard, L. (2004). How leadership is understood in early childhood education and care. *Journal of Australian Research in Early Childhood Education, 11*(1), 123–131.

Harms, T., Clifford, R., & Cryer, D. (1998). *Early Childhood Environment Rating Scale—Revised.* New York: Teachers College Press.

Heifertz, R. A., & Laurie, D. L. (1999). Mobilizing adaptive work: Beyond visionary leadership. In J. A. Conger, G. M. Spreitzer, & E. E. Lawler, III (Eds.), *The leaders change handbook: An essential guide to setting direction and taking action* (pp. 55–86). San Francisco: Jossey-Bass.

Heifertz, R. A., & Linsky, M. (2002). *Leadership on the line: Staying alive through the dangers of leading.* Boston: Harvard Business School Press.

Heifertz, R. A., Linsky, M., & Grashow, A. (2009). *Practices of adaptive leadership: tools and tactics for changing your organization and the world.* Boston: Harvard Business Publishing.

Isner, T., Tout, K., Zaslow, M., Soli, M. Quinn, K., Rothenberg, L., & Burkhauser, M. (2011). *Coaching in Early Care and Education Programs and Quality Rating and Improvement Systems (QRIS): Identifying Promising Features.* Child Trends. Retrieved from http://www.headstartresourcecenter.org/assets/files/Collab%20meeting%20OCTOBER%20Resources%20Coaching_Promising_Features.pdf

Jackson, B. W. (2005). The theory and practice of multicultural organization development in education. In M. L. Ouellett (Ed.), *Teaching inclusively: Resources for course, department & institutional change in higher education* (pp. 3–20). Stillwater, OK: New Forums.

Jackson, B. W., & Holvino, E. (1988). Developing multicultural organizations. *Journal of Applied Behavioral Science & Religion, 9,* 14–19.

Jones E., & Reynolds, G. (2011). *The play's the thing—Teachers roles in children's play* (2nd ed.). New York: Teachers College Press.

Kagan, S., & Bowman, B. (1997). *Leadership in early care and education.* Washington, DC: NAEYC.

Lave, J., & Wenger, E. (1991). *Situated learning: Legitimate, peripheral participation.* Cambridge, UK: Cambridge University Press.

Ladson-Billings, G. (1994). *The dreamkeepers: Successful teachers of African-American children.* San Francisco: Jossey-Bass.

Linsky, M., & Heifetz, R. (2007). Forward. In S. Goffin & V. Washington, *Ready or not: Leadership choices in early care and education,* pp. ix–xi. New York: Teachers College Press.

Lutton, A. (Ed.). (2012). *Advancing the profession: NAEYC standards and guidelines for professional development.* Washington, DC: NAEYC.

Mattessich, P., Monsey, B., & Murray-Close, M. (2001). *Collaboration: What makes it work (2nd ed.). A review of research and literature on factors influencing successful collaboration.* St. Paul, MN: Amherst H. Wilder Foundation.

McTighe, J., & Wiggins, G. (2004). Understanding by design: professional development workbook. Alexandria, VA: Association for Supervision and Curriculum Development

Minnesota Center for Professional Development. (2009a). *General core competencies for relationship based professional development.* St. Paul, MN: Metropolitan State University. Retrieve at http://www.mncpd.org under the tab "Relationship Based Professional Development" and scroll down to "General Core Competencies."

Minnesota Center for Professional Development. (2009b). *Guidelines for conduct and professional responsibilities.* St. Paul, MN: Metropolitan State University. Retrieve at http://www.mncpd.org under the tab "Relationship Based Professional Development" and scroll down to "Guidelines for Conduct and Professional Responsibilities."

Mor Barak, M. E., & Chernin, D. A. (1998). A tool to expand organizational understanding of workforce diversity. *Administration in Social Work, 22,* 47–64.

Mor Barak, M. E., & Travis, D. J. (2009). Diversity and organizational performance. In Y. Hasenfeld (Ed.), *Human services as complex organizations* (pp. 341–378). Newbury Park, CA: Sage.

National Association for the Education of Young Children (NAEYC) and National Association of Child Care Resource and Referral Agencies (NACCRRA). (2011). *Early childhood education professional development: Training and technical assistance glossary.* Washington, DC: NAEYC. Retrieved from http://www.naeyc.org/GlossaryTraining_TA.pdf

Noddings, N. (1984). *Caring: A feminine approach to ethics and morality.* Berkeley: University of California Press.

Nolan, M. (2007). *Mentor coaching and leadership in early care and education.* Clifton Park, NY: Thompson Delmar Learning.

Nybell, L.M ., & Gray, S. S. (2004). Race, place, space: Meanings of cultural competence in three child welfare agencies. *Social Work, 49,* 17–27.

Parlakian, R. (2001). *Look, listen, and learn: Reflective supervision and relationship-based work.* Washington, DC: *ZERO TO THREE.*

Parlakian, R. (2002). *Reflective supervision in practice.* Washington, DC: ZERO TO THREE.

Peterson, S. M., Valk, C., Baker, A. C., Brugger, L., & Hightower, A. D. (2010). "We're not just interested in the work": Social and emotional aspects of early educator mentoring relationships. *Mentoring and Tutoring: Partnership in Learning, 18*(2), 155–175.

Pianta, R., La Paro, K., & Hamre, B. (2008). *Classroom assessment scoring system (CLASS) manual K–3.* Baltimore: Paul H. Brookes Publishing Co.

Rowan, B., Camburn, E., & Correnti, R. (2004). Using teacher logs to measure the enacted curriculum: A study of literacy teaching in third grade. *The Elementary School Journal, 105,* 75–101.

Ryan, S., & Whitebook, M. (2012) More than teachers: The early care and education workforce (pp. 92–110). In R. Pianta (Ed.), *Handbook of Early Childhood Education.* New York: Guilford.

Shulman, L. S. (2004). *The wisdom of practice: Essays on teaching, learning, and learning to teach.* San Francisco: Jossey-Bass.

Spillane, J. P., Halverson, R., & Diamond, J. B. (2001). Investigating school leadership practice: A distributed perspective. *Educational Researcher, 30*(3), 23–28.

Stigler, J. W., & Hiebert, J. (1999). *The teaching gap: Best ideas from the world's teachers for improving education in the classroom.* New York: Free Press.

Sullivan, D. (2010). *Learning to lead: Effective leadership skills for teachers of young children.* (2nd ed.). St. Paul, MN: Redleaf Press.

Teaching Strategies. (2010). *Teaching Strategies GOLD.* Washington, DC: Teaching Strategies, Inc.

Vavrus, M. (2002). *Transforming the multicultural education of teachers: Theory, research, and practice.* New York: Teachers College Press.

Villegas, A. M., & Lucas, T. (2002). *Educating culturally responsive teachers.* Albany, NY: State University of New York Press.

Vygotsky, L. (1962). *Thought and language.* Cambridge, MA: MIT Press.

Webster-Wright, A. (2009). Reframing professional development through understanding authentic professional learning. *Review of Educational Research, 79*(2), 702–739.

Weiss, C. H. (1995). *Nothing as practical as good theory: Exploring theory-based initiatives.* New York: The Aspen Institute.

Wright, T. (2010). Online logs: A tool to monitor fidelity in large scale interventions. In S. B. Neuman & M. L. Kamil (Eds.), *Preparing teachers for the early childhood classroom.* Baltimore: Paul H. Brookes Publishing Co.

York-Barr, J., & Duke, K. (2004). What do we know about teacher leadership? Findings from two decades of scholarship. *Review of Educational Research, 74*(3), 255–316.

Zaslow, M., Tout, K., Halle, T., & Starr, R. (2010). Professional development for early educators: Reviewing and revising conceptualizations. In S. Neuman & D. Dickinson (Eds.), *Handbook of early literacy research* (Vol. 3) (pp. 425–434). New York: Guilford.

Index